In Service of Two Masters

In Service of Two Masters

The Missionaries of Ocopa, Indigenous Resistance, and Spanish Governance in Bourbon Peru

Cameron D. Jones

Stanford University Press
Stanford, CA
and
The Academy of American Franciscan History
Oceanside, CA
2018

Library of Congress Cataloging-in-Publication Data

Names: Jones, Cameron D., author.
Title: In service of two masters : the missionaries of Ocopa, indigenous resistance, and Spanish governance in Bourbon Peru / Cameron D. Jones.
Description: Stanford, CA : Stanford University Press ; Oceanside, CA : The Academy of American Franciscan History, [2018] | Includes bibliographical references.
Identifiers: LCCN 2017041425 | ISBN 9781503604315 (hardcover : alk. paper)
Subjects: LCSH: Indians of South America--Missions—Peru--History—18th century. | Franciscans—Missions—Peru—History—18th century.
Classification: LCC F3429 .J64 2018 | DDC 985/.033—dc23
LC record available at https://lccn.loc.gov/2017041425

Contents

Figures and Tables

Acknowledgments

Portions of this book of this book originally formed part of my doctoral dissertation. Over the past four years and with the help of numerous individuals it has morphed into its present form. Therefore, I must thank the many people and organizations that made it possible.

First, I would like to acknowledge and thank all the various organizations which during the ten years I have worked on this project helped fund my research. The U.S. Department of Education (through the Fulbright-Hays Doctoral Dissertation Research Abroad Program), the Academy of American Franciscan History, the Lynde and Harry Bradley Foundation, the Tinker Foundation, the Office of International Affairs at the Ohio State University, and the OSU Department of History all helped me arrive at the various far-flung archives I visited as well as not letting me starve in the process.

During my time abroad, I encountered many scholars who advised and help me get around Spain and Peru. In Spain, Luis Miguel Glave and José Hernández Palomo served as my guides and gave me invaluable advice. In Peru, I would have been lost without the help of professors Claudia Rosas, Margarita Suárez, and José de la Puente. I am particularly grateful to Father Jorge Cajo, O.F.M., who as the former guardian of Ocopa gave me unprecedented access to the monastery and its records. Two institutions graciously allowed me to affiliate with them—the Escuela de Estudios Hispano-Americanos in Seville, and the Pontificia Universidad Católico del Perú in Lima. In addition, I thank my fellow traveling graduate students, now professors themselves, Elizabeth Montañez and Javier Puente, who helped me navigate the intricacies of academia abroad.

At OSU, several fellow students and scholars gave me invaluable feedback and almost daily moral support during this project: Danielle Anthony, Spencer Tyce, Beau Brammer, James Weeks, Daniel Watkins, Joseph Wachtel, Daniel Vandersommers, James Bach, and Frank Blazich. I give special thanks to Steven Hyland, my academic big brother and sounding board for ideas.

Many mentors helped to make this book a reality. Alan Gallay not only served on my doctoral candidacy committee but was an outside voice of reason in the formation of this project. Joseph Miller, during his short time at OSU and throughout our correspondence, has helped me to shape this project in ways that I did not think possible. Geoffrey Parker has not only served as my teacher of the science and art of writing history but also been a consummate mentor and friend. Donna Guy provided sage advice and gentle prodding that pushed this project and me to strive to always be better. Stephanie Smith, who guided me throughout my graduate career, but especially the last, difficult years, made me a more careful and conscientious teacher and scholar. Finally, I am grateful to Kenneth Andrien, who advised me for seven long years as student and has remained a mentor since. I cannot thank him enough for his wisdom and reassurance. This book is as much a product of his skillful advising and mentoring, as it is my own hard work.

As I adapted a dissertation into a book, many came to my aid. Jeffrey M. Burns, director of the Academy of American Franciscan History, seemingly worked daily to usher my manuscript though the incredibly difficult process. John F. Schwaller has worked tirelessly behind the scenes to make this, and many other projects on Franciscan history, move forward from concept to book. Heidi Scott, David Rex Galindo, Erick Langer, Daniel Krieger all read and gave excellent feedback on my manuscript. Without their support, this book would never have happened.

At California Polytechnic University in San Luis Obispo where I currently teach, I have enjoyed excellent colleagues and students. Among my colleagues Lewis Call, Michael Carver, Margaret Bodemer, José Navarro, and Joel Orth have all served as important mentors and friends during my transition from student to scholar. As for my students, I must especially thank Blake Burgess, who was the first student to dare read my manuscript from beginning to end.

I owe a deep debt of gratitude to my family. My parents Ernest and Julie Jones provided a loving home where learning and the thirst for knowledge were always highly prized. I am grateful to my siblings Alison Sweetnam, Matthew Jones, Timothy Jones, Melinda Kunz, and Christian Jones, who put up with their annoying little brother. Finally, I dedicate this book to my wife, Carrie, and my three intelligent and beautiful daughters, Claire, Susannah, and Grace. My daughters' joy and love for life inspires me every day. Carrie stood by my side during the long ordeal of graduate school and the job market, learned a new language, and lived (and even had a baby) in foreign lands. I cannot begin to thank her enough. This book is as much hers as it is mine.

Introduction

> "The greatest desire of our sovereign in the expansion of these domains has been the conversion of the infidel Indians to reduce them into the flock of the Church."
>
> —Manuel de Amat y Junient, *Memoria de gobierno*, 1776

Frontier missions were a critical component of Spain's imperial enterprise in the eighteenth century. These missions mediated between the crown's desire to exploit the wealth of the indigenous peoples and the natives' desire for autonomy. In previous centuries, these frontier areas had served principally as buffer zones between areas of Hispanic cultural diffusion and hegemony and the sparsely populated hinterland beyond. In these borderlands, semi-sedentary indigenous groups accepted and resisted attempts by Catholic missionaries to convert them and control them in networks of mission villages, demonstrating the resiliency of both groups. By the end of the seventeenth century, many areas in the borderlands had reached a dynamic equilibrium, because religious institutions lacked the resources to force more resistant ethnic groups onto their missions. The absence of a large, exploitable pool of laborers or substantial mineral deposits made crown officials and merchants unwilling to invest in further expansions into the hinterland. By the eighteenth century, this paradigm began to shift, as other European powers exerted their influence in the Atlantic world. Spanish officials became more interested in developing their American frontiers, not just commercially but as buffer zones against foreign intrusion into territory they claimed. This brought them into contact with indigenous groups who had been spared the initial burdens of Spanish colonization.

Into this milieu came the missionaries of Santa Rosa de Ocopa.[1] In 1709, a reform movement within the Franciscan order, called the Apostolic Institute, sent half a dozen missionaries to Peru to strengthen and expand evangelization into the eastern tropical forestlands. Between 1709 and 1824, the Ocopa missionaries built an impressive network of missions throughout the Peruvian Amazon region and in southern Chile. At its height in 1802, at least in theory, the Ocopa college presided over an area of South America roughly the size of France.

During their 115-year history under Spanish rule, Ocopa missionaries interacted with numerous indigenous nations throughout the tropical forests along the eastern slopes of the Andes. These included the Asháninkas, Yaneshas, Nomatsiguengas, Piros, Cashibos, Shipibos, Conibos, Cholónes, and Hibitos (as well as the Chonos and Huiliches in southern Chile). Most of these groups had been spared Spain's initial wave of colonization (and perhaps more important, epidemic disease) and used accommodation, flight, and often rebellion to negotiate varying levels of autonomy against the impositions of missionaries. Even at the height of their power, the Ocopa missionaries lacked the resources to dominate these populations, but neither could these indigenous groups, even after, in some cases, expelling the missionaries, ignore their influence. The result was an uncomfortable accommodation that in many ways mirrored internal conflicts that existed throughout Spanish America, but which were more apparent in the frontier, far from the veneer of colonial authority.

Spanish Governance, the Bourbon Reforms, and Ocopa

Spanish America was a vast and complex space developed over centuries of negotiations with local political actors. The Habsburg dynasty that ruled Spain from 1517 to 1700 practiced a form of governance later dubbed a "composite monarchy," in which they respected the laws and even common practices of the various polities ruled by the monarchy.[2] The Americas, though an appendage of the kingdom of Castile, had their own laws, called collectively *el derecho indiano.* Even in the eighteenth century, official correspondence could spend nearly a year in transit between Madrid and Lima. To reach the missions of Ocopa from Lima could take another four months. In addition to geographic obstacles, the American landscape was a variegated patchwork of languages and cultures not clearly understood by many colonial administrators back in Spain, some of whom had never traveled to the New World. Such a complicated cultural mixture combined with the slow dissemination of information made rapid reactions from the metropolis to emerging situations difficult. Thus, crown authorities had to rely on local political actors to sort out local problems, particularly in frontier areas.

Although some of these local actors were crown officials, most were not, and they included local commercial interests, city councils, indigenous groups, freed and enslaved blacks, and religious institutions. All fell within a spectrum between accepting and rejecting Spanish authority; but one of the principal components that helped to maintain Spanish control were relatively loyal, nonstate institutions, such as the clergy. It was these semi-independent yet hispanicizing groups that in many ways mediated between local desires and crown interests. Though by 1700 this system had made governance in Spanish America increasingly unwieldy, it made the empire resilient to external pressures. Spain's involvement in the unending European conflicts and waning financial and political power, however, caused ties with its many territories to strain, particularly those outside continental Europe. The loosening bonds with its colonial masters created in many places in Spanish America a veritable colonial Golden Age, but, as more of the continent's wealth remained in local hands, from an imperial perspective something had to change.[3]

To reform Spain's decaying political system, many of the new Bourbon ministers turned to the example of France, which was the originator of the dynasty as well as the predominant European political power of the day. During most of the second half of the seventeenth century, under its "Sun King" Louis XIV, France had pursued an agenda of monarchical consolidation of state power, expressed best by one of Louis's most famous supposed utterances, "L'État c'est moi" (I am the State). France's reforms were part of a longer trend of state centralization in Europe stretching as far back as the Middle Ages, but by the eighteenth century this process was aided by the emerging European Enlightenment. "Enlightened" political thinkers began to question traditional methods of governance and sought to remove the "inefficiencies" of the old systems. This questioning of the political status quo led some philosophers to advocate republicanism or even democracy, and others championed a new, more extreme form of regalism. These new regalists believed that, as Louis was attempting to do in France, all political power should be centralized in the institution of the monarchy. They sometimes even referred to their monarchies as "absolute," a concept derived from Roman law that absolved sovereigns from being subject to their own laws. In Spain, Bourbon regalist philosophy easily took root since, despite the challenges of ruling over such vast territories, Spain already had a long history of strong monarchical authority.[4]

To implement this regalist vision, royal ministers attempted to wrest power away from any institution that rivaled crown authority. Of particular interest to Bourbon reformers was the Catholic Church. The Church had been the crown's traditional partner in the governance of its many realms. Indeed, in a practical sense the Spanish Church functioned as an arm of the government. This was in part due to the *patronato real*, or royal patronage, which allowed the Catholic kings of Spain to nominate candidates for bishops within its territories and to control the tithe.[5] This authority over episcopal appointments gave the crown great influence over the principal hierarchy of the Church, which included archbishops, bishops, and parish priests, known as the "secular clergy." As Spain began the "spiritual conquest" of the Americas, however, large numbers of "regular clergy" traveled to the Americas. Regular clergy are men and women who follow a particular religious rule, or *regula*. In the Americas, these were mostly Franciscans, Mercedarians, Augustinians, Dominicans, and later Jesuits. Regular orders, with their zeal, internal organization, and discipline, contributed much to early colonization efforts. Consequently, the crown allowed the regular clergy to fulfill many of the duties normally reserved for the secular clergy, such as operating rural indigenous parishes.[6]

Although the regular clergy helped evangelize much of the New World, their presence created a dilemma for the monarchy. Except in regards to permissions to perform sacraments, regular religious orders were supranational organizations whose members answered not to local bishops but to their own leaders in Rome. These leaders, in turn, were ultimately accountable to the pope. Furthermore, for those clergy who ministered in faraway Spanish America, even Rome's authority was limited. Long distances made effective coordination difficult and left local provincial leaders with considerable autonomy.[7] As early as the reign of Philip II (r. 1556–98) in the late sixteenth century, the influence of the regular clergy had impeded crown efforts to extend royal power over the Church in the Americas.[8] As Bourbon government ministers began to advance regalist policies in the eighteenth century, the conflict over the king's inability to control the regular clergy in the Americas escalated. One of the more extreme regalist ministers quipped in 1765 that, "from the moment they [took] vows, [regular clergy] should be looked upon as foreigners."[9]

Regular clergy, according to regalist ministers, also stood in the way of the other principal aim of the reforms, the rehabilitation of the economy of the Spanish empire. Over the centuries, devout Catholics had donated money and large tracts of land to the clergy in both Spain and the Americas. Convents and monasteries used these resources to maintain themselves. During the eighteenth century, however, royal officials began to believe that the Church's hold on these vast resources adversely affected commerce throughout the empire. They argued that, if Church property could be put in the hands of commercial interests, it would be used more efficiently and create tax revenue. Though the Spanish crown already received a percentage of Church tithes, many in the royal government saw greater potential revenue in the sale of Church property. Some ministers even began to argue that monastic life removed too many individuals from the workforce, thereby damaging the economy. Convents and monasteries labored to worship God; they did not, ministers argued, help to further industry within the empire. Moreover, because of their vows of celibacy, regular clergy had no children and thus reduced the workforce of the next generation.[10]

In attacking the Church, royal officials had to tread lightly. Most were (or at least claimed to be) devout Catholics, and because the king's power derived from divine attribution they had to be careful in attacking God's servants on earth. Indeed, though these reforms were intended to weaken the political power of the Church, most reformers did not see their actions as anticlerical or antireligious. They understood that the clergy were an integral part of the Spanish empire. As the influential Italian regalist Ludovico Antonio Muratori stated in 1749, the state would be strong if "perfect and constant harmony [existed] between the *Sacerdocio* [clergy] and the *Imperio* [state]," and if "both [strove] together to deliver the people spiritual and temporal happiness."[11] Many royal ministers engaged in reform believed that by removing clerics from political power they would be allowing the clergy to focus on their principal duty, saving people's souls.

Ocopa, therefore, presented a difficult case to those in government trying to enact reform. On the one hand, to reformers they were ideal clerics. They were disciplined, considered more loyal since the majority were Spanish-born, and did not try to stunt productivity or soak up capital by maintaining large urban monasteries. Instead, they went out into the frontier to expand Spanish dominance through evangelization, potentially opening new lucrative markets. If the crown hoped to control frontier areas more effectively, they needed groups like Ocopa. On the other hand, Ocopa had become a powerful institution, wielding political influence locally, regionally, and across the Atlantic. Reformers struggled to decide how to approach the Ocopa missionaries; was it best to curtail their rising influence, or to aid them in their endeavors? Not surprisingly, over its 115-year colonial history Ocopa experienced often ambivalent treatment from reformist royal ministers.

These shifting and contradictory stances toward Ocopa demonstrate the importance of individuals and small groups both within and outside the Spanish bureaucracy in creating the changes experienced in the Spanish empire throughout the Bourbon period (1700–1824). Ocopa's interactions with the crown exposed many of the fissures between interested groups within the Spanish bureaucracy. Ocopa's history demonstrates how both the terms and the implementation of the so-called Bourbon reforms were negotiated at all levels of society among the indigenous peoples and enslaved Africans in the missions, the missionaries themselves, local government officials in and around the College of Ocopa and its missions, the viceregal seat in Lima, and the court in Madrid. Indeed, although these historical actors were indelibly influenced by ideas circulating around the Atlantic world, such as Enlightenment-inspired regalism, it was individuals' interpretations of those ideas that ultimately decided how events in the missions and throughout the Spanish empire unfolded. If the many royal ministers wanted to increase royal authority throughout the empire, it was with this reality that they had to contend.

Historical Trends in Mission History and the Bourbon Period

Over the past few decades, the scholarly field of mission history has seen a dramatic shift in focus and tone. Most of this dynamism is due to the emergence of what has been called "New Mission History" in the 1990s. Though some excellent studies on missions preceded this period, all too many were simply triumphal Eurocentric accounts authored principally by the clergy themselves. In contrast, New Mission scholars argued for refocusing the field of mission history on the indigenous peoples and provided invaluable ethnohistorical information about the indigenous groups in the frontiers of the Spanish empire. The best of these works include Cynthia Radding's *Wandering Peoples* and Susan Deeds's *Defiance and Deference in Mexico's Colonial North*. Both works examine identity and cultural resistance among native groups in northern Mexico.[12] This ethnohistorical approach still has an important presence in the field, as exemplified by Steven Hackel's 2010 edited volume on the California missions titled *Alta California*.[13] Many of these works are masterpieces of historical interpretation and research, though in their difficult quest to uncover information on previously unstudied, often undocumented groups they have often given insufficient attention to the missionaries who interacted with them.

There are many noteworthy exceptions to more recent indigenous-focused mission histories. Most prominent, David Weber's 2005 *Bárbaros* examines the motivations of various political and religious actors for attempting to "civilize" the Spanish American frontiers during the Bourbon period. He argues that previous historians have oversimplified Spanish behavior in the frontier, in many cases overlooking their Enlightenment-inspired desire for economic exploitation of the native population.[14] Similarly, David Block's 1994 *Mission Culture on the Upper Amazon* envisions frontier Jesuit missions among Moxo people in northern Bolivia as institutions with concrete political, economic, and social goals created by the intersection of missionary teachings, government policies, and local customs. Dealing in a later period, Erick Langer's 2009 monograph *Expecting Pearls from an Elm Tree* also explores the effects of the changing intellectual and political climates on frontier mission areas. He demonstrates how political shifts between liberal and conservative governments in nineteenth-century Bolivia shaped the cultural, political, and commercial interactions between missionaries and indigenous peoples.[15] In a similar vein to these works, this book looks to understand the wider political and intellectual context of the Ocopa missionaries' activities in the eastern Peruvian jungle. It is by no means an attempt to minimize or belittle the ethnohistorical approaches, or any studies focused on the indigenous inhabitants of the region. Quite the opposite, it seeks to be a companion to such works.

Even during the colonial period, the Ocopa missionaries obsessively wrote their own history. In most cases, these histories were persuasive devices designed to extract concessions of funds and land from the crown. Foremost among these is the chronicle written in the 1770s by José Amich, titled *Compendio Histórico de las conversiones de estas Montañas de Perú* (Historical compendium of the conversions of these jungles of Peru). As would be expected, *Compendio Histórico* painted the missionaries of Ocopa as pious emissaries sent to bring the word of God to the "infidels" of the eastern Peruvian jungle.

The work downplayed any deleterious effects of any actual reforms emanating from Madrid but was critical of several colonial officials' actions regarding the missionaries, particularly the failure of Peruvian viceroys to provide money and material promised to Ocopa by the crown. Amich's account became the basis for most of the later works on the Ocopa college by Franciscan historians. It was expanded in the early twentieth century by Ocopa missionaries Fernando Pallarés and Vicente Calvo to include a narrative of the history of the institution up until 1907.[16] Even into the 1920s, historians relied almost completely on Amich's account. Bernardino Izaguirre's 1929 *Historia de las misiones franciscanas* (History of the Franciscan missions) quotes Amich extensively.[17]

A significant change occurred in the historiography of Ocopa with the rise of Indigenismo, a revisionist movement in the 1920s and 1930s that attempted to glorify Peru's indigenous past. With this movement, most works began to focus not on missionaries' pious works, as the Franciscan histories had, but on the struggles of the indigenous populations who lived in the missions. In particular, historians turned to the most remarkable event of Ocopa's history, the Juan Santos Atahualpa rebellion. In 1942, José Loayza published a collection of documents related to the rebellion, *Juan Santos, el invincible.* In the introduction and footnotes to the volume, Loayza characterized the Ocopa missionaries as simply appendages of the state who blindly adhered to the Spanish colonial project. This conflation of all Spaniards into one homogeneous group was important to his overall nationalist commentary in the footnotes that accompany the documents. Loayza contended that the rebellion was a precursor to the creole-led independence movement of the 1820s. Steve Stern's 1987 article "The Age of Andean Insurrection, 1742–1782" more correctly places Juan Santos in its larger context of the indigenous-led, anticolonial revolts of the late Bourbon period.[18] In his attempt to construct a Marxist dialectic between oppressors and the oppressed, however, Stern still overlooks the nuances of the missionaries' place within the colonial regime.

The most comprehensive works on the Ocopa missions have tended toward ethnographic examination of the peoples encountered by the missionaries. Jay Lehnertz's 1974 dissertation, "Lands of the Infidels," looked at the indigenous groups in most of the regions evangelized by the Ocopa missionaries. Lehnertz's work, unfortunately, was preliminary, without the benefit of having been refined for publication, and tended toward a conclusion that missionaries had little impact on the societies they encountered—a conclusion that later ethnohistorians and anthropologists would contradict.[19] Indeed, some of the best work that has been done on the area evangelized by Ocopa, particularly the Peruvian central high jungle, or central Montaña, has come from anthropologists. Stefano Varese's *Salt of the Mountains* looks at one of the most prominent ethnic groups that Ocopa missionaries attempted to evangelize during their early expansion (1709–42), the Asháninkas. Though Varese's work is based on fieldwork done in the 1960s, he contextualizes the Asháninkas' cultural resilience to outside impositions within a long history of resistance that began with the missionizing efforts of Ocopa.[20] Fernando Santos-Granero has published several articles on the interaction of the Ocopa missionaries with the peoples of the Peruvian central Montaña, culminating in the book *Selva Central*, coauthored with Frederica Barclay. Again, like Varese's, this book details some of Ocopa's history and discusses the Juan Santos Atahualpa rebellion, but it focuses primarily on modern ethnic, political, and economic concerns in the region.[21]

Only one work thus far has attempted to place Ocopa in the larger political context of the Bourbon reforms. Pilar García Jordan's "Frustrada Reconquista de la Amazona Andina (1742–1821)" (The frustrated reconquest of the Andean Amazon) argues that, despite the Spanish crown's lackluster response to the Juan Santos Atahualpa rebellion, it was greatly interested for geopolitical reasons in the development of the Peruvian jungle frontier zone. Ocopa worked hand-in-hand with the crown to achieve that goal but ultimately failed because of infighting within the Franciscan order over the establishment of a Catholic diocese in the Peruvian jungle (the diocese of Maynas). This article is, however, preliminary and based solely on published sources, principally the relations of the viceroys, and tends to overlook the tension and animosities between the missionaries and viceregal government. These conflicts formed part of the larger debates circulating in the Spanish Atlantic as part of the reform process.

The historiography of the Bourbon reforms in Spanish America has focused on a series of related questions: To what extent did the reforms affect Spanish America? If affected, what were the mechanisms of change? Who was involved in the process?[22] Early works on the subject saw the Bourbon reforms as a top-down process, executed by peninsular bureaucrats. John Lynch, in his 1973 classic synthesis of the Spanish American revolutions, called the reforms "the new imperialism" and the "second conquest of America." Shortly thereafter, historians began to question this paradigm. As John Fisher queried in 1982: "Did [the Bourbon reforms] really comprise the smooth, coherent masterly program of imperial change and revival that generations of commentators, from the very imperial policymakers of eighteenth-century Spain to the researchers of today, have identified? Might they not be more realistically depicted in terms of halting, uncertain, inconsistent desire for imperial modernization and centralization, characterized more by delay, contradiction, and obstruction than by decisiveness?"[23]

Fisher's doubts were soon supported by several studies, especially those by Allan J. Kuethe and Jacques Barbier, which showed the reforms to be not only "halting, uncertain, [and] inconsistent" but very much a reaction to circumstances both economic and military on the ground and therefore varied by region.[24] More recently, Barbara and Stanley Stein, in the second volume of a trilogy on the Bourbon period, *Apogee of Empire,* have questioned whether the reforms, even at their height, were ever an attempt at a profound structural change to Spain's empire, or simply "calibrated adjustments" to maintain the exploitative colonial system.[25]

To evaluate the efficacy of the Bourbon reforms, many historians have turned to examining their financial impact, particularly in regard to royal revenue. Increasing remittances to Spain was one of the reformers' principal goals and can be seen as indicative of the crown's ability to increase its control over its American possessions. Like the reforms themselves, the results of these studies are much debated and contradictory. Alejandra Irigoin and Regina Grafe argue that reforms failed to revitalize royal revenue for the metropolis. Instead, they argue, the money was simply redistributed throughout the empire from economically robust regions like New Spain to declining regions like Cuba. This system of intercolonial dependency demonstrated the reformers' inability to fundamentally change the colonial system, which needed local elites to function. Irigoin and Grafe refer to the resulting accommodation as a "bargained absolutism."[26] Rafael Torres Sánchez, however, in an exhaustive study of the General Treasury of Madrid, has shown that there existed a steady flow of income into the royal coffers, particularly from New Spain, which could have enabled the government to maintain its reform agenda during the height of the reform period (1759–88).[27] Furthermore, James Mahoney, in a study of the transition between the colonial and independence eras, argues that the Bourbon reforms had a deep impact on the socioeconomic development of Spanish America and formed an essential factor in determining the differing economic trajectories of post-independence nations.[28] Though it is not the principal focus of this study, I indeed show the importance of increasing royal revenue and commerce to the reform process and demonstrate how concern for royal coffers affected government ministers' stances toward Ocopa.

Most recently, Kenneth Andrien and Allen Kuethe, in *The Spanish Atlantic World in the Eighteenth Century*, have tried to forge an interpretative middle path between the extremes of Bourbon reforms as a "second conquest" of Spanish America and as "bargained absolutism." Although reformers wanted to enact reform, they argue, these new policies conflicted with local political actors, viceregal officials, clergymen, and even subaltern groups in the various far-flung regions of the empire, leading to heterogeneous results throughout the whole of Spain's possessions. These fights were in turn complicated by dynastic desires for military expansion, which could accelerate or retard individual aspects of the reformist agenda.

The present volume attempts to expose debates of the Bourbon reforms at all levels of the social, political, and economic spectrum through the narrative of the missionaries of Ocopa. I borrow from a conceptualization of the Atlantic world pioneered by African historian Joseph C. Miller. Miller argues that the Atlantic world should not be conceived as a few discrete hierarchical empires managed effectively by European monarchies. Instead, it should be seen as numerous smaller autonomous communities engaged in multiple, mutually reconstituting encounters, which allowed them to find new places in emerging cultural contexts of their own creation. Therefore, although no one group could completely drive the course of events, every group held enough political, economic, and cultural influence to inhibit the autonomous initiatives of the others while pursuing its own discreet agenda.[29]

The Ocopa missionaries, then, were just one of many groups in the crucible of the empire, vying for political and economic power and autonomy. Though they believed themselves to be loyal subjects of the king, they did not function simply as agents of the government sent to extract local resources or manpower for Spain; they had their own spiritual and temporal objectives. They wanted to create a spiritual utopia, as they envisioned it, sustained with state funds but free from crown interference. Crown officials, though, had other objectives. In the eighteenth century these included the consolidation of royal authority and an increase in revenue. This vision was made even more complicated by fissures within Ocopa and the Spanish bureaucracy, as smaller factions of ministers and missionaries alike acted upon and enacted policies differently, according to their individual interpretations of regalism and Enlightenment ideals. In addition, indigenous ethnic groups and enslaved Africans residing in the missions reacted diversely to the historical processes happening around them and exerted their own influence on events. What happened in the missions was the result of the interactions between the different participants, each with its own discrete agenda. This complex negotiation of political power and cultural space dominated all interactions in the Americas. The narrative of the New World, therefore, cannot be summarized in terms of European interests in conflict with indigenous peoples, or competition between different European empires, but in a complex series of compromises among various and sometimes mixed groups of Africans, Europeans, and native peoples.

Organization of the Book

This book is divided into six principal chapters. Chapter 1 examines the first three decades of the Apostolic Institute's presence in Peru. In addition to looking at the establishment of the missionaries' permanent base at Ocopa, it tracks the rapid installation of two dozen mission stations in the Jauja, Tarma, and Huánuco frontiers. As part of this narrative, the chapter delves briefly into ethnohistory to illuminate the missionaries' difficulties with "converting" the local populace. It explores the friars' initial attempts to culturally assimilate the natives of the region into mission life and how and why these ethnic groups resisted their efforts, sometimes violently. At the same time, it looks at Ocopa's emerging relationship with the Spanish colonial bureaucracy at its various levels. Though Ocopa initially received promises of funding from the crown, a series of increasingly regalist viceroys refused to fund the group consistently. The ultimate goal of the chapter is to show how these early failures to aid Ocopa's evangelization efforts, combined with indigenous resistance to the missionaries' political, economic, and cultural impositions, led to instability in the missions, which was easily exploited by Juan Santos leading up to the rebellion in 1742.

Chapter 2 focuses on the events surrounding the Juan Santos Atahualpa rebellion. Specifically, it examines how the viceregal government ultimately failed to support Ocopa against the rebels. The first part of the chapter looks at why different and sometimes competing indigenous groups joined Juan Santos, a mestizo from the Andean highlands, against the missionaries. It narrates the initial expulsion and murder of Ocopa friars and the unsuccessful attempt by local militia to end the rebellion quickly. The chapter then looks at the larger geopolitical context of the rebellion, examining how the Lima earthquake and tsunami ultimately shaped the viceroy's decision to abandon attempts to dislodge Juan Santos from Ocopa's missions. At the same time, it uncovers the role that Ocopa's support for one of its former missionaries, Friar Calixto, played in kindling the viceroy's animosity toward the college. It ultimately argues that the viceroy ordered military efforts against Juan Santos abandoned, not because of strategic concerns but to limit the influence of Ocopa, which he saw as a threat to royal authority.

Chapter 3 in part continues chapter 2 by examining the aftermath of the viceroy's decision to cede most of Ocopa's missions to the Juan Santos Atahualpa rebels. The first part of the chapter looks at Ocopa's lobbying campaign in Madrid to force the viceregal government to commit enough supplies and manpower to expel Juan Santos. The missionaries' reputation for piety and obedience convinced crown officials to grant Ocopa essentially all its demands. But the viceroy refused to honor the crown's decree, remaining intransigent on the Juan Santos question, and instead halved the missionaries' stipend. This was motivated in part by the missionaries' continued support for Friar Calixto, whom the viceroy had arrested and forcibly removed to Spain for his alleged complicity in fomenting indigenous unrest against the government. Ultimately the viceregal government relented on the issue of the college's annual stipend, but it continued to hold Spanish forces in a defensive position along the frontier. As the chapter concludes, it examines how the rebellion affected the missionaries' stance toward the viceregal government and crown officials in general. Instead of remaining obstinate to viceregal efforts to curtail its autonomy, in reaction to these events Ocopa began the process of gradually ceding control of its operations to crown authorities, in particularly the viceroy, in exchange for increased material support.

Chapter 4 explores the resurgence of Ocopa after the Juan Santos Atahualpa rebellion. The relatively more pro-Franciscan atmosphere, caused in part by the ascension of Charles III to the Spanish throne, gave Ocopa enough money and resources from the crown to restart in earnest its evangelization efforts in the Peruvian Amazon. The missionaries were aided even more when, after the expulsion of the Jesuits, Ocopa received territory and property formerly controlled by the Society of Jesus. Its attempts to evangelize were not always successful, with one of them ending in another rebellion, yet Ocopa showed itself to be one of the most powerful Franciscan institutions in the New World. Ocopa needed this influence with the rise of new ideas regarding evangelization in the frontier. The "new method," as it was called, sought to evangelize through colonization and commerce with minimal involvement from the regular clergy. Though colonization in frontier regions was almost impossible, the reformers' emphasis on commerce and increased crown control on the frontier was becoming more common. Ocopa, at least at first, avoided most of these changes.

Chapter 5 explores the weakening of Ocopa's ability to resist government imposition because of philosophical changes from within its own ranks. As some of the missionaries themselves began to embrace reformist ideas such as evangelization through commerce, viceregal officials found a way to control Ocopa more effectively, through the voluntary participation of some of its own members. The end of this chapter recounts the election of the guardian of Ocopa in 1787, a moment when missionaries more aligned with reformist goals (later known as the Aragonese faction) took control of the leadership of the college with the help of the viceroy.

Chapter 6 explores Ocopa's history during the final three and a half decades of Spanish colonial rule in Peru. In many ways this period can be seen as the apogee of Ocopa's missionary enterprise under the control of the Aragonese faction. These new leaders fervently began to incorporate many of the economic and political principles behind the Bourbon reforms in their evangelization efforts. This new emphasis was in part an outcome of the new leaders' philosophical beliefs, but it was also implemented to please crown officials, who exercised more and more authority over the college. The new propaganda worked, and Ocopa was granted its largest concession from the crown to date, almost complete pastoral control over the newly created diocese of Maynas. Ocopa's success was, however, hollow, for miscommunication and incompetence in the Spanish bureaucracy led to confusion and dissension in the new diocese. The French invasion of Spain and the wars of independence ultimately sealed Ocopa's fate.

A short conclusion explores the nature of the clerical Bourbon reforms during the eighteenth and early nineteenth centuries. The goal of this section is to suggest further implications for Ocopa's history in an understanding of the processes that shaped the Atlantic world as a whole.

Notes

1. In this work, "Ocopa missionaries" refers to the Franciscan Apostolic missionaries who began establishing missions in the central high jungle regions of Tarma in 1709 under Fray Francisco de San Joseph. Though they did not occupy the Hospice, later College, of Santa Rosa de Ocopa until 1725, they were effectively a single entity to which most historians have retroactively applied the title "Ocopa."

2. On the concept of "composite monarchy," see Elliott, "Europe of Composite Monarchies."

3. For more on the seventeenth-century "Golden Age," see Andrien, *Crisis and Decline.*

4. For more on "absolute" monarchies, particularly in the seventeenth century, see Parker, *El siglo maldito,* 101.

5. Lynch, *Bourbon Spain,* 107–9, 187.

6. Paquette, *Enlightenment, Governance, and Reform,* 57–58.

7. Tibesar, "Suppression of the Religious Orders," 205–7.

8. Ibid., 208.

9. Marchese Grimaldi in a 1765 letter to Benardo Tanucci as cited in Paquette, *Enlightenment, Governance, and Reform,* 74.

10. Ibid., 64–70.

11. Ibid., 57.

12. For a distillation of the work of New Mission historians, see Langer and Jackson, *New Latin American Mission History.*

13. As well as Hackel, see Torre Curiel, *Twilight of the Mission Frontier;* and Smith and Hilton, *Nexus of Empire.*

14. Another more recent work that looks, in part, at other interlopers in the frontier areas of northern Mexico is McEnroe, *From Colony to Nationhood.* McEnroe examines the use of Tlaxcalans from the central valley of Mexico in Spanish attempts to "civilize" the north.

15. Even in *New Latin American Mission History,* which he coedited, Langer defends the importance of continuing to look at missionaries (see "Missions and the Frontier Economy: The Case of the Franciscan Missions among the Chiriguanos," ibid., 49).

16. The chronicle in its entirety, written by Amich, Pallarés, and Calvo, is found in a volume edited by Julián Héras, O.F.M., titled *Historia de las misiones del convento de Santa Rosa de Ocopa,* published in 1988.

17. Izaguirre, *Historia de las misiones franciscanas,* 39.

18. Chapter 2 of Stern, *Resistance, Rebellion, and Consciousness.*

19. Lehnertz, "Lands of the Infidels."

20. Varese's *Salt of the Mountain* was originally published in Spanish in 1968 under the title *La Sal de los Cerros.*

21. These articles include "Anticolonialismo, mesianismo, utopía en la sublevación de Juan Santos Atahualpa," and "Epidemias y sublevaciones en el desarrollo demográfico de las misiones Amuesha del Cerro de la Sal, siglo XVIII."

22. For more thorough discussion on the historiography of Bourbon reforms, see Kuethe and Andrien, *Spanish Atlantic World.* What appears below is a summary of their discussion focused on the parts pertinent to the topic at hand. There has also been much debate about when exactly the Bourbon reforms started in Spanish America. John Fisher

uses 1750 as the starting point to his masterful *Bourbon Peru*. He argues that inconsistencies of early reform made any real impact on Peru impossible during the first half of the eighteenth century. John Elliott in *Empires of the Atlantic World* contends that the Americas were largely unaffected by the Bourbon reforms until after the Seven Years' War (1756–63). He posits that, despite the creation of the new viceroyalty of New Granada in 1717 and then permanently in 1739, commitments in Europe made it impossible for Britain and Spain to impose reform in their American possessions. Although this argument allows Elliott to make a more direct connection between reforms in Spanish and British America after the Seven Years' War, it belies the fact that reforms began after the War of Spanish Succession (1700–1713).

More recent scholarship has begun to discuss the extent to which the Bourbon state began to enact reform in the Americas prior to the Seven Years' War. In *Shaky Colonialism*, Charles Walker argues that to Bourbon reformist ministers the 1746 Lima earthquake and tsunami exposed the baroque backwardness of the city. This realization inspired Bourbon officials both in Spain and Peru to enact a series of reforms to create a more modern enlightened city. Walker, however, stops short of calling this the beginning of the Bourbon reforms. He instead argues that, although these policies foreshadowed later reform, they in themselves had little lasting effect on Peru. Probably the most promising work on the early Bourbon reforms to date is Adrian Pearce's 1998 "Early Bourbon Government." Pearce argues that the early Bourbon period is the foundation of the later reforms in the Americas. He notes that all the major administrative structures necessary for later reform, such as the Ministry of the Indies, were created during the early Bourbon period and that the crown attempted financial, mining, military, and ecclesiastical reforms within the colonies themselves. Though, like Walker, Pearce believes that early Bourbon reforms were intermittent, he argues that they "followed a consistent, enlightened agenda" (abstract). As Pearce's work suggests, in this volume I start with the initial ascent of the Bourbon dynasty in Spain in 1700 in evaluating the entire scope of the reforms. I argue that aspects of both the early and late reform periods followed the same inconsistent pattern, with implementation dependent on the efforts of individuals and interested parties at given specific moments.

23. Fisher, "Soldiers, Society, and Politics," 117.

24. Ibid.; Kuethe, *Cuba, ;* Kuethe, "La deregulación commercial"; Barbier, "Culmination of the Bourbon Reforms," 51–68; Barbier, "Peninsular Finance and Colonial Trade," 21–37.

25. Stein and Stein, *Apogee of Empire,* 27. The other two works in the series are *Silver, Trade, and War* and *Edge of Crisis.* Also see their earlier, extremely influential work, *Colonial Heritage of Latin America,* for more on their views of the legacy of this system.

26. Grafe and Irigoin, "Spanish Empire and Its Legacy," 173. See also Grafe and Irigoin, "Bargaining for Absolutism."

27. Torres Sánchez, *La llave de todos los tesoros.*

28. Mahoney, *Colonialism and Postcolonial Development.*

29. Miller, "Retention, Re-Invention, and Remembering"; and Miller, *Way of Death.*

Chapter 1
The Birth of Ocopa, 1709–1742

The first thirty-three years of Ocopa's missionizing efforts in many ways implemented the same modus operandi as missionary enterprises that came before it. This "old method" (which I have dubbed to differentiate it from what reformers will later call the "new method") was based on the writings of the famous Dominican friar and "universal protector of the Indians," Bartolomé de las Casas (1484–1566). Las Casas insisted that "the only method to call the peoples to the true religion is that of Christ: the preaching of the Gospel by missionaries escorted by unarmed soldiers, sent 'like sheep among wolves.'"[1] The concept of peaceful conversion was later sustained by two royal decrees in 1550 and finally codified in 1573 under the *Ordenanzas sobre nuevos descubrimientos y poblaciones* (Ordinances regarding New Discoveries and Settlements). Though perhaps less bloody than during the initial invasion of America, evangelization after 1550 was in most cases far from peaceful. Many mission operations had learned from experience of the necessity for at least some armed protection. The "old method" as practiced in the frontiers of Spanish America shared two essential characteristics. One was that, although many missionary operations depended at least in part on state resources, both military and financial, expansion into the frontier was led by the missionaries themselves; they generally determined where and when mission stations were to be built and how best to deal with local populations. Additionally, at least rhetorically, the first priority of these expeditions was evangelization and conversion. Though the missionaries used commercial exploitation to help fund their enterprise or even turn a profit, at least publicly the priority was to save souls.

It was this "old method" that served as a baseline for the Ocopa missionaries as they expanded their enterprise in the Peruvian high jungle east of the Mantaro Valley. And though Ocopa's parent organization, the Franciscan-controlled Apostolic Institute, was in many senses a reform of the old ways, in practice the missionaries tended to borrow heavily from previous methods. Nevertheless, from the outset their enterprise differed in two important strategies: they recruited a majority of their missionaries directly from Spain, and they relied more heavily on crown funding. This freed them from local political quagmires that had retarded the growth of frontier missions elsewhere, but it also made them vulnerable to the subtle changes in attitudes regarding the governance of Spanish America. Generous grants of funding from Madrid gave Ocopa a certain measure of autonomy and a rising influence on a transatlantic stage. The ascendancy of such a prominent religious institute in Peru, however, clashed with the pressures many viceregal officials were feeling from Madrid to increase royal revenue and exert more authority over the colonial Church. Unsurprisingly, viceregal support for Ocopa was begrudging and inconsistent.

The vicissitudes of crown support were not Ocopa's only challenge during this early period. Creating the missionary enterprise itself was fraught with difficulties. Deep canyons, fast-flowing rivers, and near impassable terrain made penetrating and sustaining missionary operations in the region difficult. Most challenging, however, was overcoming the gulf of cultural difference to convince the local native populations to convert or at least live in mission villages. The missionaries, therefore, employed every method, both persuasive and often coercive, to attract reluctant natives to their missions. These attempts obviously created resentment among the native groups in and around the missions toward the friars. The indigenous peoples were further burdened by the emergence of European diseases to which the region had not previously been exposed. The result was numerous uprisings throughout Ocopa's missions. Although these pressures from both natives and viceregal authorities forged Ocopa into one of Spanish America's preeminent religious institutions, they would leave its missionary enterprise precariously vulnerable.

The Rise of the Apostolic Institute in Mexico and Its Arrival in Peru

The Catholic Church had a long tradition of missionary work, but two events that occurred within a few decades of each other created new urgency for more effective evangelization: the discovery of the Americas in 1492 and the Protestant Reformation starting in 1517. In Europe, the Council of Trent (1545–63) attempted to reform the Church from within in order to counter the spread of Protestantism, but conflicts among and between Protestant and Catholic nations, as well as infighting between the Catholic secular and regular clergies, led to more than a century of losing adherents to "heretical" faiths. To counter these losses, in 1622 Pope Gregory XV created the *Sacra Congregatio de Propaganda Fide* (Sacred Congregation of the Propagation of the Faith) to help coordinate Catholic missionary efforts throughout the world. The Congregatio was influential in helping reconvert large populations throughout Europe, particularly in eastern Europe, but it dealt also with missionary efforts in Africa and Asia. Almost immediately after its conception the Congregatio began to establish colleges *de propaganda fide*, the first in Rome in 1628, to train more effective missionaries. In the Iberian Peninsula the burden of erecting such institutions was taken up mostly by Franciscans, and in Spain the order had built nine colleges before 1700.[2]

In the Americas, though evangelization had been an essential tool in Spanish colonization, the patronato real had prevented the Congregatio from taking control of missionary efforts after 1622 as it had done virtually everywhere else on the globe.[3] The regular religious orders, which were at least in theory directed from Rome, remained at the core of missionary ranks in the New World, but the crown jealously blocked the Congregatio for fear that it would further weaken its control by letting another foreign institution make decisions regarding Spain's American affairs. By the late seventeenth century, however, stagnation in missionary efforts throughout the Spanish empire caused a growing concern among many in the Spanish Church, leading them to believe that the Congregatio model of establishing colleges to train missionaries could help to revitalize missionary efforts in Spanish America. In 1682, Friar Antonio Llinas, a native of Mallorca with more than twenty years of missionary experience in Mexico, presented to the crown a plan to erect a series of colleges de propaganda fide in Spain's overseas territories under the auspices of the Franciscan order. The plan would create a new "Apostolic Institute" that would function in conjunction with the Congregatio in Rome but be under the Franciscan order's general leadership within the Spanish empire. The Institute's missions would also be manned principally by peninsular friars, on the argument that such Spaniards would be free of the local corruption and intrigue that had plagued local regular institutions. The king approved the measure, and on the 7 April 1682 Pope Innocent XI issued a papal bull forming the Apostolic Institute. On 15 August of the next year, the monastery of Querétero in Mexico became the first college de propaganda fide in the Americas. By 1700 the Institute had established three more colleges in Mexico.[4]

Colleges de propaganda fide in America functioned in many ways outside of the normal Franciscan leadership structure. Once a monastery received the "de propaganda fide" status, it was no longer accountable to the local Franciscan province in which it resided. Only the commissary-general of the Indies who resided in Spain had complete jurisdiction over the colleges.[5] Even before the Apostolic Institute could establish a college in a particular region, the commissary-general selected a special "commissary of missions" to direct missionary endeavors. These commissaries rarely sought the direction of provincial leadership, and, at least in Peru, a general animosity festered between the provinces and the Apostolic Institute.[6] The makeup of the Institute also caused conflicts. The Franciscan province in Peru, for example, consisted of almost 80 percent creoles by the eighteenth century, yet the Institute recruited heavily from the colleges de propaganda fide already established or founded for this purpose in Spain. From 1709 to 1823, 73 percent of the missionaries that served in Ocopa were peninsulars. These friars had studied theology at the colleges in Spain for at least two years before they were deemed worthy for American missionary service.[7]

Funding the missions also presented the Institute with particular challenges. As mendicants, Franciscans depended on the alms of the faithful to maintain their ministry. These at times included rents from property and businesses donated to the friars by local devotees. Establishing a brand new religious community dedicated to preaching to regions not yet, at least nominally, converted to Catholicism meant that the Institute could not depend solely on these traditional sources of income. Most colleges required some form of state funding, not just for the transport of peninsular missionaries from Spain to the Americas but for their day-to-day maintenance. The colleges, therefore, despite their relationship with the Congregatio in Rome, were extremely reliant on the Spanish crown.[8]

In 1708, Friar Francisco de San Joseph brought the Apostolic Institute to Peru. Francisco de San Joseph, born Melchor Francisco Jiménez in 1654 in the Spanish village of Mondéjar near Toledo, served six years as a soldier in the Spanish army in Flanders as a young man. It is not known whether he saw action, but Spain's involvement in the Franco-Dutch War (1672–78) during roughly the same period that he was in Flanders suggests the possibility. Upon returning to Spain, young Melchior found his vocation, taking the habit as a Franciscan in the monastery of San Julián near Burgos and renaming himself Francisco de San Joseph. In 1692 at the age of thirty-eight, San Joseph sailed to Mexico in the service of the Apostolic Institute. He stayed two years at Querétero before leaving for Guatemala City, where he aided in establishing a community of missionaries that later became a college de propaganda fide. San Joseph stayed in Guatemala City only a few months before he left to proselytize among the "infidel" nations of the Urinamas, Chaguenes, and Terrabas in what is now Costa Rica. In 1708, Friar Francisco Esteves, commissary of propaganda fide missions in the Americas, made San Joseph his vice-commissary and sent him to Lima with six other missionaries to extend the Apostolic Institute into Peru. Once in Peru the missionaries traveled through the central sierra region near Huamanga (modern-day Ayacucho) for a year, preaching to the local population. It was during these travels that the missionaries learned about several abandoned missions in the high jungle east of Tarma. In 1709 the intrepid group entered the high jungle through the Chanchamayo River valley and established two small mission reductions at Quimirí and Cerro de la Sal (figures 1, 2).[9]

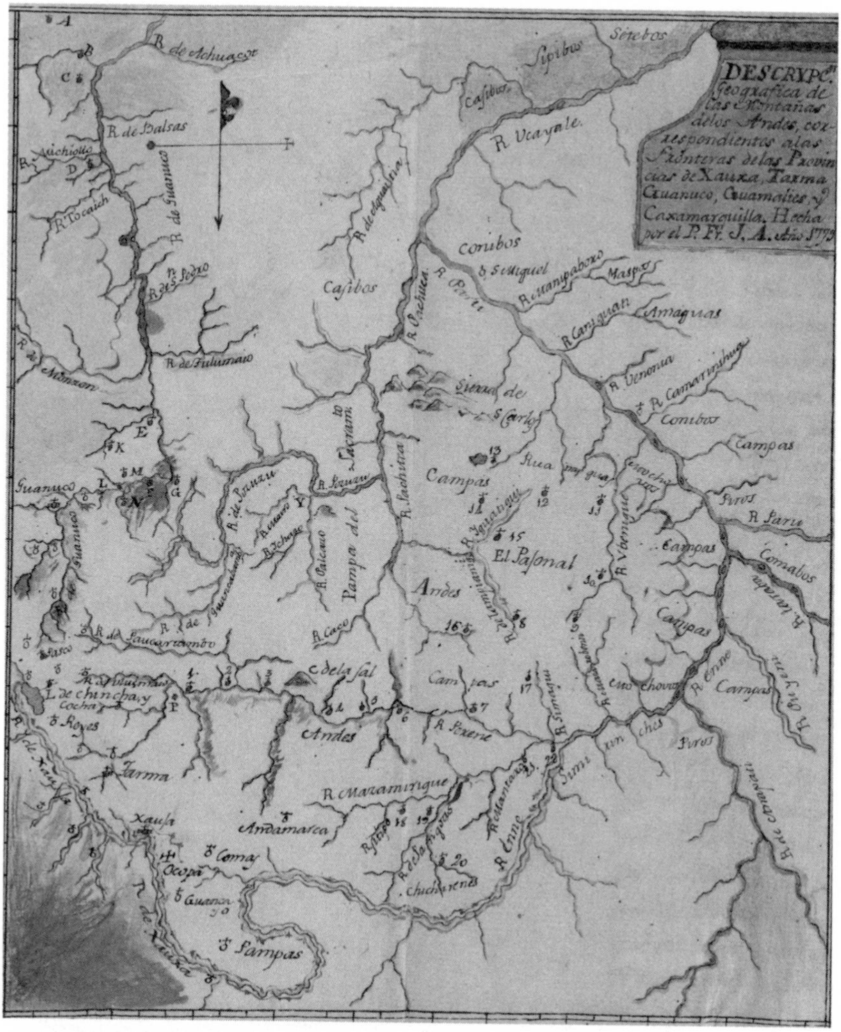

FIGURE 1. José Amich's map of the Montaña, 1779. 1, Quimirí; 2, Nijándaris; 3, La Sal; 4, Metraro; 5, Eneno; 6, Pichana; 7, Autes (San Tadeo); 8, Tampintaqui; 9, Aporoquiaqui; 10, Tiguanasqui; 11, Camansqui; 12, Cuichasqui; 13, Pixintoqui; 14, Caretequi; 15, Capotequi; 16, Savirosqui; 17, Quispango; 18, Sonomoro; 19, Savini; 20, Parua; 21, Catalipango; 22, Jesús María H. Pozuzu. "Descripción Geografía de las Montaña de los Andes," RAH, 9-9-1731, f. 433 (613).

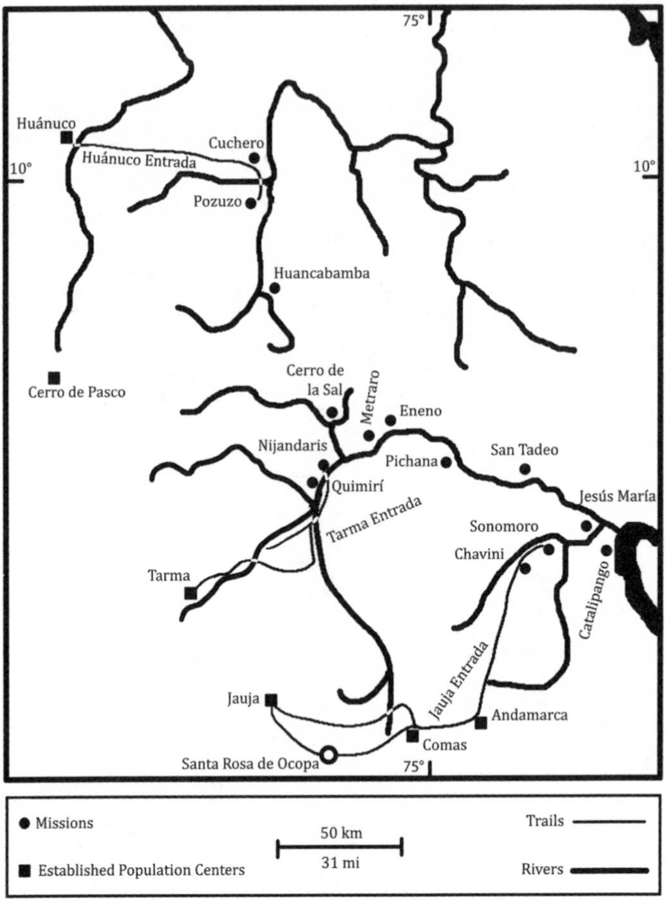

FIGURE 2. The missions of Jauja, Cerro de la Sal (Tarma), and Huánuco. Map courtesy of William G. Silva. Reproduced with artist's permission.

The Challenges of the First Mission Stations

The area in which Francisco de San Joseph and his companions entered was considered at the time to be one of the most inhospitable regions of the Americas. A viceroy in the mid-eighteenth century described the region as a "vegetated hell."[10] The eastern arm of the Andes mountain range made access to the region extremely difficult. Only where relatively large rivers transected this rocky curtain wall could the missionaries enter. These river valleys were commonly referred to as *entradas* (entrances) and were generally named for the closest provincial capital. As time went on these entradas became synonymous with the missionary zones that were accessed through them, and consequently many colonial writers alternatively refer to them by the name of the most important mission in the region.[11] Both in the modern and colonial vernacular, Peruvian (as well Spanish) officials used the word *Montaña* (Mountain) to describe the eastern jungle region of Peru, where the rocky, sparsely vegetated highlands give way to densely forested tropical landscapes. Most of the Montaña is dominated by river plains with high arboreal canopies. Only the regions closest to the Andes are marked by mountainous terrain. This *ceja de selva,* or eyebrow of the jungle, as it is commonly known, is probably one of the most impassable geographic areas in South America. Not only does its verticality make its rivers unnavigable, but its lack of high tree canopies allows for a dense ground cover of smaller trees and bushes. Only its proximity to the highlands made it an attractive site for attempts at evangelization during the eighteenth century.[12]

If the terrain of the region was not enough to dissuade the missionaries from entering the Montaña, the oppressively hot climate and hazardous animal life presented more difficult challenges. Daytime temperatures in the Peruvian jungle hover around 90°F with an almost constant humidity of 90 percent. Because of its proximity to the equator, daily temperatures vary little throughout the year, giving its inhabitants no seasonal reprieve as in higher latitudes. Seasons are marked by the yearly rains that begin in November and continue through March. During the rainy season the jungle receives more than one hundred inches of rain, making any sort of travel during these months virtually impossible. Therefore, missionaries in distant mission stations could expect to be isolated from the outside world for nearly half of the year.[13] The hot, wet conditions also were a breeding ground for mosquitoes. José Amich, Ocopa's chronicler who experienced the Montaña firsthand complained, "The infestation of the mosquitos is a very great torment; because . . . they do not permit a moment of rest, especially in the swampier valleys. It is necessary to cover yourself completely . . . [and with] luck the heat will not suffocate you."[14] Other fauna of the Montaña also proved difficult to manage. In several missives the missionaries complained about the "wild beasts" of the jungle, including poisonous ants and snakes.[15] In the burial records of one of their mission stations, the friars even recorded that one of their converts had been killed by a "tiger," probably a jaguar.[16]

Even before the arrival of the Spanish, however, the border between the highland and the jungle had been extremely porous. Trade flowed between the two regions. In particular, coca, used in highland Andean rituals as well as to fortify workers for daily labor at high altitudes, formed the basis of commerce between the regions. After the Spanish colonization of the Americas, the crown did not have an official presence in much of the Montaña, and networks of commercial and cultural exchanges persisted.[17] The crown's relationship with Montaña nations in most cases was mediated through the highland Andeans, as evident in the Spanish vocabulary to describe the Montaña and its inhabitants. Colonial correspondence, for example, frequently used the word *chuncho,* which is Quechua for "monkey," to describe particularly aggressive nations.[18]

Despite this long-standing relationship between the highlands and the Montaña, there were few organized attempts to colonize the area of Ocopa's first missions before the seventeenth century. This was most likely due to a lack of motivation to overcome the obvious physical and cultural barriers the region presented. Though coca plantations functioned in the margins between the highlands and the Montaña and trade did trickle through, there was no real financial incentive to do much more. According to anthropologists Fernando Santos-Granero and Frederica Barclay, interest in the region was spurred during the seventeen century by the rise in silver production in the nearby Cerro de Pasco mines. The relative prosperity created by the mining boom, they argue, allowed local elites to exploit their interests in the high jungle, particularly the expansion of coca farming. Nonetheless, Santos-Granero and Barclay concede that expansion was not solely due to financial incentives but to the missionaries' religious fervor as well.[19]

Indigenous resistance did, however, assure that what few expeditions attempted to penetrate the region in the seventeenth century failed to establish a continuous missionary presence. In 1635 a lay friar named Jerónimo Jiménez, most likely following existing trade networks, entered the Montaña through the Tarma entrada and founded a small chapel in the village of Quimirí along the banks the Chanchamayo River. Two years later members of the Asháninka nation killed Friar Jerónimo as he tried to penetrate farther into the high jungle. Four years later two other Franciscans attempting to enter the Montaña through the Tarma entrada met the same fate. In 1673 the Franciscans made a second attempt to establish a mission at Quimirí but were forced to retreat a year later when a local cacique named Mangoré attacked the missionaries. Mangoré also destroyed a burgeoning Franciscan mission at Sonomoro in the Jauja entrada established that same year by Friar Manuel Biedma. Biedma returned to Sonomoro in 1681 but was killed six years later by members of the Conibo nation, leading to the Franciscans' eventual withdrawal from the mission. In 1689, Franciscan friar Blas Valera attempted once again to establish a mission in the Tarma entrada at the Cerro de la Sal, but this mission had disappeared by 1694.[20] All in all, by 1716 the friars were claiming that missionary work in the region had created fifty-five martyrs.[21] Although these patterns of missionary expansion, native unrest, and retreat foreshadowed events in the eighteenth century, in 1709 the Franciscans hoped that the Apostolic Institute's political connections and singular focus on missionary work would have a more lasting impact on the region.

The Franciscans were not the only regular order to attempt to evangelize the region. The Dominicans had long-standing ties to the Chanchamayo River valley (which formed part of the Tarma entrada) since they maintained a sugar plantation along the upper part of the valley.[22] In 1699 they attempted to take up where the Franciscans had left off, establishing missions in Quimirí, Cerro de la Sal, and farther down the river at Eneno. They hoped that these reductions would serve as a barrier to raids on their plantation. Like the Franciscans, however, the Dominicans were forced to retreat.[23] Nevertheless, even as late as 1717 the Dominicans had not given up on their designs for the region, requesting funds from the crown to recommence missionary work in the Chanchamayo River valley.[24]

Within four years the Franciscan Apostolic missionaries were well entrenched in the region. In a letter to the crown in 1713 requesting funds for his new enterprise, San Joseph claimed that in the Tarma entrada they had 585 montañeses living "under the bell" at Quimirí, 112 of who were already baptized, not counting those who had died of smallpox. They also had a permanent settlement at Cerro de la Sal and another with six hundred inhabitants at Eneno, though they had temporarily abandoned Eneno because of rumors of native unrest. They had reentered the Jauja entrada as well, establishing mission stations at Sonomoro, Chavini, and El Carmen (see figures 1, 2). The missionaries also had begun evangelizing farther north in the Montaña, pushing into an entrada north of the highland city of Huánuco. San Joseph claimed that previous missionaries had baptized in excess of 30,000 natives in the Huánuco entrada, but that they currently had only three hundred in one mission station at Pozuzu, and only forty-seven of those were baptized.[25] The expansion of the Apostolic Institute's missions was enough to convince the archbishop in 1716 to grant the Ocopa missionaries the faculties of a parish priest, allowing them to administer the sacraments of the Eucharist and marriage within their congregations.[26]

Despite several studies on the subject, the exact ethnographic makeup of the region during the eighteenth century is difficult to discern. This is due principally to a failure of the missionaries themselves to categorize the indigenous nations they encountered in any standardized manner. Missionaries and other external colonial observers alternatively differentiated groups using ethnic, linguistic, and geographic denominations. One Montaña nation could have three separate names used interchangeably throughout the documents, though in all fairness to the missionaries modern academics still debate just how to categorize some Montaña ethnic groups. Frequently missionaries used names that ethnographers cannot match to known groups, perhaps through a misunderstanding of the ethnic composition of the group, or because that particular ethnicity was subsequently obliterated by disease or war, or simply as a mistranslation or alternate spelling of a given ethnic designation. Though at times missionaries tried to identify the ethnicity of the groups they encountered, more often they categorized the natives by their status within the Catholic faith.[27] Missionaries referred to those who had accepted the friars' teachings as "converts" or "Christians" and those who resisted the missionization as "infidels" or "chunchos."[28]

According to Friar José Palos, the provincial minister in Lima who visited the newly formed Apostolic missions in 1716, in the region lived "Amages, Campas, Autes, Siminche, Callisecas, Coñinos, Citipos, Carapachos, and Mochonos Indians."[29] Census records, however, demonstrate that the early mission stations were inhabited almost completely by two jungle nations, the Ande or Campa nation (known today as the Asháninkas) and the Amuesha, Amage, or Mage nation (known today as the Yaneshas). Both Asháninka and Yanesha peoples spoke dialects of the Arawak language family, which had penetrated the Amazon basin from the Caribbean in about the first millennium B.C.E.[30] It seems that at least in some cases Asháninkas and Yaneshas cohabited the same mission. In a census taken in the mission of Eneno probably around 1737 by the cacique Mateo Quillmoch de Assia, of the 151 inhabitants of the mission sixty-two are identified as Yanesha and fifty-one as Asháninka. The remaining thirty-eight inhabitants' ethnicity was not declared. The cacique Assia, a Yanesha, listed his wife as Asháninka, whom he may have chosen to better lead the biethnic community.[31] As the missionaries began to expand deeper into the Jauja and Tarma entradas, however, they encountered other jungle Montaña nations, such as the Piros (another Arawak-speaking group). In the Huánuco entrada most of the inhabitants were Yaneshas, but as the missionaries neared the floodplain of the Ucayali River they began to encounter Cashibos, Shipibos, and Conibos who spoke dialects of the Panoan language family.[32]

The missionaries recorded very little about the appearance, social interactions, or culture of the people of the Montaña. According to what scarce records exist on the subject, the natives were short by European standards, with dark skin and black hair. They commonly painted their faces and wore a *cushma*, a type of cotton tunic usually dyed with achote. In describing their culture, the missionaries tended to emphasize their "sinful" behavior, stating that the montañeses practiced incest, excessive drinking, and devil worship among other "pernicious" acts. Many times these enumerations of the natives' cultural poverty were discursive tools to draw contrasts between Christianized and non-Christianized natives and to demonstrate the superiority of Hispanic Catholic culture.[33] Even among the converted, some "vices" were difficult to root out, in particular polygamy. Montaña nations also tended to have dispersed populations. Poor jungle soil made it difficult for large numbers to live in one centralized village, so most of the year they lived in small family groups and came together with others only for trade or mutual protection.[34] This way of life was anathema to the town-dwelling Spaniards. In particular, the missionaries feared that if converts lived too far from the missions they would easily slip back into their previous "idolatries."[35]

Methods of Conversion

In 1718 the Franciscan procurator-general over the Indies, Friar Francisco Seco, marveled at the rapid growth of the Institute's missionary enterprise:

> [The missionaries have] baptized one thousand and seventy-seven people between adults and infants. They have two hundred and sixty-five catechumens, which consist of two hundred and nine families. They penetrated and opened more than eighty leagues of land into [the jungle]. They have made three large bridges, one with two spans. They fabricated nine churches and three hermitages or chapels. To sustain their dependents, they have two hundred and forty-six sheep; also birds [probably chickens], and lesser cattle, as well as planted fields: almost fifty thousand feet of bananas, whose fruit serves as bread.[36]

Such an impressive growth within only ten years raises the question how the missionaries drew so many people into their missions. For one, the missionaries maintained strategic control of the salt deposits at the aptly named Cerro de la Sal (Mountain of Salt). Salt was a vital resource for native groups throughout the entire jungle. Since the rainy season made fishing in the swollen rivers impossible six months of the year, jungle inhabitants needed to preserve and stockpile fish during the dry season to maintain a supply of protein year round. The only preservative to which they had access was salt, and without it they suffered from severe starvation. Salt was so important that some ethnographers have dubbed it the currency of the jungle.[37] Though many, including the first Franciscans to the region, knew of the Cerro de la Sal's existence and importance, it was not until 1645 that a military expedition led by Captain Francisco Bohorquez was sent in an attempt to control it. This force was able to subdue the indigenous population around the Cerro de la Sal for a short time, but the local montañeses eventually forced them out. In 1685, Manuel Biedma wrote extensively on the importance of controlling the salt depots militarily. To control the deposits, he advocated that the crown donate an *encomienda,* a grant of indigenous labor, to a wealthy Spaniard who would sell the salt only to Montaña nations who had obtained licenses from the missionaries.

The natives of the Montaña were not ignorant of either the strategic importance of this resource or the missionaries' plans for cornering the market. According to San Joseph, when the Apostolic Institute first arrived in the Tarma entrada in 1709, its initial efforts to find the salt deposits were thwarted by local caciques who instructed their followers not to reveal its location.[38] As San Joseph writes, however, "After two years, in which we suffered immense labors, exploring various regions, evangelizing numerous nations, we fortunately discovered this desired mountain, and reduced, with our Catholic doctrine, its inhabitants, so that we could communicate with the rest of the gentile nations, which appear in copious troops and many fleets of rafts to carry the salt down the river."[39] After the mountain's discovery, San Joseph moved quickly to secure the deposits and constructed two forts at Quimirí and Cerro de la Sal. Indeed, it was no coincidence that the first three missions the Institute established in the region were at Quimirí, located along an access road from the salt deposits to the highlands; Cerro de la Sal, the actual site of the deposits; and Eneno, the river port closest to the deposits where most indigenous traders moored their boats.[40] With the construction of these three missions, in theory, native parties coming up to extract salt or trade had to interact with the missionaries. Some crown officials, however, doubted that the missionaries did or could ever effectively control the deposits, because of the large area over which they were spread.[41] Certainly not every native group in the area was forced to receive the missionaries in order to gain access to salt, but their presence was probably enough to disrupt indigenous commercial networks.

Another way the Apostolic Institute attracted the Montaña natives to live in their missions was by distributing steel farming implements to them. As one friar stated, the missionaries had found a "docile people, easily impressed with the Catholic faith," but their conversion was aided "with the assistance of giving them tools for the cultivation of their fields."[42] Steel tools, particularly machetes, axes, and knives, were invaluable for the type of slash-and-burn agriculture prevalent in the jungle. The poor jungle soil made farming in one field year after year impossible. Montañeses had to clear new fields every few years, cutting down the trees and underbrush and burning them to fertilize the soil. Steel implements greatly increased the speed of preparing fields and the size of fields that could be cultivated, allowing for a greater abundance of food. The missionaries allowed those who came to the missions to use the tools for several weeks during the planting season, thereby attracting more settlers who they hoped would eventually convert.

The missionaries were careful to lend the tools only temporarily to the montañeses, likely for two reasons.[43] The Franciscan leadership feared that this type of quid pro quo relationship would lead to false conversions; the Franciscan province of the Twelve Apostles of Lima prohibited friars from giving gifts to potential or recent native converts over this very concern.[44] Additionally, though it seemed to contradict the prior reasoning, was that missionaries wanted the indigenous inhabitants of the missions to remain dependent on them and therefore stay in the mission communities. The missionaries' policy of lending tools, of course, did not always work.[45] Several missionaries complained that the montañeses would come to the missions and give obedience to the missionaries, perhaps even be baptized, in order to obtain tools and then simply leave. They cited the natives' great "greed" for the tools as one of the reasons that seemingly docile mission Indians rose up in rebellion against the missionaries. Missionaries claimed that rebel leaders incited the people of the Montaña against them so that they could steal their tools. Certainly the value of these tools in providing food for their families was a powerful incentive to obtain them by whatever means necessary.[46] Despite these concerns, however, the Apostolic Institute continued this method of attracting souls to its missions throughout the colonial era.[47]

It is likely that the missionaries did not actually draw such large numbers of montañeses to the missions as they claimed, at least living ones, since one of the other ways the missions augmented the number of people they reported to have baptized was the compulsory baptism of dying natives. Baptism *in artículo mortis* (at the moment of death) was a common practice among Catholics throughout the early modern world. They believed that without baptism cleansing the soul from sin (in the case of children the original sin of Adam and Eve) the soon-to-be departed would most certainly go to hell. Though the missionaries were trying to build spiritual utopias on earth, they believed that such deathbed conversions were, in the eternal perspective, just as important as the salvation of those destined to live on. These "numerous" imminent-death conversions were certainly a factor in missionaries' arithmetic that claimed they had converted 10,000–12,000 souls, though this still was certainly an exaggeration.[48]

These supposed conversions did little to build up the mission communities. Nevertheless, the missionaries tried to use such death-bed conversions as a discursive tool to convince government officials to fund the missions. They could then claim not only that had they brought hundreds into the "Christian life" in the missions in a short amount of time, but also that they had saved thousands from the fires of hell, fulfilling the empire's goal of converting its inhabitants to the "true faith," dead or alive. Although this argument was probably lost on many Spanish officials, claiming that they had baptized tens of thousands was much more impressive than the several hundred supposed converts that actually lived in the missions.[49]

Delineating the missionaries' coercive methods, however, begs the question of whether any of the montañeses were convinced by the friars and truly converted to the Catholic faith. The debate about whether the native population of the Americas could be completely converted to Catholicism had a long and tortured history, especially in the Andes. Spanish officials had early on in the colonial period made the native population of the Americas immune from prosecution by the Inquisition because they believed them incapable of "true conversion"—which presumably meant practicing the faith just like a Spaniard, a contested concept itself but certainly devoid of any native tradition or practice. In Peru, however, a series of rather doctrinaire archbishops ignored this directive, and several attempts to root out "idolatries" by force were attempted over the seventeenth century.[50]

The Ocopa missionaries certainly thought that some of the conversions resulting from their evangelization efforts were at least sincere if not complete. To prove it, in 1713 San Joseph sent a letter to the crown recounting several stories of natives' miraculous conversions and stalwart devotion. He claimed that when he arrived in the Montaña he encountered a group of Christians who had been baptized by a previous expedition and had hidden themselves in the remote village of Potocuatros because of fear of the "tyrannies" of the other montañeses. There they had a church and continued to practice baptism on each other. He also recounted that, in another village when the small chapel the missionaries had built caught fire in their absence (though he does not say how the fire started), the village women, at great risk to their own lives, saved the altar and all the images of the saints. Then he told the story of a cacique who, having broken his leg, asked for his men to find a missionary so he could be baptized, presumably so that if he died his soul would not go to hell.[51]

Demonstrating that any Montaña natives were completely and honestly converted to Catholicism because they were convinced by the friars' message is of course impossible. No personal writings of any montañés from the period survive (and probably never existed). Certainly even the most devout converts did not understand Catholic Christianity in the hispanicized manner that the missionaries would have wanted; they retained a hybridized belief based on their own previous religion and cultural environment. What can be demonstrated, nonetheless, is a preference among some the people of the Montaña for the missionaries. Missionaries spent months or years alone in isolated villages, where in many cases the local population fed and maintained them, even through several famines. According to the missionaries some montañeses died for their beliefs as well; they claimed that 233 Christianized natives were "martyred" between 1634 and 1737.[52] Certainly at least some of these "martyred" could have joined rebel groups attacking the missions but instead chose to die with the missionaries. In several rebellions between 1709 and 1742, after groups of discontented natives attacked the mission, other mission converts formed war parties to go after the rebels.[53] Even during the Juan Santos Atahualpa rebellion (1742–52) many Christianized montañeses died in defense of the missions. Also, many of the inhabitants of the Sonomoro mission relocated to the highlands so that, according to Amich, they did not have to abandon their Catholic faith.[54] Whether these actions were completely free of any sort of coercion is, of course, unknowable. Social pressure within each village from Christianized caciques or some type of dependency on the missionaries certainly informed their decisions.[55] In difficult, life-threatening moments, however, some chose to stay with the missionaries and be identified as Christians.

Life in the Missions

The Ocopa friars attempted to control most aspects of life in the missions, concentrated on religious activities. The municipal laws of the Yanesha mission of Pozuzu, probably written in the 1760s but most likely in effect much earlier, laid out a rigid schedule of church attendance and devotion. Every morning the community gathered and the missionary designated as the mission's priest led them in the rosary. On Sundays, Wednesdays, Fridays, and Saturdays every native in the community was required to attend mass in the afternoon. The procession of the *Capac Eterno* (probably another name for Jesus Christ; *capac* means "powerful" or "prince" in Quechua, and *eterno* is Spanish "eternal") preceded each mass, which ended with a sermon.[56] The missionaries took attendance at each ceremony and whipped those who were absent without permission—three lashes for the first offense, six for the second, and twelve for the third. If the truancy continued, the offending person was placed in stocks. The mission natives were also charged with the care and maintenance of the church and the main square. Every Saturday the married men and widowers brought firewood to the church. Those who did not were to be punished by whipping. The married women cleaned the plaza and the widows the church, while the young women set out flowers on the sacristy and crosses. In Pozuzu there were three principal feast days: the mission's patron saint, St. Anthony of Padua (13 June), Corpus Christi (sometime between May and June), and the Assumption of the Virgin Mary (15 August). The singing of hymns, mass, and other religious festivities celebrated these feasts. Other holy days such as Christmas, Ash Wednesday, Good Friday, and Easter were also observed with religious ritual. Though the temporal aspects of the community were in theory run by the community leaders, at least according to the laws of Pozuzu, the missionaries chose those leaders.[57] How closely the community adhered to these guidelines remains uncertain. Detailed explanations of what punishments the mission inhabitants received for each omission, however, suggest that punishments were meted out regularly and that the Montaña converts resisted the rigid mission lifestyle.

The sole surviving confession manual from the Ocopa missions, written in Pozuzu in 1764, also reveals the missionaries' concerns for their flock's eternal soul. They encouraged the inhabitants of Pozuzu to confess their sins once a week on Sundays, which the Yaneshas probably did in their own language, since the manual, written in both Spanish and Yanesha, was devised to help the missionaries learn the questions in the local dialect. Though the manual was written in 1764, the author claimed that it was an update of an older version that had contained Yanesha terms that had fallen out of use (perhaps as the friars learned more about the Yanesha language and culture).[58] Many of the questions in the manual were rather standard for confession: "Do you lie?" "Do you steal?" "Do you desire to kill your spouse?" The missionaries were, however, particularly concerned with sexual sins. These questions certainly reflected the vast gulf between Catholic and native Montaña sexual mores, which it seems the Yaneshas of Pozuzu struggled to bridge. The manual instructed the priest to ask whether the women stared at men at church or made signals to them with their tongues, eyes, or mouths. One question even asked women, "Have you ever uncovered your breasts to appear good [more attractive] to a man?" Confessants were asked if they had committed adultery and to detail with whom and the number of times. The manual's author seemed particularly preoccupied with incestuous sexual relationships, which missionaries believed to be prevalent in Montaña cultures.[59]

The confession manual also attempted to confront potentially destructive beliefs and behaviors to mission life. Some of these threatening elements included "heretical" beliefs that resulted either from the persistence of Yanesha culture or a hybridization with Catholicism. Mission priests asked confessants whether they believed in dreams; if they heard a bird cry did they think someone was going to die, or if they spat on their hand to know the truth of something, or whether they worshiped the moon. Most important, however, the priests were instructed to press the villagers about their relationships with the Cimarrones, the rebellious montañeses outside the missions.[60] This was particularly important in Pozuzu since the missionaries moved many of the most faithful converts to establish another mission at Cuchero in 1753, leaving those whom they feared would "escape" into the jungle. The mission priest was also to ask the confessant whether he or she had considered joining the rebels or communicated with them or gave them "axes, knives, or machetes."[61] Not only were the farm implements important to the friars' strategy of keeping the montañeses in the mission communities, but friars knew all too well that these tools could be easily used against them as weapons of war.

The missionaries themselves, of course, did not see their actions as being malevolent or oppressive. Indeed, as in so many other instances in the colonial world, Spanish missionaries saw themselves as benevolent "fathers" to their native "children." Missionary leaders instructed missionaries that they should not treat the mission natives as "children of the whip" but treat them with "affection."[62] Of course, corporal punishment for children in the eighteenth century was not uncommon, and when carried out "in moderation" they believed it was simply an extension of this paternalistic relationship.

In many ways the order that the missionaries attempted to impose in the missions paralleled the monastic life that they themselves had embraced. In the monastery they attended mass multiple times a day, so they did not see it as unreasonable that the montañeses do so four times a week. Discipline, obedience, order, and even martyrdom were integral parts of the missionaries' lives, and, though it could be unpleasant in the short-term physical sense, in the eternal perspective, they believed, these things were beneficial for the natives' souls. For example, in a petition to the crown describing an epidemic in Eneno in 1713, San Joseph, instead of lamenting the actual native deaths, exclaimed "how many children have died *without baptism*?"[63] Similar sentiments were shared by several Ocopa friars over the next hundred years.[64] Although the montañeses dying of disease or starvation was lamentable, the real tragedy, in the minds of the missionaries, was that so many died without the sacrament of baptism.

Indeed, one of the unintended consequences of the missionaries' presence in the Montaña was virgin-soil epidemics. Because of their relative isolation from Europeans, Montaña nations had been spared the great pandemics that killed many of the inhabitants of the Americas. This isolation, however, meant that they still lacked any sort of immunity to the European diseases. In the Tarma missions, epidemics of smallpox killed large numbers of converts in 1711, 1713, and 1715, in some cases reducing the mission stations' populations by more than half. Other outbreaks of unknown diseases hit the Ocopa mission stations in 1721, 1724, and 1736–37.[65] Anthropologist Fernando Santos-Granero argues that there was a distinct correlation between these epidemics and violent uprisings among mission populations. The outbreaks particularly infuriated mission natives, he argues, because they disproportionately affected children (under fourteen years). Indeed, uprisings in 1712, 1719, 1724, and 1737 occurred in mission villages recently decimated by disease.[66]

Disease undoubtedly was a spark for unrest, but it was not the only factor stirring up the natives' enmity toward the missionaries. The epidemics were exacerbated by the cultural impositions of the missionaries. During times of disease, peoples of the Montaña had the custom of scattering into smaller family groups, even leaving infected individuals alone in the jungle with supplies to arrest the spread of the disease. The missionaries, however, believed this practice to be an example of the natives' "barbaric, pitiless" nature and argued that scattering would actually lead to more deaths since these small family groups had less people available to care for the sick. They consequently exhorted the natives to stay in the mission communities during outbreaks.[67] The missionaries also feared that if montañeses were out of the mission too long they would return to their "idolatries."[68] Maintaining mission communities concentrated during times of disease most likely accelerated the rates of infection, turning outbreaks into epidemics.

Other Settlers in the Missions

Missionaries and native montañeses were not the only inhabitants of the mission stations. To build up the missions' infrastructure and maintain order, the friars incorporated other ethnic groups and Spanish institutions into their missionizing project. Enslaved and free blacks became an integral part of the missionary enterprise. The missionaries employed the Africans generally in two ways: to supplement indigenous labor to produce food for the missions and as a disciplinary force. In the Hispanic world using blacks in a martial capacity was less taboo than in British North America. Blacks, including slaves, were taught to fight and were armed as personal security for elites. Because of a lack of a military or police presence in the missions, the friars turned to their enslaved Africans to mete out punishments. San Joseph commented in 1719 that "the Indians already have much fear [of the blacks]: because they are the ones that whip [the natives] when they do not attend mass or catechism."[69] Three years later San Joseph again commented that the montañeses thought the blacks to be "children of hell."[70] The missionaries even entrusted blacks to stay in the missions while they were absent. It is possible that missionaries were attempting to create divisions between the Africans and the montañeses as part of a strategy to control the missions' populations. The missionaries perhaps hoped that when rebellion broke out the ire of the montañeses would fall upon the blacks just as much as on the friars, forcing blacks to join in the protection of the missionaries. During most of the uprisings in the Ocopa missions, blacks sided with Spanish forces.

Pitting blacks against montañeses, however, did not always guarantee loyalty. One exceptional example was African Antonio Gatica, who became one of the Juan Santos Atahualpa rebellion's principal commanders against the missionaries. Gatica was a free black from Mina (west coast of Africa) whom the missionaries brought to the Montaña, perhaps at first as a slave, to serve as a laborer in the Tarma entrada. Over time Gatica was able to integrate himself into the local Montaña culture. He married the sister of an important local leader, Mateo de Assia, the cacique of Metráro and Eneno who would also later become a principal figure in the rebellion. Gatica, who lived in Eneno, also became the godfather of many of the converts in that mission.[71] According to Viceroy Villagarcia, this cultural duality gave Gatica, as well his biethnic children, "great authority."[72] When the rebellion broke out, seven other blacks followed Gatica against the missionaries, possibly suggesting more cultural integration of Africans into the communities of the Montaña.[73]

Other groups of highland Andeans and Europeans had also settled in the region. The fragile but persistent commercial ties between the highland and the jungle, as well as a small trickle of Spaniards, mestizos, and highland Andeans escaping justice, had brought with it at least a few immigrants. One missionary was even surprised by the number of "Europeans" who had come to the region in search of the legendary lost Inca city of gold, Paititi.[74] The missionaries were not necessarily opposed to the presence of such settlers since, although many were far from being ideal Catholics, they could help to acculturate the "barbarous" Montaña nations. In 1718, San Joseph even requested that the crown create a program for poor Andean and Spanish families to settle in the jungle alongside the missionaries' new converts, a program later adopted by Bourbon reformers under the "new method" of evangelization.[75] The missionaries also used highland Andean labor to help build up the roads, bridges, and structures necessary for their endeavor. In 1717 the crown gave the missionaries *mita* rights (a corvée labor draft to which most natives in the viceroyalty of Peru were subject) for one hundred men in the frontier villages Chinchao and Pillao.[76] These villages dutifully fulfilled this labor every year, probably because the alternative was either a fine of seventy pesos (a sum much higher than most natives' annual earnings) or service in the mercury mines of Huancavelica.[77]

Over time, Spanish troops began to protect the missions. In reaction to small rebellions in the Tarma entrada, as early as 1718 the missionaries began petitioning the crown for soldiers. These most often took the form of a handful of regular army troops out of Tarma or Jauja, supplemented by militia during times of rebellion. Most of the troops were concentrated in the forts at Quimirí, Cerro de la Sal, and Sonomoro, but later they began to accompany the missionaries on their expeditions deeper into the Montaña. The presence of soldiers in frontier missions was not uncommon. Though the "old method" of evangelization was for the most part mission-led and intended to be peaceful, conditions on the ground had long taught missionaries throughout the Spanish American borderlands of the need for military support. The justification for troops was not forceful conversion but to protect the montañeses against possible reprisal for converting. As one viceroy explained to the king: "His Excellency should not reprimand [the missionaries] for building a fort against the attacks of the barbarians, because this does not oppose, according to all modern writings on this point, the freedom [of the natives] to accept the Gospel. It does not constrain their free will, but repels cruelty."[78] As the eighteenth century wore on, however, the protection justification began to fade as the militarization of the frontier became a hallmark of reformist rhetoric under the "new method" of evangelization.

Acquiring State Funding and Conflicts with Early Bourbon Reformers

To maintain the expansion of its newly formed missions, the Peruvian Apostolic Institute needed a steady source of income. Building up this new network of mission stations required a large investment in material not available in the Montaña. The missionaries needed steel tools to attract montañeses to the missions as well as the various vestments, ornaments, and objects to adorn the new chapels and perform Catholic rites, such as images of Christ, Mary, and the saints; sacramental chalices; and fine linens for the altars. To transport these goods from their base of operations in the highland Mantaro Valley to the missions was also costly.[79] Furthermore, maintaining montañeses concentrated in one location accelerated soil depletion in the immediate vicinities of some of the mission stations, forcing the missionaries to import food at great cost in order to stave off starvation.[80] As with other Apostolic Institute operations, the Ocopa missionaries at first could not rely on local alms around their base of operations for support. The newly converted montañeses did sustain the missionaries in many locations with food and labor, but they could not provide the type of hard currency necessary to import European goods. Even in their base of operations in the Christianized highland Mantaro Valley, the missionaries were newcomers, making the wealthy local elite reluctant to donate alms to the Institute. Perhaps they wanted to wait until the Institute had a permanent presence in the region before they exchanged their worldly wealth for prayers to release their souls from purgatory. No notary records exist for mortmain donations during the first two decades of Ocopa's operations in the region. The first such donation in 1729 demonstrates the local elite's reluctance to "invest" in the missionaries. Don Sebastian Nieto left the missionaries (at that point based at the monastery of Santa Rosa de Ocopa near Jauja) an annual payment of twenty-five pesos from his estate in exchange for saying two masses for his soul per year. He stipulated, however, that if the missionaries failed to do so the money would be given to the parish church of Jauja for the same service.[81] The only substantial donation that was recorded during this period came in the form of five hundred pesos from the archbishop of Lima.[82] There are also some indications that some institutions in the local Franciscan province gave the missionaries money, but these donations do not appear to be significant.[83] Crown funding, therefore, was vital to the missions' ability to grow.

In 1713, just five years after founding the first missions in the Tarma entrada, Friar Francisco de San Joseph petitioned the crown for funds. San Joseph requested that the crown provide 6,000 pesos per year, 2,000 pesos for each of their three entradas at Jauja, Tarma, and Huánuco, and also for the transport of twelve new missionaries from Spain. He argued that he needed this money to pay for "tools and wages, the transport of provisions, and guards." In his attempt to persuade the crown to fund the missions, San Joseph recounted several stories of the miraculous conversion of several of the Montaña caciques and their followers, at the same time warning that if Ocopa was not provided with the funds many hundreds of native children would die in the Montaña without baptism. He also, of course, mentioned the numerous missionaries who had paid with their lives to bring about this great conversion.[84]

This type of deeply religious language was typical of the rhetoric used by Ocopa in these early years, but it would subtly begin to change as ideas about governance in Spanish America began to shift. Just three years later, for example, San Joseph's companion Fernando de San Joseph amended the Institute's reasons for missions receiving funding to appeal more to Spain's imperial interests in expanding its influence into the frontiers. He added that with the funding the missionaries could "clear trails a distance of 100 leagues and build bridges over the large, fast flowing rivers, which serve as a barrier to the barbarians," and that such work would lead to the "expansion of new dominions" for the king.[85] On 12 March 1718, King Philip V issued a royal decree confirming previous promises to send more missionaries and granted the Peruvian Apostolic Institute the 6,000 pesos per year that San Joseph had requested. The decree was also written in a pious tone and recounted most of the miraculous stories of San Joseph's initial petition, while omitting the more worldly arguments made by Friar Fernando. Unfortunately for the missionaries, the decree did not resolve how the crown would pay for these concessions; it simply shifted responsibility for payment of both the stipend and the travel expenses of the new missionaries to the treasury in Lima.[86]

Getting viceregal officials to release the 6,000 pesos annually to the missionaries proved more difficult. The advancement of regalism in the New World during the first twenty-five years of the eighteenth century was limited, but the crown had made significant gestures toward religious reform. Probably the most significant reform during this period for the regular clergy was the crown's attempts to eliminate small convents (*conventillos*). The regular orders used these conventillos as bases of operations for their rural indigenous parishes, from which the orders notoriously stripped funds to pay for their large urban convents instead of reinvesting the tithes back into the parish. By officially listing these friars as part of the convent, they were putting them under the control of their own order's hierarchy rather than secular church authority. In 1703, King Philip V issued a decree that all convents have at least eight friars in permanent residence to be considered official. The decree was most likely ignored, since it was reissued in 1708, 1727, 1731, and 1739.[87] Nonetheless, the elimination of conventillos demonstrated a burgeoning desire to reform the Church, particularly the regular clergy.

The inability of the Institute to convince viceregal authorities to pay the stipend, at least for the first decade, perhaps had less to do with reform and more to do with political instability in the viceroyalty of Peru. Between 1705 and 1724, Peru had eight viceregal administrations. Only during two of these administrations was someone named viceroy; the other six were considered interim appointments. Three of these administrations were headed by clerics, but they were little suited for the office, and their tenures were plagued with corruption and incompetence. The last such viceroy during this period of uncertainty was the Trinitarian friar and archbishop of Charcas, Diego Morcillo Rubio de Auñón, who was seventy-four when he became viceroy in 1720. During his four years as viceroy, Archbishop Morcillo became so rich from corruption and contraband that he was able to endow a church in Rome (where a monument to him still stands) with 200,000 pesos.[88] Other factors also delayed the missionaries receiving their payment. In 1720 funds destined for the mission were diverted to bolster the viceregal capital's port of Callao against the English privateer John Clipperton. Clipperton had taken the president of the audiencia of Panama captive, inspiring a rush to rebuild the port's aging fortifications.[89] The result was that, although the decree giving the missionaries their stipend was ratified in 1718, they did not receive their first payment until 1726.[90]

After 1724 viceregal officials' anticlerical attitudes became more of a barrier to missionaries receiving their stipend. The new viceroy, José de Armendáriz y Perurena, marqués de Castelfuerte (r. 1724–36), was authoritarian by nature, which made him, from the Church's perspective, come across as a "highly aggressive" regalist. As historian Adrian Pearce summarizes:

> The language he used to justify his actions was that of an extreme form of regalism and it was this view which informed his attitude toward the exercise of the *Real Patronato* (the royal patronage). It is quite clear, however, that his aggression exceeded that of a dispassionate servant of the crown: his criticism of the clergy was expressed in violent and even crude language, and he was deliberately confrontational in his dealings with them.

Castelfuerte exerted the full authority of the royal patronage, which generally went underutilized under the Habsburg viceroys, by exercising his privilege to veto ecclesiastic elections and to remove summarily priests from their parishes. His relationship with the Franciscans in particular became so embittered that the commissary-general of the Indies attempted to have him excommunicated. Though at times these attacks were obviously personal in nature, officials in Madrid rarely challenged Viceroy Castelfuerte's reforms, and his actions in many cases formed the basis for changes in colonial policy toward the Church.[91]

In regards to the Apostolic Institute, Castelfuerte seemed less antagonistic but still attempted quietly to erode the largesse that the crown had awarded the missionaries. Like many of his successors, the viceroy openly praised the missionaries and ostensibly agreed to pay the 6,000 pesos they had been granted, sending them a full payment just a year and a half after taking office.[92] Castelfuerte, however, eventually exploited the vagaries of two clauses of the 12 March 1718 decree that granted the missionaries their stipend to allow him not to comply fully. The decree charged the viceroy with finding funds within his own jurisdiction to pay the missionaries. Castelfuerte interpreted this responsibility as giving him arbitrary authority to decide whether the missionaries needed the funds or whether such need was a priority to the viceroyalty's limited financial resources:

> I ordered that several payments be made to [the missionaries], such as the one of 6,000 pesos they received at the beginning of the year 1726 . . . and the one of 2,000 that was designated for them in the year 1729, because it seemed that the amount [was] proportional to the needs of them that received it and to the state of the royal treasury which gave it to them, being sufficient for the maintenance and advancement of the missions.[93]

In addition, the decree specified that the funds come from the royal treasury in Lima. So instead of transferring the payment to the closest treasury to the missionaries' base of operations (which after 1725 was only eighteen miles away in Jauja), the viceroy required that at least one missionary make the rugged overland journey from Ocopa to Lima (174 miles away) to appear in person and collect the funds. This essentially meant that every time the missionaries wanted payment at least one (usually two) friars had to travel for several weeks from their highland base to Lima to justify to the viceroy the necessity for more money. Then, if the viceroy agreed to pay the stipend, they would have to send one or more friars back to Lima several months later to collect the funds.[94] Early on this was particularly disruptive to missionary work because the missionaries lacked sufficient manpower to spare even one friar. Before 1734, the number of active missionaries, those who were not too infirm or old, rarely exceeded a dozen.[95] It seems that some years the Institute simply did not try to collect the funds.

Castelfuerte's successor, José Antonio de Mendoza Caamaño y Sotomayor, Marques of Villagarcía, maintained the same policies. Villagarcía personally proved less ardent than Castelfuerte in attacking the clergy.[96] Regarding the Apostolic Institute, however, he was equally neglectful and maintained the same policy of forcing the missions to come to Lima in person and justify, then later collect, their stipend. Consequently, payments to missions between 1724 and 1745 were few and almost always incomplete.[97] During this period, the royal treasury registered only eight payments, and only one, the first in 1726, was for the full amount (see table 1).

TABLE 1. Payment of annual stipend to the Ocopa missionaries, 1724–1739

Year	Amount (pesos)
1726	6,000
1729	2,000
1731	1,000
1732	2,000
1736	4,000
1737	4,000
1738	4,000
1739	4,000

Source: Lehnertz, "Lands of the Infidels," 316.

The missionaries, of course, strongly disagreed with the manner in which Castelfuerte and Villagarcía handled their annual stipend, and they flooded the Council of the Indies with petitions to force viceregal officials to pay the money promptly and in full. They also demanded that the funds be distributed from the royal treasury at Jauja rather than Lima to avoid having to travel to Lima every time they needed to collect the funds.[98] Crown officials in Madrid agreed, and the royal decree of 12 March 1718 was reissued twice, in 1729 and 1734. By 1734 pressure from Madrid made ignoring the missionaries' request more difficult, and in response Viceroy Castelfuerte further complicated the process by requiring that local governors in the region report on the state of the missions before issuing payments.[99] Even this tactic, however, could not delay payment indefinitely; Villagarcia, though he still made the missionaries come to Lima to collect, issued steady payments to the missionaries from 1736 to 1739, though at the reduced amount of 4,000 pesos per year.

The viceregal government was not the only institution that impeded the growth of the Apostolic Institutes' missions in Peru. The leaders of the Franciscan Province of the Twelve Apostles, which oversaw the order in most of the audiencia of Lima including the Institute's three missionary zones, seemed to see the rise of the Institute as a threat to their own power. Once the missionaries could establish a college de propaganda fide, according to the 1686 Innocent bulls, they would be virtually independent of provincial leadership. Therefore, the Province attempted to delay the establishment of a permanent base of operations for the Institute as long as possible. The Innocent bulls stipulated that the Province surrender to the Institute two religious houses to be converted into seminaries and eventually colleges of missionaries. Almost immediately upon his arrival in Peru in 1709, San Joseph petitioned the Province to release two such localities. He specifically requested the monastery at Huánuco, which was a relatively large facility, well situated at the trailhead of one of the Institute's entradas and easily accessible to the other two.[100] The Province rejected this proposal and after several more years of petitioning tried to grant the missionaries a monastery in Huaraz, nearly 180 miles from Huánuco (320 and 350 miles from Tarma and Jauja, respectively). The site was impractical, for it would take weeks for the missionaries to travel to and from this location and their missions (including a climb over a 15,000-foot pass), and San Joseph refused to take possession of it. He continued to insist and began petitioning directly to Madrid and Rome.

Finally, in 1724 the Province was forced to compromise and ceded to the missionaries the small *hospicio* (refuge) of Santa Rosa de Santa Maria de Ocopa.[101] Ocopa was located in a remote corner of Mantaro Valley at an altitude of 11,100 feet. The physical facilities included only two small cells for living quarters and a small chapel dedicated to Saint Rose of Lima.[102] Though Ocopa lay relatively high in the mountains and its small facilities were less than ideal, its proximity to Jauja (only eighteen miles away) and Tarma (forty-six miles) meant that it had ready access to the Institute's missions.[103] For the next twenty-five years Ocopa was the Peruvian Apostolic Institute's only base of operations in the viceroyalty, and the name Ocopa became virtually synonymous with the Institute's until it began to expand into other areas of operation in the 1750s. The provincial leaders' delay in establishing a permanent base of operations for the Institute even earned them the reproach of Pope Benedict XIII, who emphasized that "we [the Pope] order, desire, and command, that [the Province] indubitably and inviolably observe" the command to aid in building colleges de propaganda fide in Peru.[104]

The conflict foreshadowed a complex love-hate relationship between Ocopa and the Province. Certainly both organizations were Franciscan and desired the advancement of the work of their order, an increased piety among the faithful, and the evangelization of nonbelievers. Because the Apostolic Institute was independent from the Province, however, this naturally meant that they competed for money and resources. Ocopa, for example, attracted alms from donors who potentially would have given to the Province. Furthermore, crown donations to Ocopa were seen by at least some government officials as contributing to the order in Peru as a whole and therefore diminished the Province's capacity to lobby for its own royal contributions.[105] Nonetheless, Ocopa's piety and discipline were helping to rehabilitate the order's notorious reputation for laxity and corruption, which could help them to increase donations from both the populace and the state. These underlying tensions between the two entities complicated their relationship over the next century.[106]

Outside groups were not the only factor in delaying aid to the growing Ocopa missions. Though the 12 March 1718 decree granted the Apostolic Institute funds to transport twelve new peninsular friars to Peru, these missionaries did not arrive until 1730. The delay was actually at the request of

Ocopa missionaries, who required that one of their own travel to Spain to escort the new missionaries to Peru.[107] They took this extreme measure because of problems associated with the policy called the *alternativa*—a system devised in the late sixteenth and early seventeenth centuries and used by several religious orders in the Americas to maintain peace between peninsular Spaniards and creoles within religious communities. As early religious communities began to grow in the New World, creole and mestizo clerics began to dominate religious houses numerically, causing resentment among the small but still powerful peninsular contingents. This discord tended to flash into open hostility during the elections of new community leaders, roughly every three to four years, leading to several notable schisms. To avoid conflicts, religious communities began to devise a system whereby leadership positions alternated between peninsulars and creoles. The crown later codified the practice into colonial law.

By the eighteenth century, the small number of peninsular regular clerics in the New World forced religious communities to recruit peninsulars in order to meet the demands of the alternativa. This meant that any regular peninsular cleric who could afford passage to the New World would almost certainly be rewarded with a leadership position, which could lead to opportunities once he returned to Spain.[108] The Ocopa missionaries so feared that the large monasteries in Lima would snatch up their new missionaries that, in addition to the new missionaries being escorted, they demanded that the 1730 group completely avoid the viceregal capital, land at the port of Paita, and proceed directly to Ocopa.[109] In some ways the delay in the arrival of new missionaries was more damaging to the expansion of the missions than viceregal interference in the dissemination of the missionaries' annual stipend.

Expansion of the Missionary Work and Demographic Collapse

The desperate need for manpower was created by a seemingly rapid expansion of the Ocopa missionary enterprise. From 1709 to 1727 in the Tarma entrada the missionaries built six mission stations along the Sal and Perené rivers. Farther below, at the confluence of the Perené and Ene rivers, the Tarma entrada effectively merged with the Jauja entrada, which by 1727 also had three missions (see figures 1, 2). Just north of the confluence of these two rivers, the missionaries encountered an elevated, temperate zone called the Gran Pajonal. This region, according to the missionaries, was heavily populated and had a more temperate climate, making it seem to have a greater potential for more permanent settlement. Friar Juan de la Marca entered the Pajonal in 1727 and established the first mission at Catalipango in 1729. La Marca was aided in his journey by the cacique of Eneno, Mateo de Assia, and his brother-in-law, the missionaries' African servant Antonio Gatica. Assia seemed to have been the missionary's greatest asset in the journey, using his "great authority" to "persuade the Ande [Asháninka] habitants of the Pajonal to receive the law of God." It was these actions that perhaps made the Assia and Gatica defections to Juan Santos Atahualpa more bitter. The missionaries continued to return to the region and by 1739 had at least officially established ten missions in the Pajonal.[110]

In Huánuco the missionaries had less success. By 1739 they had established only two missions, which later merged into a single station. These small advances were not for a lack of potential converts or effort. Starting in 1726 the missionaries sent several expeditions farther east into the jungle with little success. In 1731 their Yanesha converts from Pozuzu guided missionaries to the Mayro River valley where the Yanesha fished during the summer. The friars named it the Pampas de Sacramento since they arrived on Corpus Christi. In 1732 an expedition to the Pampas under Friar Simon Jara encountered an Amerindian nation that his Yanesha guides called Carapachos, and though their encounter was peaceful no one in the party could communicate with them. Carapachos, a group ethnographers have been unable to identify, probably spoke a Panoan dialect, distinct from the Arawak languages the missionaries had previously encountered. Language became a significant barrier to evangelization in the Pampas, with several expeditions over the next decade failing to establish any sort of permanent missionary presence in the region. Language, however, was not their only impediment; disease and famine in the Huánuco missions as well as a lack of manpower made expeditions to the Pampas more difficult.[111]

These rapid expansions in territory in which the missionaries operated, of course, strained Ocopa's human resources. By the time the ten new missionaries arrived at Ocopa in 1730 (two of the original twelve died in transit), they could do little more than replace the aging friars who manned the existing mission stations. According to Viceroy Castelfuerte, in 1734 death and abandonment had whittled the number of active full Ocopa friars down to only six.[112] After 1734 missionaries from other monasteries in Peru helped to bolster their numbers so that by 1736 the missionaries claimed sixteen full friars, two lay friars, twenty-three oblates, and six alms gathers. As the missionaries began to establish mission station after mission station, however, they still did not have enough missionaries to service them.[113] Ideally at least one full friar (meaning that he was also an ordained priest) and a companion (lay friar or oblate) resided in and ministered to each mission community. Additionally, at least a handful of friars had to reside at Ocopa both to administrate the missionary enterprise and to train new missionaries. As the missionaries expanded their enterprise in the mid-1730s, only one friar (sometimes just a lay friar) serviced two or more demographically disparate mission stations. Between 1736 and 1737, the missions of Eneno, Cerro de la Sal, and Metraro had only one friar among them.[114] Also, missionaries did not always stay in their designated missions, since as part of the "old method" they were charged with finding new areas to evangelize; when they heard rumors of new population centers, they left their posts to explore surrounding territories.[115]

The problem of manning the missions was further exacerbated by the exhausted jungle soil finally forcing mission communities to spread out over larger and larger areas. Despite the missionaries' efforts, over time mission communities could no longer live "under the bell" but had to divide into small family groups called *ayllos* that radiated out from a central mission station hub, where the missionaries and other outside settlers lived. One of Eneno's ayllos, Epillo, was some thirty miles from the mission church.[116] In response to this lack of manpower, Ocopa once again petitioned the crown for more missionaries, this time thirty, which the crown agreed to support in 1734. Unfortunately, eleven died in transit and even the remaining nineteen who arrived in Peru 1737 were still insufficient to man all of Ocopa's supposed mission stations.[117]

Viceregal officials soon became suspicious of this rapid proliferation of Ocopa's mission stations. If Ocopa had so few missionaries, how could it possibly claim mission stations in so many locations? Were these viable, substantial religious communities or simply places where missionaries had at one time visited and possibly baptized some of the population? In 1736 the missionaries presented a census of the missions that claimed that the Jauja, Tarma, and Huánuco entradas contained twenty-four mission stations populated by 4,835 inhabitants.[118] Only three years later a census conducted by Franciscan commissary Friar Lorenzo de Nuñéz during an official inspection of the missions (*visita*) recorded only nine mission stations: San Fermín de Parua, Sonomoro, Quimirí, Nijandaris, Cerro de la Sal, Metraro, Eneno, Pichana, and Los Autes (San Tadeo), with 851 inhabitants.[119] Nuñéz seems to have omitted the missions of the Huánuco entrada, Pozuzu and Trilligo, though the 1736 census claimed that these villages had a combined total of 437.[120] Jorge Juan y Santacilia and Antonio de Ulloa, explorers and reformers who were gathering information for a confidential report on the state of Peru for the crown, estimated that the Ocopa missions had roughly a thousand inhabitants, based on information they gathered in Lima during the late 1730s—still less than half of what the friars claimed.[121] Therefore, although Ocopa presented its missions to the crown as a continually expanding enterprise that flourished miraculously despite problems with manpower and funding, independent census numbers and even Ocopa statistics indicate a less positive outlook.

The change in population in the few mission stations where the missionaries were able to take multiple censuses demonstrates stagnation and even decline in mission populations over time. Between 1722 and 1739 censuses of four mission stations—Quimirí, Cerro de la Sal, Eneno, and San Tadeo (los Autes)—indicated modest but steady declines in populations (figure 3). Only in two instances, in Eneno between 1732 and 1735 and in Quimirí between 1735 and 1739, were there actual increases in mission populations, and only one was significant: Eneno's population nearly doubled during that period, perhaps through Mateo de Assia's influence. Ocopa touted to the crown an expansion of the number of its mission stations, but individual mission station populations were in decline.

Indeed, the two existent baptismal registries from the Ocopa mission stations of Eneno and Pozuzu demonstrate the missionaries' inability to sustain the missions through baptism and the retention of converts. In Eneno (figure 4), although there was a predictable spike in baptisms when the mission was initially established, the overall trend was negative. This appears consistent with a community that at first accepted the missionaries but because of epidemic disease began to decline. The sudden increase in burials, for example between 1736 and 1738, corresponds with a known outbreak. There was, however, no abnormally high influx of baptisms at this location after 1734, suggesting that missionaries were no longer attracting new converts there.

The mission of Pozuzu perhaps better demonstrates the long-term outlook for Ocopa mission populations (figure 5). Since Pozuzu did not fall to the Juan Santos Atahualpa rebels in 1742, Ocopa missionaries maintained a community there until 1788. Its surviving baptismal registry, for 1736–87, though it included only infants and children shows a trend similar to that at Eneno. Baptisms steadily declined over fifty-one years, going from an average of 21.6 baptisms during the first five years to an average of 2.6 during the last five. This negative trend was probably exacerbated by the missionaries removing over a hundred converts in 1753 to found another mission nearby. As in Eneno, Pozuzu experienced periods of high mortality, particularly in 1744, but overall high mortality rates cannot account for marked population decline in the missions. Though mortality rates over time were slightly higher than baptismal rates, the rate of depopulation tended to be much higher. In Eneno, for example, while baptismal rates from 1732 to 1742 declined slightly from a yearly average of eleven to an average of nine, and burial rates remained virtually flat, if not slightly elevated, and the population of the mission community was almost halved, going from 287 to 153. As anecdotal evidence from the Pozuzo's confession manual suggests, converts must have simply chosen to flee the mission communities. Some montañeses in the missions, however, rather than leave their homes attempted to remove what they probably saw as the underlining problem—the missionaries.

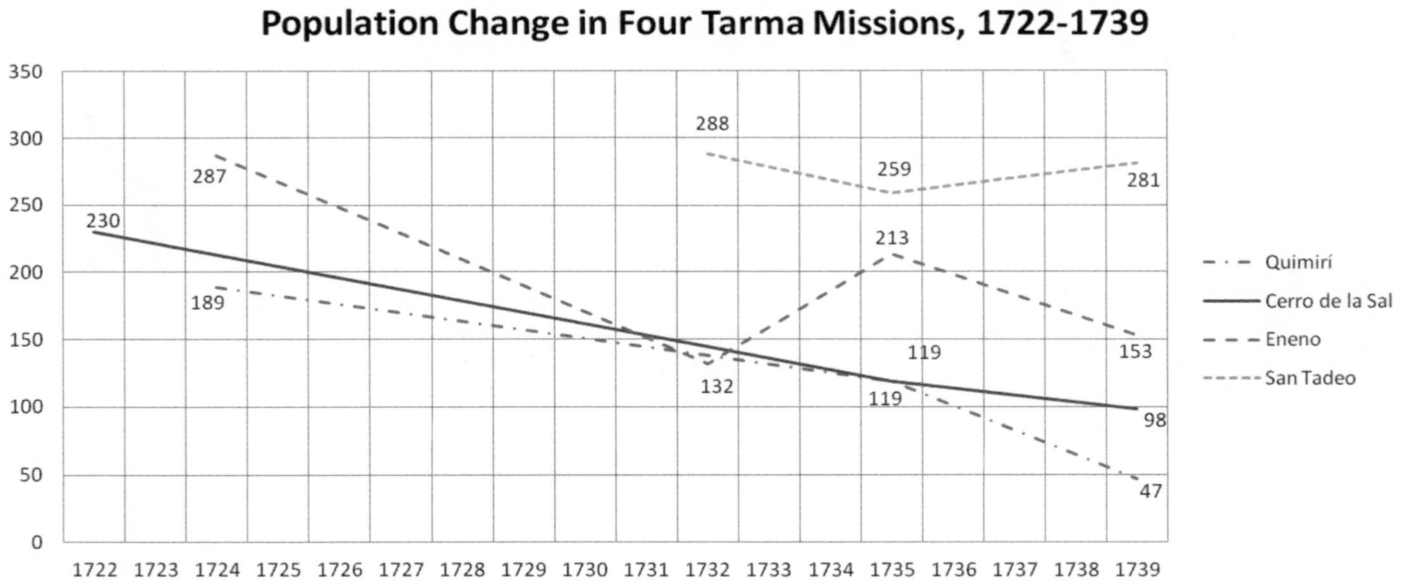

FIGURE 3. Population change in four Tarma missions, 1722–1739. Data from Heras, *Comienzos de las misiones de Ocopa* (published version of BNP, C. 342).

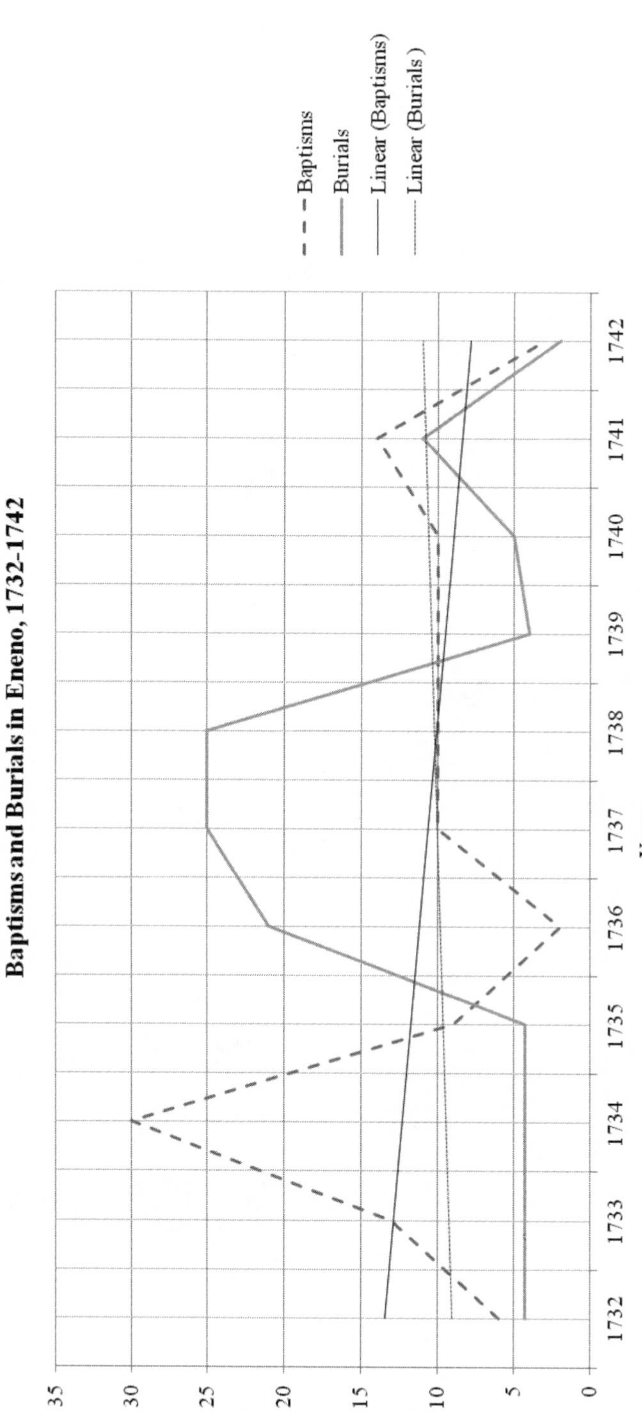

FIGURE 4. Baptisms and burials in Eneno, 1732–1742. Data from AGN, Sección Republicana, Ministerio de Hacienda, Libro 567.

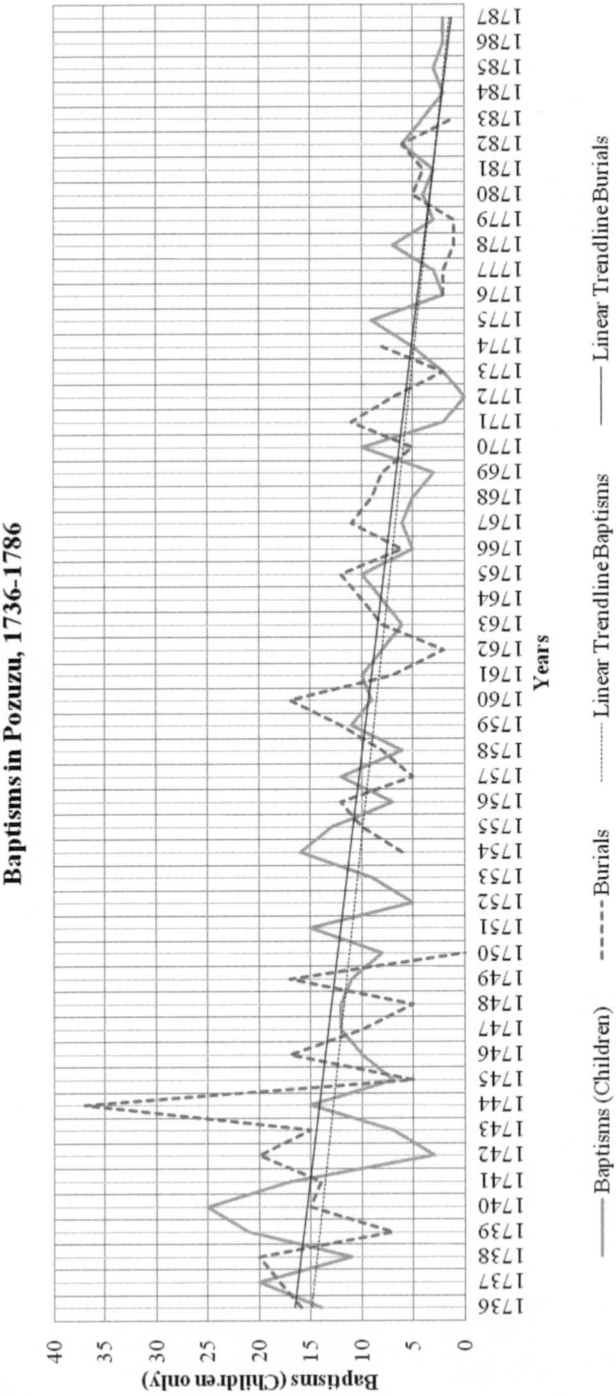

FIGURE 5. Baptisms in Pozuzu, 1736–1786. Data from AL-MRREE, LEB-12-4, Caja 94.

Rebellions

Between 1709 and 1742 the Ocopa missions experienced four rebellions—in 1712, 1719, 1724, and 1737. Most of these rebellions were small affairs in which montañeses rose up against the local missionaries. All involved some contingent of disaffected converts, usually led by the local cacique, though many missionaries, perhaps shocked by the betrayal, claimed that the rebels were always aided by some group of "gentiles" from outside the missions. These rebellions usually consisted of a brief flash of popular anger, resulting in the massacre of local missionaries and other colonists followed by the rebels retreating into the jungle to avoid recriminations.[122] These four resulted in the deaths of eleven missionaries (full friars, lay friars, and oblates) and several dozen enslaved blacks, highland Andeans, and Spanish soldiers. The deaths, of course, proved excellent material for subsequent petitions to the crown that detailed the missionaries' holy sacrifice. One example was the death of Friar Fernando de San Joseph, one of the original Apostolic missionaries in Peru. After the Asháninkas of the village of Choquizoqui tossed the missionary into a large bonfire, he miraculously emerged holding his crucifix aloft, preaching the word of God before he succumbed to his burns. All of these rebellions were suppressed locally, usually by a force of mission Amerindians who remained loyal to friars, later joined by a militia contingent from Tarma. Generally, however, by the time outside forces arrived there was little left to suppress, since rebels usually had already escaped into the jungle.[123]

The last and largest of these four rebellions, the Torote rebellion in 1737, closely follows this model but demonstrates an escalation in size and scope. Ignacio Torote was the cacique of the village of Catalipango and also the son of Fernando Torote, who had led a rebellion against the missionaries in 1724. In early March 1737, Ignacio gathered twenty-one warriors, seventeen "bad Christians" and four "infidels," from his home village of Catalipango. There they murdered anyone connected to the missionaries, an oblate who had been stationed there in the absence of a friar, an African who presumably worked for the missionaries, his Indian wife, two orphans being raised by the missionaries, and the wife of the cacique of Sonomoro, who must have had some connection to the village. After destroying and burning the church they made a rapid march to the mission station of Sonomoro, normally a four-day journey which they made in two and a half. On 20 March they surprised the three missionaries at Sonomoro, peppering them with arrows. According to Amich, when the dying missionary Manuel Bajo asked Torote why he was killing them, the cacique revealingly responded, "Because you and yours are killing us every day with your sermons and doctrines, taking away our liberty. Preach then Father, for we are the Fathers now," after which they bludgeoned Bajo to death with clubs. The rebels razed the church and stayed in the village until

1 April, when a contingent of eighty highland Andeans from Comas, led by their parish priest and Ocopa missionary Cayetano Rodríguez, arrived and forced the rebels to retreat. Friar Cayetano could do little but bury the dead.[124]

The Ocopa missionaries could not let such open and violent defiance stand, since Torote had not only massacred their brothers but turned a local dispute into a regional one. They begged viceregal authorities for more resources to help capture rebels and completely quash resistance. They petitioned the viceroy through Friar Cayetano himself, who went to Lima bearing not only the tale of possible general insurrection but the arrows pulled from the corpses of the martyred friars. This symbolic gesture worked, and Viceroy Villagarcía released 4,000 pesos for an expedition of 150 men led by the frontier governors, Pedro Milla y Campoy and Benito Troncoso Lira. This force did not, however, leave the highlands until the middle of October 1737, and, by the time they arrived in Catalipango, Torote had retreated deeper into the jungle. The expedition encountered only three suspected members of the Torote's raiding party, whom they executed two days before Christmas 1737 in Eneno. They placed the heads and hands of the rebels along the paths between the mission stations as a warning to any potential subversives. The warning would go unheeded.[125]

The Torote rebellion, like the uprisings before, exposes the systemic problems with the Ocopa missions that made them inherently unstable. The reduction of the Asháninka and Yanesha peoples into the missions, the desired result of those "sermons and doctrines," was indeed killing the native population. Catalipango, where the rebellion had begun, had just suffered an outbreak of an unknown bleeding disease, which had increased the mortality rate of the neighboring mission station of Eneno by a factor of five (see figure 4). Though the "old method" of evangelization was intended to be peaceful, demographic collapse combined with outside control and restrictive living conditions inevitably led to resentment and rebellion. Furthermore, the missionaries' zealous overextension of their manpower had created a space for resistance. Only one oblate and one African servant manned Catalipango at the time the rebellion broke out. Perhaps a more substantial presence in the area could have at least warned the missionaries of the brewing discontent of the village's cacique.

Viceregal failure to supply the missionaries with their annual stipend, however, undoubtedly was a factor in the fragile state of the missions at the end of the 1730s. Lack of funds meant slower development of mission facilities, fewer resources to attract montañeses to the missions, and less protection for missions and expeditions. At this time these effects were perhaps only secondary, but they were a portent for later viceregal neglect. As in this early period, Ocopa's fate would be shaped by various groups on the ground who competed over the shifting meanings and practice of governance throughout Spanish America.

Notes

1. Marcel Battaillon, *Estudios sobre Bartolomé de las Casas,* as cited in Santos-Granero and Barclay, *Selva Central,* 19.

2. Saiz Diez, *Los colegios,* 27–38.

3. The *patronato real* (royal patronage) was a series of concessions made by the papacy to the Spanish crown starting in late fifteenth century that granted the monarchy sweeping powers over the Spanish Church, particularly in the New World. Under the patronage, for example, the crown collected tithes and had control over major clerical appointments such as bishops.

4. Saiz Diez, *Los colegios,* 39–60.

5. The commissary-generals in New Spain and Peru also could intervene in the affairs of the colleges, but these offices were abolished in 1768; see ibid., 39–53, 176.

6. This is evident in the conflicts over the elevation of Ocopa to a college in Peru; see Rodríguez Tena, *Crónica de las misiones franciscanas,* 220–23.

7. Tibesar, "Alternativa," 242; Lehnertz, "Land of the Infidels," 328; Saiz Dies, *Los colegios,* 29–35.

8. San Antonio, Petition to the crown, 12 February 1757, Madrid, AGI, Lima 808. A similar pattern of funding developed for the College of Chillán in Chile.

9 . This information on Francisco de San Joseph is contained in a biography by friars Fernando Pallarés and Vicente Calvo that was included in the 1870 version of José Amich's writings titled *Noticias históricas de las misiones de fieles e infieles del Colegio de Propaganda Fide de Santa Rosa de Ocopa.* It was also included in the most recent edition of Amich's work, edited by Julián Heras, *Historia de las misiones,* 27–35. Though the source of the information is not known, many of the details coincide with Amich's own account as well as with letters from Francisco de San Joseph himself found in AGI, Lima 536, 537.
In this context, a reduction was a village or town where indigenous populations were concentrated. The term comes from the early colonial period when the Spanish colonial government forced native populations who had been "reduced" by epidemic disease to concentrate themselves into designated towns and villages.

10. José de Armendariz, "Relación que hizo de su Gobierno," BNE, mss. 3109, f. 77r.

11. For example, the Tarma entrada became commonly known as the missions of Cerro de la Sal, but the terms were still virtually interchangeable and at times the old term was still used. For clarity in this text, only the provincial capital names are used.

12. Amich gives an excellent description of the Montaña in the first chapter of his *Historia de las misiones,* 53–56; Rodríguez Tena dedicated an entire volume to the flora and fauna of Peru and in particular the jungle in *Crónica de las misiones franciscanas,* bk. 1; see also Lehnertz, "Land of the Infidels," 1–15.

13. Lehnertz, "Land of the Infidels," 1–15.

14. Amich, *Historia de las misiones,* 54.

15. A good example of these types of complaints are found in Friar Joseph de San Antonio, Petition to the crown, Madrid, AL-MRREE, LEB-12-19, Caja 95.

16. This was found in the burial records for the mission of Eneno, AGN, Ministerio de Hacienda, Libro 567.

17. See Saignes, *Los Andes orientales.*

18. Both missionaries and colonial officials alike use this term: San Antonio, Account of the rebellion of Juan Santos, 8 May 1747, Ocopa, AGI, Lima 541; Villagarcia, Report the crown, n.d., Lima, AGI, Lima 415; Friar Bernardino de Mathias, Letter to San Antonio, 15 November 1756, Lima, AGI, Lima 808.

19. Santos-Granero and Barclay, *Selva Central,* 17–18.

20. Accounts of these expeditions are found in several locations: Amich, *Historia de las misiones,* 57–129; Izaguirre, *Historia de las misiones,* bk. 1. There is also a brief summary in Royal decree, 12 March 1718, San Lorenzo de el Escorial, AGI, Arribadas 591.

21. San Joseph, Report to Fr. Joseph Sanz, commissary-general of the Indies, 24 January 1716, AGI, Lima 541.

22. San Antonio, Petition to the crown, 11 May 1758, Madrid, AGI, Lima 808.

23. Royal decree, 12 March 1718, San Lorenzo de el Escorial, AGI, Arribadas 591.

24. "Manifiesto que haze la provincial del Perú de el Orden de Predicadores, sobre la justificacion con que procedio de Rmo. P. M. Fr. Antonio Cloche su General, en la expedicion, y providencia de prorrogar el Capitulo Provincial futuro, que se avia de celebrar en 24 de Julio de 1718 hasta dicho Julio de 1720 en la Persona del M.R.P.M. Fr Juan Moreno Doctor en la Real Universidad de los Reyes, Prothonotario de la Camara Apostolica, y actual Prior Provincial de dicha Provincia," December 1717, AGI, Lima 537. I am grateful to Luis Miguel Glave for bringing this reference to my attention.

25. San Joseph, Petition to the crown, 8 July 1713, Lima, AGI, Lima 536.

26. San Joseph, Letter to Antonio de Soloaga, archbishop of Lima, 1716, CVU, Papeles Varios, Mss. Tomo 20, no. 4; response 6 April 1716.

27. Both Varese (*Salt of the Mountain,* 1–6) and Lehnertz ("Land of the Infidels," 21–29) discuss these problems at length.

28. Examples of this categorization of montañeses by their status within the Catholic faith are ubiquitous, but probably the best is Amich, *Historia de las misiones.*

29. Friar Jose Palos, Report to the crown, 16 November 1716, Lima, AGI, Lima 537.

30. Varese, *Salt of the Mountain,* 1–6; Lehnertz, "Land of the Infidels," 21–29.

31. Census of Eneno, AGN, Ministerio de Hacienda, Libro 567.

32. Lehnertz, "Land of the Infidels," 21–29.

33. Ibid., 32.

34. Varese, *Salt of the Mountain,* 6–31.

35. See Causa contra Fray Domingo Garcia, 8 October 1745, JSEI, 106–9.

36. Friar Francisco Seco, Report to the crown, n.d., AGI, Lima 537. A note from 10 October 1719 at the end of the copy of the royal decree (12 March 1718, San Lorenzo de el Escorial, AGI, Arribadas 591) dates this document sometime between when the decree was issued and when the copy was made, probably 1718.

37. Varese, however, argues that such a comparison is inappropriate (*Salt of the Mountain,* 34–35).

38. Ibid., 56, 70, 83.

39. San Joseph, Letter to Fr. Joseph Sanz, 24 January 1716, Tarma, AGI, Lima 541.

40. Tibesar, "San Antonio de Eneno," 24.

41. Probably the best example of this is Viceroy José Antonio Manso de Velasco, "Relación que hizo de su Gobierno," BNE, mss. 3108, f. 118v.

42. Fr. Lucas de Quenca, Procurador de Indias, Petition to the crown, n.d., Madrid, AGI, Lima 536.

43. This process is described in San Joseph, Letter to Friar José Sanz, commissary-general, 24 March 1721, Tarma, AGI, Lima 538. A copy of this letter is also found in a volume of San Joseph's letters edited by Heras (*Cartas e Informes,* 55–60), which was taken from the Propaganda Fide Archive in Rome.

44. The provincial minister had to reissue this order in 1717, which indicates that it was not being followed. Friar Joseph de Palos, Order, 5 May 1717, ASFL, r. 6, n.1, doc. 231, ff. 501v–502v.

45. San Joseph, Letter to Fr. José Sanz, commissary-general, 24 March 1721, Tarma, AGI, Lima 538.

46. Amich, *Historia de las misiones;* Friar Paulo Alonso Carballo, Letter to Bartolomé Maria de la Heras, archbishop of Lima, 11 September 1818, San Buenaventura de Chaviri, AAL, Sección San Francisco XI-28; Friar Lego Juan de San Antonio, Report to the crown, 28 February 1757, Lima, AGI, Lima 808; Joseph Antonio Manso de Velasco, "Relación que hizo de su Gobierno," BNE, mss. 3108, f. 120r.

47. Gil Muñoz, Vice-commissary of the Franciscan province of San Antonio de Charcas, Petition to the crown, 12 May 1752, Cuzco, AGI, Lima 541.

48. This particular number was mentioned numerous times, so much so that it found its way into a royal decree, 13 March 1751, San Lorenzo de El Escorial, AGI, Lima 542.

49. This type of discourse is obvious in San Joseph, Petition to the crown, 8 July 1713, Lima, AGI, Lima 536; Friar Juan Higinio de Ibarra, visitor-general of the missions, Report, 30 March 1715, Lima, ASFL r. 6, n. 1, 223, ff. 490v–491r; and Friar Fernando de San José, Report to crown, 20 March 1716, Lima, AGI, Lima 537.

50. Mills, *Idolatry and Its Enemies,* 24–28.

51. San Joseph, Petition to the crown, 8 December 1713, Lima, AGI, Lima 536. These same stories were repeated in the royal decree that resulted from this petition (12 March 1718, San Lorenzo de El Escorial, AGI, Arribadas 591).

52. "Mapa de los Mártires," 1737, AGI, Mapas y Planos, Perú y Chile 32.

53. Friar Lorenzo Nuñés de Mendoza, commissary-general of the Ocopa missions, Letters to the viceroy, 13 May 1736 and 14 April 1737, Ocopa, AGI, Lima 539; Friar Alonso Lopez de Casas, commissary-general of the Franciscan order in Peru, Report, 19 May 1737, Lima, AGI, Lima 539; Real Acuerdo, Act, 16 April 1737, Lima, AGI Lima 539.

54. Amich, "*Historia de las misiones,*" 183.

55. Varese argues that because of the influence of its cacique the mission of Sonomoro did not back Juan Santos Atahualpa (*Salt of the Mountain,* 87–96). In one of the few baptismal records that exist for the missions, the cacique of Eneno, Mateo Assia, engaged in the traditional Catholic patron-client relationship of becoming the godfather to many of the children in the village. Assia was, however, one of the principal commanders against the missionaries during Juan Santos Atahualpa rebellion, casting serious doubts on whether his previous devotion to Catholic ritual was a factor in the montañeses supporting the friars.

56. Loan words from Quechua, considered the common tongue in Peru, were embedded throughout Catholic rhetoric in the Andes. It is unclear whether the term was brought to Pozuzu by the missionaries or adopted independently by the Amueshas. For more information on Quechua in Catholic rhetoric, see Alan Durston, *Pastoral Quechua.*

57. Friar Domingo de la Cruz, Municipal Laws of the Mission of San Antonio de Pozuzu, n.d. (probably 1760s), AL-MRREE, LEB-12-4, Caja 94, ff. 177r–222v. A special thanks to Joan Manuel Morales Cama for helping me obtain a copy of this document, which includes the registry of baptisms, marriages, and burials for Pozuzu for 1734–87 as well as a confession manual from 1764.

58. The author of the confession manual remains unknown, but it was probably Friar Domingo de la Cruz, who arrived in 1764 and whose handwriting in the mission's registry of baptisms, marriages, and burials matches that in the manual. Confession Manual, AL-MRREE, LEB-12-4, Caja 94, ff. 33v–55r; Registry of baptisms, marriages, and burials for the pueblo of Nuestra Señora de la Asumpcion de Yanahuanqui [Pozuzu], AL-MRREE, LEB 12-4, Caja 94, ff. 1r–105v.

59. Confession manual, AL-MRREE, LEB 12-4, Caja 94, ff. 33v–55r.

60. *Cimarrón* is a general term in Spanish for any group of Amerindians or Africans who have escaped Spanish society to form their own communities. It is from this word that the English term "maroon" was derived.

61. Confession manual, AL-MRREE, LEB 12-4, Caja 94, ff. 33v–55r.

62. Friar Domingo de la Cruz, Municipal laws of the Mission of San Antonio de Pozuzu, n.d. (probably 1760s), AL-MRREE, LEB 12-4, Caja 94, ff. 177r–222v.

63. San Joseph, Petition to the crown, 25 November 1713, Lima, AGI, Lima 539 (emphasis added); also found in San José, *Cartas e informes*, 33. San Joseph expresses a similar sentiment almost twenty years later in another petition to the crown (12 July 1732, Lima, AGI, Lima 539).

64. These include Friar Francisco Seco, procurator-general, Report, 30 November 1732, Madrid, AGI, Lima 539; Friar Manuel Gil, commissary of the missions in Peru, Report to the crown, 7 September 1764, Lima, AGI, Lima 834; and Friar Paulo Alonso Carballo, Report to the archbishop of Lima, Bartolome Maria de la Heras, 11 September 1818, San Buenaventura de Chaviri, AAL, Sección San Francisco, XI-28.

65. Santos-Granero, "Epidemias y sublevaciones," 33–35.

66. Ibid., 36–52. Whereas Santos-Granero proves this correlation through a thorough examination of the missions' censuses, the missionaries themselves reported these connections: San Joseph, Report of the missions de propaganda fide, 12 June 1732, Ocopa, AGI, Lima 539.

67. Amich, *Historia de las misiones,* 76.

68. See Causa contra Fray Domingo Garcia, 8 October 1745, JSEI, 106–9.

69. "Ya a estos [los negros] tienen mucho miedo los Indios: porque son los que Azoten [a los amerindios] quando hazen notable faltas a Misa o Doctrina." San Joseph, Letter to José Sanz, commissary-general of missions, 19 September 1718, Tarma, AGI, Lima 537.

70. San Joseph, Petition to the crown, 23 March 1721, Tarma, AGI, Lima 538.

71. Baptismal record for the mission of Eneno, AGN, Sección Republicana, Ministerio de Hacienda, Libro 5, ff. 1–22; Villagracia, Letter to Manso de Velasco, 1745, Lima, RAH 9-9-3 1699, f. 190v.

72. Joseph Antonio Mendoza, "Relación de Marques de Villagarcia," BNE, Mss. 3108, f. 22r; Joseph Antonio Manso de Velasco, "Relación que hizo de su Gobierno," BNE, mss. 3107, f. 114r.

73. Amich, *Historia de las misiones,* 169.

74. There are accounts of several highland Andeans entering the Montaña, including that of Juan Santos, but others include Royal decree, 12 March 1718, San Lorenzo de el Escorial, AGI, Arribadas 591; and Friar Fernando de San José, Letter to Fr. Joaquin, Tarma, June 1730, AGI, Lima 541.

75. San Joseph, Letter to José Sanz, commissary-general of missions, 19 September 1718, Tarma, AGI, Lima 537.

76. Real Acuerdo, Act, 13 September 1756, Lima, AGI, Lima 808.

77. Sebastian de Mendizabel, captain of military forces in Tarma, Petition to the viceroy, 24 March 1721, Tarma, AGI, Lima 538.

78. Castelfuerte, "Relación que hizo de su govierno," BNE, mss. 3109, f. 80vr.

79. San Joseph, Letter to José Sanz, commissary-general of missions, 19 September 1718, Tarma, AGI, Lima 537; San Joseph, Petition to the crown, 23 March 1721, Tarma, AGI, Lima 538.

80. Friar Christorial de Molina, procurator for the Dominican province of San Juan Bautista del Perú, Letter of support for the apostolic missions, n.d., Lima, AGI, Lima 536.

81. Will of Don Sabastian Nieto, ARJ, Protocolos Notariales, Tomo 18, Scribe Juan de Mesa Valera, f. 327vr.

82. Friar José Palos, Provincial minister for the Franciscan Province of Doce Apostles of Peru, Report on the missions, 16 November 1716, Lima, AGI, Lima 537.

83. Rodríguez Tena, "Crónica de la misiones franciscanas," 220–34.

84. San Joseph, Petition to the king, 25 November 1713, Lima, AGI 539. There is also a copy of this letter in San José, *Cartas e Informes,* 31–33.

85. Friar Fernando de San Joseph, Petition to the crown, 20 March 1716, Lima, AGI, Lima 537.

86. Royal decree, 12 March 1718, San Lorenzo de el Escorial, AGI, Arribadas 591.

87. Andrien, "Coming of Enlightened Reform," 188.

88. Pearce, "Early Bourbon Government," 26–28.

89. San Joseph, Petition to the crown, 23 March 1721, Tarma, AGI, Lima 538.

90. Lehnertz, "Lands of the Infidels," 316.

91. Pearce, "Early Bourbon Government," 197–99.

92. Castelfuerte, Report to the king, 8 November 1734, Lima, AGI, Lima 539.

93. Castelfuerte, "Relación que hizo de su Gobierno," BNE, mss. 3109, f. 79r.

94. Joseph de Salazar y Monatoneo, syndic-general of the Franciscan missions, Petition to the crown, n.d., Lima, AGI, Lima 539.

95. In 1734 they had only six; see Castelfuerte, Report to the king, 8 November 1734, Lima, AGI, Lima 539.

96. Pearce, "Early Bourbon Government," 200.

97. Fiscal's comments in regards to a petition to the crown from Friar Diego Joseph de la Fuente, Franciscan procurator-general for the Indies, 14 June 1738, Madrid, AGI, Lima 539.

98. There are multiple petitions from multiple sources, including Joseph de Salazar y Monatoneo, syndic-general of the Franciscan missions, Petition to the crown, n.d., Lima, AGI, Lima 539; San Joseph, Petition to the crown, 6 June 1726, Ocopa, AGI, Lima 539; and Friar Diego Joseph de la Fuente, Franciscan procurator-general for the Indies, n.d., but postscript from 14 June 1738, Madrid, AGI, Lima 539.

99. Audiencia of Lima, Writ, 27 August 1736, Lima, AGI, Lima 539.

100. San Joseph, Letter to the provincial minister of Lima, 12 August 1709, Lima, AGI, Lima 541, copy.

101. This negotiation is detailed in Rodríguez Tena, *Crónica de las misiones Franciscanas,* 220–37.

102. *Ocopa* literally means "corner" in Quechua.

103. Amich, *Historia de las misiones,* 140.

104. Pope Benedict XIII, Edict to Franciscan provincial ministers in Peru, 17 June 1728, Rome, AGI, Lima 541.

105. "Plan de las contribuciones anuales, y limosnas que se deven hacer a los conventos de San Francisco en este Reino del Perú," 8 July 1773, Lima, RAH 9-9-3 1680, f. 55rv.

106. Andrien, "Coming of Enlightened Reform," 188.

107. Francisco Díaz de Román, Report, 29 November 1729, Madrid, AGI, Arribadas 538.

108. Tibesar, "Alternativa," 229–83; San Antonio, Petition to the crown, 2 May 1751, Madrid, AGI, Lima 541.

109. San Joseph, Letter to José Sanz, commissary-general of missions, 19 September 1718, Tarma, AGI, Lima 537.

110. Amich, *Historia de las misiones,* 151–54 (quote, 152); Marquez de Soto Hermoso, governor of Tarma, Report on the missions, 4 July 1736, AGI, Lima 536.

111. Amich, *Historia de las misiones,* 145–50.

112. Castelfuerte, Report to the king, 8 November 1734, Lima, AGI, Lima 539.

113. "Mapa de los Mártires de Santa Rosa de Ocopa," original 1736, copied 1746, AGI, Mapas y Planos, Perú y Chile 32. Four of those sixteen full friars came from the monastery of Pisco; Amich, *Historia de las misiones,* 141.

114. Lehnertz, "Lands of the Infidels," 75–76.

115. These types of impromptu expeditions by mission friars were prevalent in the expeditions to the Pampas de Sacramento; Amich, *Historia de las misiones,* 145–50.

116. Tibesar, "San Antonio de Eneno," 27. *Ayllo* is most likely a hispanicization of the Quechua word *ayllu* (kin group).

117. Lehnertz, "Lands of the Infidels," 399; AGI, Arribadas 538.

118. "Mapa de los Mártires," 1736, AGI, Mapas y Planos, Perú y Chile 32.

119. Heras, *Comienzos de las misiones*, 156–92 (published version of BNP, C. 342, ff. 154–202); Lehnertz, "Lands of the Infidels," 116, 424n.

120. "Mapa de los Mártires," 1736, AGI, Mapas y Planos, Perú y Chile 32.

121. Juan and Ulloa, *Discourse and Political Reflections*, 166–67.

122. Such short, localized but violent rebellions were common in colonial Spanish America; see Taylor, *Drinking, Homicide.*

123. Miguel de Rementeria, lieutenant general of Tarma, Report on the rebellion at Metraro, 2 September 1720, Tarma, AGI, Lima 538; Royal decree, 12 March 1718, San Lorenzo de el Escorial, AGI, Arribadas 591; Santos-Granero, "Epidemias y sublevaciones," 26–52. The story about Friar Fernando is found in Francisco de San Joseph, Report to the crown, 12 June 1732, Ocopa, AGI, Lima 539.

124. Much of this account is taken from Amich, *Historia de las misiones*, 155–63, but is corroborated by Friar Lorenzo Nuñes de Mendoza, commissary-general of the Ocopa missions, Letters to the viceroy, 13 May 1736 and 14 April 1737, Ocopa, AGI, Lima 539; Friar Alonso Lopez de Casas, commissary-general of the Franciscan order in Peru, Report, 19 May 1737, Lima, AGI, Lima 539; and Real Acuardo, Act, 16 April 1737, Lima, AGI Lima 539. The dialogue is probably invented, but I think it reflects some concerns about the Ocopa enterprise that the missionaries and perhaps the montañeses were feeling. See also Santos-Granero, "Epidemias y sublevaciones," 41–42; Lehnertz, "Lands of the Infidels," 112–13.

125. Amich, *Historia de las misiones*, 155–63.

Chapter 2
Rebellion, Religion, and Reform

In June 1742 the Juan Santos Atahualpa rebellion erupted from the mission of Quisopango. It eventually led to the destruction of all but two of Ocopa's twenty-three mission stations. Despite a recurring pattern of violent resistance in the high jungle mission stations serviced by the friars, the rebellion took the missionaries almost completely by surprise. By this time, whispers of indigenous unrest (and actual uprisings) had become a common facet of missionary service in the Ocopa enterprise and throughout the Montaña, but the size and scope of the rebellion were unmatched by earlier revolts. Like the Torote rebellion five years before, most uprisings in the missions had been limited to a single village or group; the Juan Santos Atahualpa rebellion, though, spread over a large swath of the central Montaña and involved multiple ethnic groups. Furthermore, the rebellion was led not by a local cacique but by a highland Andean interloper, Juan Santos, suggesting that it had the potential to spread beyond the remote jungle missions.

For centuries, missionaries and scholars alike have focused on the Juan Santos Atahualpa rebellion when discussing the history of the missions of Santa Rosa de Ocopa. The Ocopa missionaries used the rebellion, particularly the stories of the martyrs it produced, as a tool of propaganda to acquire more support for their missionary enterprise.[1] Later, nationalist Peruvian historians, particularly during the Indigenismo movement of the 1920s–40s, erroneously linked the rebellion to the creole-led independence movement some eighty years later.[2] More recent scholarship has focused on characterizing the rebellion as the beginning of a series of indigenous-led, anticolonial uprisings that culminated in what historians have dubbed the "Great Age of Andean Insurrections" (1780–82).[3] Although such a direct link to these later uprisings is tenuous at best, the Juan Santos Atahualpa rebellion was of sufficient size to warrant the attention and concern of high-ranking royal ministers in Lima and Madrid, including the viceroy and the minister of the Indies. Indeed, royal officials attempted to connect Juan Santos to conspiracies and civil disturbances throughout the viceroyalty of Peru.[4]

This previous historiography identifies the local and perhaps regional political implications of the rebellion but tends to ignore its larger transatlantic ramifications. The uprising revealed the complex problems that created the nascent centralization initiatives of the Bourbon reform process. To many regalists, the Ocopa missionaries were ideal clerics, helping to expand Spanish hegemony into a region previously unincorporated into the empire. For this reason, the missionaries gained unprecedented support for their endeavors from crown authorities in Madrid during the first half of the century. At a regional level, however, Ocopa's power and size threatened viceregal authorities, who were attempting to consolidate royal control in Peru. This struggle between local and empire-wide interests sometimes motivated reformers and nonreformers to act in ways that seemed to contradict their own goals. Bureaucrats in Lima desired to exploit Amazonian resources, yet they were willing to neglect and even obstruct the missionaries in their efforts in order to attenuate their influence in Peru. This tension and confusion affected events throughout the viceroyalty, ultimately aiding the Juan Santos Atahualpa rebels to realize their aspirations for autonomy.

Juan Santos Atahualpa

Little is known about Juan Santos before the outbreak of the rebellion in June 1742. The Franciscan chronicler José Amich described him as a mestizo from Cuzco who was taller than average with pale skin, muscular limbs, a beard, and hair cut short like "the Indians of Quito," but one who dressed in the traditional cushma of the Montaña.[5] Another source said that Juan Santos was about thirty years old when the rebellion broke out. He spoke or had knowledge of at least four languages: Spanish, Latin, Quechua, and Asháninka. Juan Santos claimed to have been the servant of a Jesuit priest, whom he had accompanied to Europe and Africa. He maintained that sometime during this journey he had met with "the English," who had agreed to support him by sea in his rebellion against the Spanish.[6] According to Amich's account, written several decades later, Juan Santos then entered the Ocopa missions in May 1742 in an attempt to flee justice after he had killed a man in Huamanga (modern-day Ayacucho). According to this account, while wandering through the high jungle he encountered the cacique of Quisopango, Mateo Santabangori, who guided him to his village, where he began his rebel movement.[7] A more contemporary account written by royal officials in 1744 refutes Amich's version, instead saying that in 1729–30 Santos traveled along the Peruvian Andes "from Cusco to Cajamarca" claiming to be the legitimate descendant of the Incas and attempting to "restore his kingdom from the power of the Spanish and free his vassals from the tyrannies that they suffer." After this attempt to rally support in the highlands, perhaps some ten years before the outbreak of the rebellion, Santos made his way to the missions.[8]

Considering Santos's fluency in the local dialect and his widespread local support, it is more likely that he had spent considerable time among the montañeses before the outbreak of hostilities in 1742. Several years before the rebellion, according to another Franciscan chronicler, Francisco Rodríquez Tena, a lay friar from Cusco named José Vela prophesized that "in seventeen forty-two an abominable monster will rise up in this kingdom who will attempt, filled with arrogance, to crown himself king of all this kingdom and new world of Peru," suggesting that rumors of a rebellion in the region had already reached the highlands.[9] What is certain, however, is that a year before the rebellion the commissary of the missions in Peru, Friar Joseph Gil Muñoz, noted that "infidels" were meeting with converts in "secret conferences," which made the converts "vacillate in their fidelity" so as to want to "insult the father missionaries and take away their lives."[10] By June 1742, missionaries in both the Tarma and Jauja entradas as far out as the Gran Pajonal started reporting that people, mostly young men, were fleeing their missions, headed, according to those who remained, to Quisopango to see the "Apu-Inca," or Lord Inca Juan Santos Atahualpa.

Santos created the fervor that fueled his rebellion by combining Catholic theology with highland Andean and Montaña millenarianism. For example, when the first Ocopa missionary, Friar Santiago Vázquez de Caicedo, arrived in Quisopango from the neighboring mission of Autes, he found people gathered in the center of the village. As he approached he called out "hail Mary" to the crowd, who responded with the perfunctory "without sin conceived." After Santos appeared wearing a silver cross, Friar Santiago asked him questions about Christian doctrine, to which Santos responded in Spanish in a satisfactory manner (at least to the friar), and then he recited the Creed in Latin. According to most accounts, Santos claimed that God had told him to reconquer Peru from Spain. Amich went so far as to state that Santos claimed he was the Son of God.[11] Juan Santos also seems to have borrowed ideas from Mosaic law, learned perhaps during his years serving a Jesuit priest, ordering that the villagers slaughter all the pigs, deeming them to be unclean.[12]

Although Juan Santos outwardly practiced Christian rites, he incorporated rhetoric that appealed particularly to highland Andean cultural sensibilities. According to the few existing descriptions of Santos's ideology, all of them secondhand, Santos continued to rail against the abuses of the Spanish colonizers, as he had reportedly done in the highlands between 1729 and 1730. For example, he ordered an end to *obrajes* (workhouses) and the mita, neither of which existed in the missions. He also invoked Andean millenarian rhetoric. He conceived of the world as having only three kingdoms: Spain, the Congo, and his kingdom, which he should rightfully rule as the direct descendant of the last Inca emperor, Atahualpa.[13] He took the name Atahualpa to emphasize his claim to royal Inca lineage. One scholar has argued that his choice was an attempt to invoke the Andean myth of Incarrí, a messianic tradition that held that the Incas would return from the dead to retake control of Peru.[14] According to Amich, Santos promised that he would expand his rebellion into the heavily populated highlands and even sent a "spy" to try to convince the highland Andeans to join his cause. From all accounts, his goal was not simply local control but to march on Lima, where, aided by the British navy, he would force the viceroy to surrender Peru.[15]

Both the Ocopa missionaries and viceregal officials used fears that Santos's rebellion would somehow spread to the highlands to urge the crown to support their plan for action against his followers. In both sets of correspondence to the crown there are vague references to highland Andeans going down to the jungle; however, there are no examples of such a movement happening en masse. Though many highland Andeans may have sympathized with Santos, they seem to not have recognized his leadership. As part of the long process of colonization in Peru, the Spanish had divided most of the Andeans along kinship groups. Andeans usually only recognized the leadership of their immediate *kuraka* (ethnic lord). Larger indigenous hierarchies, for the most part, had been long since dismantled. Consequently, most rebel groups in the colonial period were extended kinship communities such as in the Tupac Amaru rebellion. Therefore, neither Juan Santos's anticolonial nor his millenarian rhetoric seems to have been enough to convince large numbers from the highlands to join him in the jungle.[16]

Juan Santos's military force actually was composed almost entirely of indigenous nations from the Montaña, although he made no reference to them in his statements recorded by contemporaries. Anthropologist Stefano Varese argues that Santos was able to command jungle Amerindian forces because of key alliances he had forged with the local caciques in the Tarma entrada.[17] Santos maintained a close relationship with Mateo de Assia, the cacique of Metraro and Eneno, who served as one of his principal generals.[18] Varese, similarly, contends that the community of Sonomoro did not join the rebellion because of its cacique's positive disposition toward the missionaries, though he ignores the fact that the Torote rebellion had razed the village only five years earlier, perhaps making them apprehensive to join another rebel group.[19] Certainly, the support of local caciques was vital in initiating the rebellion. But the size, duration, and multiethnic composition of the rebellion suggest that Santos's appeal to the Amerindians' cultural and economic interests were more important in mobilizing supporters than any traditional ethnic or familial alliances.

Santos possibly invoked anticolonial or religious themes among the montañeses similar to those he did with the highland Andeans, though no written account of this remains. Montaña cultures contained millenarian traditions like those among the highland Incarrí that Santos certainly exploited. The Asháninkas had the Kesha, a cultural hero with messianic characteristics, and the Yaneshas had the Yompor Ror, a messianic figure who was supposed to return to give the people the gift of immortality, a belief possibly derived from the hybrid mixture of local beliefs with Christianity.[20] After Santos's arrival, the Yaneshas alternatively began to call the Yompor Ror the Yompor Santo, giving credence to Santos utilizing a deeper socioreligious connection to the Montaña cultures. Similar beliefs were shared by all the other nations that purportedly participated in the rebellion.[21]

The peoples of the Montaña had other socioeconomic reasons for rebelling against the missionaries. Well before Juan Santos Atahualpa arrived in the missions, the montañeses had rebelled violently against the missionaries (see chapter 1). They probably rose up with Santos for the same reasons they had before: the rigid missionary lifestyle, increased intrusion of commercial interests, and, most important, demographic collapse caused by successive waves of epidemics, which the montañeses blamed on the missionaries. This time, however, Juan Santos coordinated their efforts more effectively. The missionaries, for their part, attributed Juan Santos's popularity to his promises of steel tools, which the montañeses "search[ed] for with great covetousness,"[22] a gross oversimplification of complex resistance to missionaries' cultural and commercial impositions.

Juan Santos also drew a third group into the rebellion: Africans who served the missionaries. Enslaved and free blacks had become an integral part of the missionary enterprise. Ironically, Juan Santos specifically vilified Africans as functionaries of their Spanish masters in accounts of his speeches. In Quisopango, as the forces of Juan Santos took control of the mission, villagers savagely attacked three blacks left behind by the Ocopa friars. At the same time, Santos claimed to oppose slavery, prohibiting it in his new kingdom, though his rhetoric also suggested that Africans would be driven out of Peru with the Spaniards.[23] Despite these contradictions, some blacks joined and even served in leadership positions in Juan Santos's forces. African Antonio Gatica was one of Juan Santos's principal commanders alongside his brother-in-law, the cacique Mateo de Assia. He was joined by at least seven other blacks. Since some Africans had worked as soldiers for the missionaries (Gatica himself had been named sergeant major of the mission station of Eneno), they must have proved invaluable to the rebellion, most likely wielding and perhaps training montañeses to use European weapons that Santos's forces had acquired.[24]

Juan Santos's rhetoric also aimed at pitting the Catholic regular orders against each other, particularly Jesuits against Franciscans. Santos stated that once in power he would send the Franciscan friars back to Spain and obtain permission from Rome to ordain natives to be priests. He then stipulated that the only priests allowed in his kingdom would be Jesuits. Although Santos's preference for Jesuits certainly stemmed from his relationship with his former master, the Society of Jesus was the only regular congregation at this time that frequently allowed non-Europeans into its ranks. Almost from its arrival in Peru in 1568, the Society had included mestizos among its ranks, arguing that their knowledge of local languages made them more effective missionaries. Furthermore, according to Santos's own alleged statements, he had witnessed Africans saying mass among the Jesuits in Angola and added, "Even though they were not white like the Spaniards they could be good fathers and priests."[25] Santos certainly, therefore, used this rhetoric to exploit existing animosities between the Franciscans and the Jesuits, who had been vying for missionary territories in the frontiers of Peru since the late sixteenth century.

At the time of Juan Santos's rebellion, King Philip V favored the Jesuits, even selecting one as his confessor, leading to their ascendency in Spanish imperial politics during the early eighteenth century and causing anxiety among the Franciscans.[26] Furthermore, the idea of ordaining natives to the priesthood was hotly debated during this period both within the Franciscan order and among regalist ministers, who opposed such deviations from orthodox social hierarchies. Ocopa was one of the earliest proponents among the Franciscans of Peru of the ordination of native clergy, and at the same time Ocopa missionaries were battling Juan Santos their support of this cause was eroding their already tenuous standing with the viceregal government. Perhaps Santos hoped this declaration would spark conflicts both within and among the orders and the Bourbon government that would give him time to establish himself in the central Montaña.

Santos did not wait passively for his rhetoric to inflame imperial rivalries or incite a general insurrection. By the time Friar Santiago arrived in Quisopango, Santos's band had already overpowered the loyal blacks, stolen their weapons, and constructed a crude fort. Over the next few months Santos's forces, commanded by Assia and Gatica, expelled converts and missionaries alike from most of the missions in the Tarma entrada. By September 1742 most of the missionaries had gathered in the last mission left in the entrada, Quimirí. Meanwhile, word of the rebellion had reached Lima, where Villagarcía and the audiencia voted to provide 6,000 pesos and one hundred muskets to the frontier governors of Tarma and Jauja, with orders to subdue the rebellion.[27] Governors Benito Troncoso and Pedro de Milla met in a war council early in September and devised a plan to take Juan Santos in a pincer movement. Troncoso would lead his troops through the Jauja entrada behind where they believed Juan Santos to be encamped at Metraro or Eneno. Meanwhile, Milla would make a more direct advance through the Tarma entrada down the Chanchamayo River valley (see figure 2). They hoped to trap Juan Santos so that he could not retreat into the jungle, as Ignacio Torote had done a few years before. To prepare for the arrival of troops from Tarma, the presiding missionary at Quimirí ordered one of their oblates to go with several local converts to clear a path for the soldiers. He returned without success, reporting the presence of many "infidels" blocking the path. Two missionaries who had fled to Quimirí from their assigned missions, Domingo García and

José Cabanes, volunteered to lead another expedition to clear the paths. As their party attempted to repair the bridge over the La Sal River, they were ambushed and killed along with one oblate.[28]

By mid-September 1742, Troncoso and Milla had begun to prepare for their advances toward Juan Santos's encampment. On the seventeenth, Troncoso gathered his forces at Sonomoro, the first mission in the Jauja entrada, but with no word from Milla he waited ten days before departing. The two commanders never successfully coordinated their attacks. On the twenty-seventh, Troncoso began his march, and with the aid of sixty local Amerindians they arrived at the birthplace of the rebellion, Quisopango, two weeks later. Troncoso attacked the makeshift fortress Juan Santos had erected and killed the local cacique with no losses to his own troops. As he suspected, the bulk of Juan Santos's forces had moved on and were now at the mission villages of Eneno and Nijándaris. Unable to communicate with Milla, he probably realized that he could not face such a large host so far from his line of supplies in the harsh conditions of the high jungle and decided to retreat in good order back to Sonomoro. Milla, meanwhile, was delayed because of a lack of supplies, and he did not leave Tarma until 1 October. In mid-October, Milla arrived at Cerro de la Sal, but he remained there for two more weeks to wait for reinforcements from Tarma. Fearing that disease would ravage his troops, on 1 November he decided to attack Nijándaris before help from Tarma could arrive. At Nijándaris, however, fierce resistance and the fear that the rebels would cut off his retreat forced Milla to withdraw under the cover of darkness back to Cerro de la Sal and, ultimately, Tarma. By the summer of 1743, with the exception of Sonomoro, the missionaries had abandoned all the missions in the entradas of Tarma and Jauja for the shelter of the highlands.[29]

Once word reached Lima of Troncoso's and Milla's failure to crush the rebellion, Viceroy Villagarcía ordered the construction of a new fortress at Quimirí in order to "subjugate the apostates and infidels, hinder the transit of Indians from the sierra to the jungle, and also to serve as a staging area for the formal expedition which he considered launching to capture the rebel."[30] To assure success, he sent two companies of soldiers from Callao, under captains Pedro Alamora and Fabricio Bartuli, along with four four-pound cannons and four swivel guns. In mid-October 1743 the expedition left Tarma under the command of the governor of the province, Alfonso Santa, and accompanied by three Ocopa missionaries, including Friar Lorenzo Núñez. Fortunately for the expedition, their departure coincided with Juan Santos's attack on Huancabamba farther to the north, and they arrived in Quimirí without incident on the twenty-seventh. There they resupplied and garrisoned the fort with seventy men under the command of Captain Bartuli, with Friar Núñez attending to the soldiers' spiritual needs, before marching back to Tarma on 11 November. Though Santa armed the fort with the weapons and munitions from Callao, he left only a small amount of food, with the promise to resupply those remaining later. Two days after the expedition returned to Tarma, a party was sent to resupply the fortress. Because the initial expedition had not encountered any resistance, in all likelihood because of the absence of rebel forces in the area, the resupplying party was lightly armed. When they reached the Chanchamayo River, rebels ambushed them, killing seventeen men and taking possession of the supplies so desperately needed at the fort. As the lack of supplies became desperate in the fort, the commander sent Friar Núñez back to Tarma to beg for relief. Despite the real threat of capture and death, he and another missionary made their way to Tarma but found Santa unwilling to help relieve the fortress, probably because of the fate of the resupply party. Santa's intransigence forced the friars to travel to Lima for aid. Upon meeting with Núñez, Viceroy Villagarcía ordered the governors of Jauja and Tarma to relieve the fort "with the promptness that [this] urgency required."[31]

By 28 December, three hundred men had left Tarma under the command of frontier governor Benito Troncoso. Sometime before the beginning of January, however, the rebels had breached the fort and massacred the garrison. As a result, when Troncoso's expedition arrived at the Chanchamayo River on the third, they were met with artillery fire from the cannon and swivel guns left at the fort as well as a display of the bloody shirts taken from its fallen defenders. Seeing no way to cross the river under fire and no purpose in relieving the now-dead garrison, Troncoso withdrew his men back to Tarma, marking the last armed expedition to attempt to end the rebellion under Viceroy Villagarcía.[32]

After the fall of Quimirí, Friar Núñez began negotiations with the rebels through intermediaries to allow missionaries to reenter the Jauja and Tarma entradas. According to Amich, however, this negotiation failed because Villagarcía prohibited Núñez from personally entering the Montaña to conclude the peace agreement. Seemingly unconvinced of the Franciscans' ability to deal with Juan Santos, Villagarcía turned to the Jesuits to mediate an end to the rebellion. The Jesuits had petitioned the viceroy to allow one of their society, a Father Irusta, to enter the Montaña and negotiate a cessation of hostilities. Almost certainly, these Jesuits believed that since Juan Santos favored the Society over the Franciscans they would have success and quite possibly take over the missions from Ocopa. In the summer of 1745, Irusta, who seems to have had some experience in the central Montaña, though no Jesuit expeditions had entered the region in the previous fifty years, met with several principal caciques and claimed that the cacique Mateo de Assia had agreed to help royal troops capture Juan Santos. But news of this possible break in Juan Santos's alliance did not reach Lima before Villagarcía had left office in 1745.[33]

Viceroy Villagarcía's inability to crush the rebellion did not make him reluctant to blame the Ocopa missionaries for instigating it. He traced the outbreak of the rebellion to the heavy-handed behavior of one of the Ocopa missionaries, the then-deceased Friar Domingo García. García had ordered Mateo de Assia whipped for interfering with the punishment of his brother Bartolomé, who had been accused of adultery. Villagarcía judged this action to be of "indiscrete immoderation" that made Assia feel "notable insult," causing him to lead his people "to rise up against the obedience" of the friars.[34] To counter the viceroy's attacks, the Ocopa missionaries appeared before Governor Troncoso to present testimony on the matter. They probably hoped to present this evidence to the crown to exonerate themselves from any rumors of malfeasance that might have reached Madrid. They most likely selected Troncoso because he had significant personal and economic ties to Ocopa. In 1750, for example, the governor donated the entirety of his deceased wife's estate, totaling more than 16,000 silver pesos, to Ocopa.[35] Thus they believed he would be a sympathetic mediator. From the testimony, Troncoso concluded that Bartolomé de Assia had indeed committed adultery and that in trying to interfere with his brother's punishment Mateo de Assia had broken the law; therefore, García had every legal right to whip both brothers in an attempt to teach Catholic sexual morality to the "infidels" under Mateo's leadership. Governor Troncoso was further persuaded in his ruling by the discovery of Friar Domingo's decapitated head, which, despite being buried almost a month in moist jungle soil, was apparently "fresh, without corruption or bad odor," a well-known sign of sainthood.[36] Whether these testimonies ever even reached Villagarcía or other government officials is unclear.

Villagarcía's overall assessment of the missionaries was divided between his private opinion and his official statements. In a private letter of advice to his successor, he admitted that "experience will manifest to his excellency that nature [in the Montaña] has placed an impenetrable bar to arms and that this is a conquest of hearts [*ánimos*] that the wisdom of the missionaries will make [against] the backwardness of the Barbarians."[37] Even publicly, Villagarcía did not place complete blame on the missionaries for the rebellion, recognizing that obviously the "Indios Chunchos" (nonmission Amerindians) who had supported the "pretend Incas" and actually rebelled had ruined the missionaries' work.[38] His official report to the crown on the rebellion, however, was also bitingly critical. He considered the restoration of the missions to be "very difficult," and though he said he could not deny the zeal of the missionaries he questioned their ability to administer their missions. He complained that though his government had given the Franciscan missionaries 16,000 pesos they had little to show for it, and he questioned whether it would be "convenient if those missions remained under the power of those friars."[39] Perhaps the viceroy's attack against Ocopa to the crown was an attempt to create a scapegoat for his administration's inability to deal with Santos. A later viceroy, Manuel de Amat, hinted that the king had removed Villagarcía as viceroy for that failure, although he was seventy-nine years of age at the time and due for relief.[40] In many ways, however, Viceroy Villagarcía's attacks of ineptitude against the Ocopa friars echoed previous criticisms, which would be repeated in later years as Bourbon reformers made their case against Ocopa.

King Philip V replaced Villagarcía with José Antonio Manso de Velasco y Sánchez de Samaniego, then captain-general of Chile. Manso de Velasco was an up-and-coming figure in the Spanish bureaucracy. Born in the northern Spanish province of La Rioja in the city of Torrecilla in 1689, José Antonio Manso de Velasco had risen through the ranks of the Spanish government through a combination of military success and political skill. In 1705 he joined the Spanish royal guards and saw combat in the War of Spanish Succession (1700–13) and subsequent conflicts. In 1736 he was named captain-general of the Philippines, but the assignment was later changed to Chile, where he served from 1737 to 1745. In Chile, Manso de Velasco gained invaluable experience when he oversaw the reconstruction of Valdivia after an earthquake destroyed the city in November 1737. But Manso de Velasco's 1744 appointment as viceroy of Peru was not based on his experience alone. Manso de Velasco was closely aligned in court with his fellow *riojano,* Zenón de Somodevilla y Bengoechea, the first marqués de la Ensenada.[41] The two men had become friends when serving as officers during the successful siege of Oran in 1732.[42] Somodevilla, like Manso de Velasco, was not of noble birth. Having started as a clerk, he advanced his way through the Spanish civil administration. After helping to orchestrate the coronation of King Philip V's youngest two sons as kings of Naples and Sicily and Parma, Somodevilla received the Neapolitan title "marqués de la Ensenada." In 1743, because of Ensenada's adept administrative skills, King Philip appointed him minister of finance, war, navy, and the Indies as well as secretary of state and superintendent of revenues—or, in the words of one historian, "secretary of everything."[43] Ensenada's correspondence with Manso de Velasco is peppered with flowery odes of brotherhood, such as referring to each other as "countryman of my soul," and demonstrates a close friendship and political alliance.[44] Both were dedicated to reform and hoped to revive Spain's ailing overseas empire by increasing royal control. Having the patronage of Ensenada, who by 1745 had become the most powerful man in Spain, gave Manso de Velasco unprecedented latitude in reforming the viceroyalty, or at least so the new viceroy believed.

Ensenada ordered that Manso de Velasco's first task be to "assure the pacification" of the rebellious provinces in the east. Ensenada suggested that Manso de Velasco could even bring in troops from Chile to quell the Juan Santos rebellion.[45] Ensenada's concern in quashing the rebellion had more to do with assuring the viceroyalty's security than with helping Ocopa. Also in July, just as Manso de Velasco became viceroy, Father Irusta arrived in Lima with word of Mateo de Assia's defection to the royalist cause. Manso de

Velasco acted quickly, ordering troops from Callao to Tarma, placing them under the command of General José de Llamas. Llamas arrived in Tarma in February with orders from the viceroy to enter the Montaña immediately with the aid of Governor Troncoso. Troncoso warned against an expedition during the rainy season, which made the Montaña roads impassable and fostered disease. Not wanting to contradict his orders from the viceroy, however, Llamas pressed on, and in March his troops left Tarma in two separate parties, with two hundred men-at-arms and three hundred baggage carriers commanded by Llamas himself, and one hundred and fifty men-at-arms with two hundred baggage carriers under Troncoso—the largest expedition ever launched against the Juan Santos rebels.

The expedition was an utter failure. Troncoso's warning about mounting an expedition in the rainy season proved prophetic. Damp conditions rotted provisions and caused the troops to suffer from disease and fatigue. Pack animals slipped and got stuck in soft mud; most had to be abandoned. Both parties had small skirmishes near Nijándaris, but neither achieved victory, as the rains saturated their powder supplies to the point that they were unusable. The alliance with Mateo de Assia that the Jesuits claimed to have forged never materialized, and after a few weeks both parties returned to Tarma. In his official correspondence with the crown on 21 June 1746, Manso de Velasco claimed victory for the Llamas expedition, asserting that despite their losses they had at least pushed Juan Santos deeper into the jungle, thereby securing the borders.[46] Whether the expedition actually accomplished this or Juan Santos simply retreated on his own accord is not known. In all of Manso de Velasco's correspondence about the expedition, there is no mention of attempting to reclaim the lost Ocopa missions. For the viceroy, fighting Juan Santos was about security, not religion. In October 1746, however, events in the viceregal capital temporarily diverted the viceroy's attention from the eastern jungles of Peru.

The Lima Earthquake and Reforms

On 28 October 1746 at 10:30 in the evening, a massive, estimated 8.4 magnitude earthquake rocked Lima, instantly killing about 1,500 in the viceregal capital. The worst of the disaster came at 11:00 when the sea around Lima's port, Callao, began to retreat. Suddenly, a wall of water, approximately fifty feet tall, bulldozed the bustling port town, killing all but a few hundred of its roughly six thousand inhabitants. Many ships belonging to the large merchant fleet in the harbor survived the initial wave but were subsequently destroyed by the backrush of debris-filled water from the leveled port city. Most of the viceregal government buildings collapsed; both towers of the cathedral fell, and parts of the viceregal palace were uninhabitable. Lima lay in ruins and Callao essentially no longer existed.[47]

José Manso de Velasco saw opportunity in the ruins of the viceregal capital. Along with his allies, in both Lima and Madrid, he planned to rebuild Lima, both physically and spiritually, on an enlightened regalist model. Of particular importance to this project was divesting the regular clergy of their influence within the city and in the viceroyalty as a whole. Starting in December 1746, just two months after the earthquake, Manso de Velasco wrote a series of letters to the crown regarding the state of the regular clergy in Lima. Although numbers of clergy in the city were comparable to that of most Spanish cities during this time, the earthquake's destruction of the convents and monasteries had exposed just how many regular clerics there really were. The viceroy criticized the severe overcrowding of the major convents and monasteries, which he believed caused laxity in the regular orders' religious piety. The viceroy even posited that "Divine Providence" had sent the earthquake to facilitate the reformation of the Lima convents. Manso de Velasco also targeted the regular clergy's control of the rural Indian parishes, which had become a significant source of income for the regular orders in the viceroyalty. Manso de Velasco lamented that rather than reinvest tithes back into the parishes the regulars stripped these parishes of all their funds to pay for their large urban convents.[48]

In the intervening weeks and months after the earthquake, Manso de Velasco began enacting reforms aimed specifically at reducing the power of the clergy. For example, the viceroy targeted the city's *censos,* liens and loans that monasteries and convents made to private citizens, other religious institutions, and even the state. The interest charged on the censos was set below market rate to avoid the appearance of usury, which was considered a sin by the Catholic Church. These loans usually were couched in terms of "contracts of purchase and sale in which the [religious houses] purchased the right to collect an annuity."[49] By the eighteenth century, however, this distinction began to fade as the use of terms such as principal (*principal*) and interest (*rédito*) came into normal parlance. To facilitate the rebuilding of the city, in January 1747 the viceroy froze all censo payments for two years, cut the principal of all censos in half, and reduced the rates of interest from the standard 5 percent to 2 percent or 1 percent, depending on the type of censo. Manso de Velasco argued that by doing this he would allow Lima residents to rebuild their homes quicker, since many limeños still owed money to the Church for their old residences that now lay in ruins.[50] This was helpful for most limeños, but more important to the viceroy it was helpful to the crown, which was also in debt to the religious houses. Manso de Velasco even froze all payments to religious orders from the crown during the months immediately after the earthquake. The reduction of censo interest rates, of course, impaired the orders' ability to rebuild their religious convents and monasteries, which Manso de Velasco hoped to reduce in number and size in his enlightened regalist Lima.[51]

Manso de Velasco surrounded himself with like-minded limeños, but not everyone in the viceregal capital agreed with his reforms, particularly his anticlerical policies. Many of his supporters were prominent citizens of the city, including members of the audiencia, who shared his regalist vision for the Spanish empire. But the viceroy's critics, including many members of the clergy, saw this group as a *pandilla,* or street gang, devoted more to making themselves rich than to restoring the well-being of Lima. The archbishop of Lima, Pedro Antonio Barroeta, a particularly vocal critic, claimed that Manso de Velasco's men were immoral, prone to gambling, and promiscuous, and that one was even a homosexual. He even went so far as to accuse one of the viceroy's closest associates, Judge Juan Marín de Poveda, of having leprosy. Some sources indicate that the archbishop also considered excommunicating the viceroy. In stark contrast, royal officials in Madrid praised Manso de Velasco as an efficient administrator. The court ministers were particularly impressed with his continual remittances of silver back to Spain, even immediately after the disaster. In 1748 his efforts earned him the title Conde de Superunda, (Count over the Waves).[52]

Consequently, when Superunda's reports on the fallen state of the regular orders after the earthquake reached Madrid, the powerful marqués de la Ensenada worked quickly to back his recommendations. In 1748, Ensenada and then-secretary of state José de Carvajal y Lancaster met at the Escorial Palace with the archbishops-elect of Lima and Mexico as well as the heads of all the religious orders. Ensenada and Carvajal reached an agreement with the prelates to reduce the number of regular clergy. Ensenada convinced the king to form a *junta particular de ministros* (special council of ministers) with the archbishops-elect of Lima, Bogotá, and Mexico City; four members of the Council of Castile; and three members of the Council of the Indies to expedite the reform process. Between 29 November 1748 and March 1749, Carvajal along with the king's confessor, Jesuit father Francisco de Rávago, convened the junta on Carvajal's estate. Based on the reports of several government observers, including Manso de Velasco, the junta agreed that the crown should allow only licensed convents and monasteries to rebuild, and that every order in the city should be limited to one religious house for each gender. These three men, Ensenada, Carvajal, and Rávago, constituted what many called the "Jesuit party." Due to their, and the king's, proclivity for the Society of Jesus, it was exempt from or unaffected by most of the reforms.

Disagreements within the government on the exact details of the recommendations delayed action. In the end, the crown produced a vaguely worded royal decree in 1751, almost five years after Superunda's initial complaint. When the decrees reached Lima, they were too little and too late. The vagueness of the official guidelines allowed the religious orders to contest or ignore them, and in the end most convents were rebuilt.[53] In part, the recommendations for rebuilding the convents were so mismanaged because the junta had spent most of its time discussing the removal of the regular orders from their rural Indian parishes. These parishes had been a concern well before the earthquake, and the junta was eager for decisive action. Upon the junta's recommendation, on 4 October 1749 the crown ordered the gradual removal of the regulars from the rural parishes in the archdiocese of Lima. The guidelines in the decree stipulated that when a regular cleric vacated an Indian parish a secular priest would fill the position. At first this rule pertained only to the archdioceses of Lima, Mexico City, and Bogotá; a later decree in 1753 extended it to include all of Spanish America.[54] One of the reasons the crown wanted to remove regulars from their parishes was so that the religious orders could concentrate on missionary work in the frontiers of the Spanish empire rather than in their large urban convents and monasteries.[55] In principal, therefore, Ocopa was fulfilling the express will of this new wave of reformers.

Even before the Juan Santos Atahualpa rebellion broke out, however, a current of distrust and hostility against Ocopa existed within reformist circles within the viceroyalty of Peru. These negative sentiments were evident in the famous report on the state of the viceroyalty commonly known as *Noticias Secretas de América*, written by two young Spanish naval officers and dedicated regalists, Jorge Juan y Santacilia and Antonio de Ulloa. In 1735, Juan and Ulloa accompanied an officially sanctioned French scientific expedition to measure one degree on the equator. They stayed in the Andean region for eleven years, taking notes on both its natural wonders and its political intrigues. Upon their return to Spain in 1749, Ensenada commissioned a report of their observations on the general state of the colonies. Intended only for a small group of crown officials, their report was damning, citing gross abuses by both government officials and the regular orders.[56] Except for the Jesuits, Juan and Ulloa painted the regular clergy as an undisciplined, greedy rabble who "rival[ed] the rural governors in extracting wealth from the blood and sweat of the people."[57] Juan and Ulloa accused the friars in the frontier missions of colluding with local Spaniards to exploit the Amerindians' labor, which in turn incited the natives to revolt. As a prime example of missionary abuses causing revolts, the young reformers cited the Ocopa missionary involvement in the Juan Santos Atahualpa rebellion:

> To clarify the basis for our opinion, one can simply turn to the latest revolt of the newly converted Indians in the provinces of Jauja and Tarma. Here forty years have been wasted reducing a group of only 2,000 Indians. When the revolt began, the Indians' principal aim was to flee the abuses and excesses of the clergy, since they still did not have to pay tribute. To gain adherents, the rebel leader preached that he was going to free the Indians from Spanish oppression. If the Indians were rebellious by nature, could any Indian from any village—since they are

> treated so cruelly and contemptuously—have failed to take sides against such tyrannical abuse? Certainly not.[58]

Although these words seem to justify the Amerindians' actions, they were written out of political expediency rather than sympathy for the rebels. In truth, Juan and Ulloa never even traveled to the Ocopa missions, or to most of the other places of which they claimed to have intimate knowledge.[59] Most likely these reflections on the Ocopa missionaries were based on reports they had received from like-minded regalists during their stay in Lima. The report, therefore, demonstrated that, at least among some of Lima's political elite, a sentiment existed that Ocopa's missionary efforts were not only unproductive but detrimental to the advancement of royal authority in Peru.

The Lima Conspiracy, the Huarochirí Rebellion, and Friar Calixto

In 1750 the atmosphere of crisis in the city of Lima deepened when, on 21 June, a priest came to the viceroy with the news that during confession he had learned of a conspiracy to overthrow the government by the city's indigenous population. The next morning, another priest came forward with a similar story from a confessant. According to the informants, on 20 September, Saint Michael's Day, a group of the city's Indians would use the day's celebration as a cover to burn the thatched roofs of the temporary houses in the outskirts of the city. A later account claimed that conspirators even had plans to dam the Rimac River so that the fires could not be extinguished. While the citizenry was distracted by the fires, other conspirators would storm the viceregal palace and take control of the armory. As soon as the city was taken, all important Spanish officials would be executed, save a few members of the regular orders to celebrate Catholic rituals in the city. According to Manso de Velasco, the natives were fulfilling a prophecy given by Santa Rosa of Lima that in 1750 Peru would be returned to its original rulers. Some rebels, the viceroy claimed, even wanted to summon Juan Santos and crown him king, though he seriously doubted they had actually communicated with the distant rebel leader. After a brief investigation confirmed the priests' story, Manso de Velasco acted quickly to arrest most of the people involved in the conspiracy. Ultimately, he executed six of the principal conspirators in the main square of Lima; others received lesser punishment, and he issued a general pardon for the rest of the populace.[60]

These executions did not stop the conspiracy from spreading outside the city. While Manso de Velasco arrested suspects in Lima, one of the conspirators, Francisco Jiménez Inca, was attending his daughter's wedding in the adjacent highland province of Huarochirí. During the wedding festivities,

Jiménez Inca recruited several more people to the conspiracy. So when rumors of his impending arrest arrived in Huarochirí after the collapse of the conspiracy in Lima, he was able to secure the protection of two local *kurakas* (indigenous chieftans), Juan Pedro de Puipuilibia and Andres de Borja Puipuilibia. Local Spanish officials were initially unconcerned, believing that when royal troops arrived to arrest Jiménez Inca the local populace would simply hand him over. The Spaniards' feeling of security was confirmed when Borja Puipuilibia agreed to deliver Jiménez Inca. Unfortunately for the Spanish forces, it was a trap. On 19 July, as they waited in the village of Huarochirí for Borja Puipuilibia to arrive with Jiménez Inca, Andeans attacked the Spanish forces by surprise, killing several in the initial assault. Some, including the Spanish commander, José Antonio Salazar y Ugarte, barricaded themselves in the town hall but were killed when they tried to escape the next morning. The rebels' successes did not, however, last long. Within a few weeks, the viceroy dispatched more than four hundred regular army troops and more than one hundred and fifty militiamen to Huarochirí. This Lima force was joined by conscripted indigenous workers from the nearby mining region, and the uprising was eventually crushed.[61]

In his report to the king, dated 24 September 1750, Manso de Velasco blamed the Lima conspiracy and the Huarochirí rebellion on two causes. For one, the viceroy noted that the conspirators denounced the abuses of corrupt *corregidores* (rural governors), judges, and priests—complaints common throughout colonial Spanish America. Principally, however, Manso de Velasco claimed that the Lima conspirators were "exasperated" over the exclusion of natives from the priesthood. The viceroy attributed the "patronage [of] this sentiment [to] two friars of the order of San Francisco" whom he described as possessing "indiscrete piety and poorly allocated zeal."[62] Although he did not mention them by name in the document, the viceroy was referring to two former Ocopa missionaries, who at the time were in residence in Madrid, Brother Calixto de San José Túpac Inka and lay friar Isidoro de Cala y Ortega.

Brother Calixto was born in Tarma in 1710 to Pedro Montes, a Spaniard, and Dominga Estefania Tupac Inca, an Andean of noble Inca descent. According to records procured by the missionaries of Ocopa, he was the eleventh descendant of the Inca Túpac Yupanqui. In 1727, Calixto entered the Franciscan order in Lima as a *donado* (oblate). In colonial Latin America, donados were usually natives, mestizos, or in some cases illegitimate Spaniards who lived in Franciscan communities but worked essentially as servants. They generally could not hold office or lead liturgical or evangelizing activities. A lack of skilled manpower within the order, however, particularly in regards to speaking native languages, forced many Franciscan institutions to allow donados to act in capacities normally reserved for friars. Records of who served in the Ocopa missions before 1755 are incomplete, but anecdotal evidence suggests that the Peruvian Apostolic Institute relied heavily on donados to man its enterprise both in the jungle and at Ocopa.[63] Calixto spent almost two decades in Lima working for various Franciscan institutions principally as a *procurador*, a clergyman charged with soliciting funds from private donors or the crown and with managing those funds for a particular community.[64] At some point, he also spent a few years working as a missionary for Ocopa.[65] In 1744, Calixto accompanied Friar Joseph Gil Muñoz, the commissary of missions in Peru, to Guatemala on his way to Spain to advocate support for the Apostolic Institute. The Cabildo de Indios (indigenous municipal council) of Lima also gave them license to appear before the pope on its behalf to petition for natives to receive full membership in religious orders and to be able to take vows as priests.[66] While waiting to sail, however, Calixto received orders from Friar Mathías de Velasco, commissary-general of the order over all Spanish territories and a former Ocopa missionary, to return to the viceroyalty of Peru to serve in the missions being started by the Apostolic Institute in the audiencia of Charcas (modern-day Bolivia).

During this same period, the procurador of Ocopa in Lima, Friar Juan de San Antonio, began the process of securing documents to prove Calixto's status as a member of the indigenous nobility so that he could be elevated from a donado to a lay friar. Although by law American natives were not allowed to become friars, a royal decree in 1691, later ratified in Peru by Viceroy Castelfuerte in 1725, granted natives of noble birth the privilege of becoming full members of religious orders.[67] Calixto's baptismal records from Tarma had, however, been lost some time after his birth, which forced Friar Juan de San Antonio to meet with his relatives, many of whom had been "elevated" to positions of "Sergeants, Captains, and *Maestros de Campo* [acting field commanders]," in order to verify that he was of Inca royal descent, which the viceroy later ratified.[68] This dispensation for noble American natives was rarely granted and according to the commissary-general, Friar Mathías, the Franciscan order as a general rule banned people of "infidel ancestry" to rise above the level of donado. Nonetheless, he believed the order should make an exception for "Brother Calixto Túpac [because] he had served in the missions, and the College of Ocopa, with much edification and example to the missionaries."[69] After returning to Peru, Calixto traveled to Charcas as Friar Mathías Velasco had ordered. On his way there Calixto passed by Quillabamba (on the frontier of Cusco) where, according to Juan de San Antonio, his indigenous nobility, combined with his language ability, enabled him to build relationships with local caciques, leading the missionaries to have great success.[70]

Despite Calixto's success as a missionary, he continued his advocacy of an indigenous clergy. Historian Jorge Bernales Ballesteros has suggested that after 1744 Calixto began to meet with "discontented Indians" who were upset that natives were not allowed to "embrace the priestly state," though the Cabildo de Indios of Lima's license in 1744 for Calixto and Muñoz to discuss the matter with the pope suggests that Calixto's involvement with this issue perhaps began much earlier.[71] Sometime before 1748, Calixto returned to Lima, where he illegally printed a polemic treatise against the established colonial order, known as the *Representación Verdadera*.[72] Calixto's name appears on the cover letter, but the actual author of the *Representación* is unknown, though Manso de Velasco identified him as Franciscan friar Antonio Garro.[73] As historian Charles Walker points out, although the *Representación* was ostensibly about allowing American natives to become full members of religious orders, at its core it was a pointed criticism of the Spanish colonial system. The author of the *Representación* dwelled at length on the vast gulf between the theory of Spanish colonial rule and the actual practice. In particular, he condemned local viceregal ministers for failing to implement crown policies. He even criticized the colonial policy of not allowing indigenous people to hold government offices. Though the *Representación* contained a condemnation of the Juan Santos Atahualpa rebellion, the author argued that the uprising was caused by a lack of indigenous clergy in the missions as well as "the same Spaniards, soldiers and corregidores, with their exorbitant harassments and lack of modest charity in their treatment of the uncivilized barbarians and the recently converted."[74] The *Representación* utilized the rhetoric of the Lamentations of Jeremiah, which tells the story of the destruction of Jerusalem by the Babylonians, to intone an apocalyptic vision typical of late baroque thinking. The invocation of Lamentations in the *Representación* was a clear message from the author to the reader (the king) that failure to implement its demands would result in the destruction of the viceroyalty.[75]

The *Representación* was not well received by many Spanish regalists, since the campaign to allow American natives into the higher ranks of the clergy would have occasioned a fundamental change in natives' status within the Spanish colonial system. Early on during the colonial period the Spanish had deemed Indians neophytes, new Christians, too inchoate in their understanding of Catholic doctrine to be allowed to teach, give mass, or even be culpable of heresy before the Inquisition. As historian Juan Carlos Estenssoro argues, though the division between European and Amerindian was essentially the justification for race-based discrimination, legally it was American natives' spiritual inferiority that served to justify Spain's colonial hierarchy. Spaniards had to rule because the indigenous population could not understand the true religion and therefore could not be trusted to hold high spiritual or government office.[76] Most Bourbon reformers feared that, if the distinction between old and new Christians were erased by allowing these men to have equal rank with Spaniards in religious communities, it would lead to the breakdown of social boundaries, which undermined the orderly regalist social hierarchy. At the same time, crown officials had to deal with the reality that many clergymen in the Americas, whether peninsular or creole, lacked the language skills necessary to teach the native people of Peru, where Quechua, along with other local languages, still dominated. Therefore, government ministers allowed for certain exceptions, such as the 1725 edict in Peru that ratified the royal decree of 1691 allowing the indigenous nobility to take religious vows.[77]

It is unsurprising, then, that Manso de Velasco lambasted the *Representación,* stating that giving universal permission for American natives to take such vows was against "the nature and condition of the Indians." He blamed the document for stirring up anticolonial sentiment that led to the Lima conspiracy and the Huarochirí rebellion: "The indiscrete expressions with which the [*Representación*] is filled reflect on, more than is just, the [natives'] pain at seeing their own lands possessed and governed by foreigners. [This] has influenced, not a little, [their ability] to avoid disloyal thoughts which they conceive during the drunkenness to which their meetings are reduced, [and] has produced the effect of their reckless machinations." For this reason, even before the Lima conspiracy was discovered, the viceroy had refused to give license to Calixto, to let the *Representación* be published, or to give Calixto permission to travel to Spain to present it before the king.[78]

Calixto persisted in his cause, despite Manso de Velasco's disapproval. After illegally printing the *Representación,* he began sending copies to kurakas throughout the viceroyalty in order to solicit funds for his journey to Spain, where he hoped to present the document before the king. After Manso de Velasco rejected his request for a license to travel to Spain, Calixto decided to take the cheaper, illegal route to Europe through Portuguese Brazil. In September 1749 he left Lima for the overland journey to Buenos Aires, accompanied by Isidoro Cala y Ortega. Friar Isidoro was a creole from Lima and fellow former Ocopa missionary who had served with Calixto in Quillabamba. Isidoro carried an additional petition intended for the pope. It was written in Latin and of unknown authorship but possibly also penned by Garro. Titled *Planctus Indorum* (Indian's Lament), like the *Representación* it advocated an Amerindian clergy and condemned the abuses of the Spanish colonial system.[79]

From Buenos Aires the two Franciscans crossed into Brazil and later sailed to Lisbon. In Lisbon they initially decided to go first to Rome, to present the *Planctus Indorum* to the pope, but when other Franciscans told them that the journey was too expensive they entrusted it to a banker bound for Rome and continued their journey on to Madrid. On 22 August 1750, they arrived in the capital and that night immediately made their way to the royal palace, where they were told that they could not present their petition without it being first sent to the Council of the Indies. Fearing perhaps that the Council might not send the *Representación* to the king, the next morning they waited outside the king's rural estate for his carriage to emerge. As the carriage went by them, they passed the *Representación* to the king through the open carriage window, without, according to Calixto, it even stopping. The following day, they received word that the king had read the petition with great interest and was passing it on to the Council of the Indies for further consideration.[80] The sudden appearance of the *Representación* seems to have caught some ministers by surprise, particularly Ensenada, who sent a series of frantic letters to various people looking for a copy of the manifesto.[81] Over the next several weeks Isidoro and Calixto met with several members of the Council of the Indies, thanks to commissary-general Friar Mathías Velasco's connections at court. Friar Mathías had encouraged the clerics to travel to Spain, despite not having permission from the viceroy. The king, for his part, seems to have received the petition favorably.[82] In January 1751 the king even sent a royal decree to Manso de Velasco instructing him to not block petitioners, particularly kurakas and natives of noble ancestry, from coming to Madrid if they had the correct recommendations, and to even help them finance their journey if necessary.[83]

One of Calixto's most ardent advocates before the crown was Ocopa's representative in Madrid, Friar Joseph de San Antonio. In a long petition to the crown San Antonio touted Calixto's service in the Ocopa missions, saying that he had served with "fidelity" and was a "good example to all." He stated that he and Calixto were there on the same mission, to advocate saving the missions of Ocopa, a grave necessity because it would ultimately save Peru from the unrest of its indigenous population who, without recourse to the king, were oppressed by local governors. He hoped that the king would allow Calixto not only to be made a lay friar but to take those vows at Ocopa and continue there as a missionary. He believed that allowing noble natives like Calixto to take vows as friars would give the indigenous population hope that someday their children "could obtain the same benefit," thereby calming the unrest. San Antonio also argued that the ordination of indigenous clergy would provide the missionaries with sufficient manpower to complete their missions of saving the souls of the "infidels" as well as the baptized and thus avoid the total destruction of the viceroyalty that the *Representación* implied. San Antonio's lobbying, along with others', must have been persuasive, because on 17 May 1751 Calixto was made a lay friar in Valencia. Though he was not ordained at Ocopa, San Antonio still hoped he would return to work there.[84]

Calixto was not the only donado who had been traditionally barred from taking up the friar's habit but whom Ocopa's leadership had supported for elevation. In 1755 the guardian of Ocopa allowed Manuel Maria from Tangiers to wear the habit of a lay friar despite being of Muslim descent. Friar Manuel argued to the archbishop of Lima that the guardian allowed him to do so because it had been many generations since his ancestors had been Muslims.[85] Most likely the missionaries were permissive about allowing those with the "stain" of heretical ancestry to serve as lay friars out of pragmatism. As San Antonio had argued in the case of Calixto, they needed missionaries in the frontier. The Apostolic Institute had been founded in part to service these borderlands. Since most creoles were unwilling to leave urban centers because of familial and communal ties, they relied on peninsular Spaniards to fill their ranks. Transporting these friars from Spain, however, had been, and continued to be, a problem for the missionaries. Therefore, they needed these often non-white, non-European clerics to swell their ranks. Furthermore, like Friar Mathías Velasco, the highest-ranking Franciscan in the Spanish empire, many both within and outside the Church recognized that indigenous clergy might be more effective in servicing native populations. It is no wonder that such discourses were prevalent in this distant corner of the Spanish empire, including from Juan Santos himself.

In light of the Lima conspiracy and Huarochirí rebellion, Ocopa's position in favor of indigenous clergy and its support of Friar Calixto only further strained the mission's relationship with Manso de Velasco. Although the viceroy had always been an ardent critic of the regular clergy, in 1747 he, at least officially, praised the missionaries as having "endeavored with such determination" to "reform the customs, vices, and abuses in all of the cities, villages, and places they have been" and having "continue[d] to be a benefit for the public cause, for religion, and for the royal service of his majesty."[86] After the Lima conspiracy, however, the viceroy's support for the missionaries completely eroded. Though he never admitted to this acrimony publicly, his actions displayed not only a personal distrust of Ocopa but a complete disregard for its work in the eastern frontier.

Final Retreat from the Jauja and Tarma Entradas

While the commotion created by the Lima earthquake and tsunami diverted the viceroy's attention away from the Juan Santos Atahualpa rebellion for a time, the missionaries of Ocopa were continuing their efforts to reoccupy their lost missions. In early 1747, Friar Lorenzo Núñez, newly elected commissary of missions over Ocopa, decided to send an expedition of missionaries to once again negotiate a peaceful end to the rebellion. Manso de Velasco granted the missionaries permission to reenter the Tarma entrada, and in May four missionaries, led by friars Francisco Otazuo and Salvador Pando, left for Quimirí. According to Amich, there they found Juan Santos, who received them "with great respect." Santos seems to have enjoyed discussing a range of topics with the missionaries. He even allowed the missionaries to celebrate mass, but he would not agree to peace. According to the friars, he responded with "ambiguous words" on the topic, saying that he would not end hostilities until the kurakas of the highlands came down and promised him their obedience.[87]

Whether this incident of the missionaries' meeting with Santos in 1747 actually took place or Amich invented the story is unclear. Only one other source corroborates that missionaries entered the central Montaña in 1747.[88] If this incident actually occurred, however, Santos's reasons for refusing to talk peace demonstrated a keen understanding of his situation. The Montaña provided a physical obstacle for colonial forces, but if he hoped to have any significant influence on Spanish colonial policy he had to have the support of the highlands, where most of the population of the viceroyalty resided. Without it, the rebellion would simply remain a local uprising in a marginal corner of the Spanish empire. According to Amich, after eight days the missionaries left Quimirí, with the exception of Otazuo, who stayed with a donado to try to reconvert the montañeses. The missionaries could not convince the natives to rejoin the Catholic flock, however, because, according to the missionaries, they feared Santos's wrath. Santos finally had them arrested and the donado tortured. They were freed only when Núñez entered the Montaña to plead for their release, though Santos refused to meet personally with him to come to terms.[89]

Within a few years, the viceroy began once again to take an interest in ending the Juan Santos Atahualpa rebellion. In 1748 he ordered José de Llamas to form an expedition to enter the Montaña. Llamas, however, was not opposed to finding a peaceful solution to the uprising. Before his expedition left, a native claiming to be Santos's emissary met with him to negotiate a general pardon for Juan Santos and his forces. He stated that the rebellion had been caused by internal problems in the Montaña, and that they did not want to continue fighting the crown. Hoping to save himself from the possible losses and probable failure of another expedition, Llamas halted preparations to enter the high jungle. Though he was suspicious of Santos's intentions, with the viceroy's permission he sent a delegation to Santos's camp to try to finalize a peace that would return the entire region to Spanish rule. After almost two years the delegation had not returned, and their fate is unknown, though presumably they were killed. In the meantime, in anticipation of the coming peace, highland Andeans began to enter the margins of the Montaña to sow coca fields. Sometime before 1750, however, a Montaña raiding party, assumed to be under Santos, surprised a group of coca farmers and killed as many as thirty. This event, along with his delegation's failure to return, convinced Llamas that Santos was acting "in bad faith," and in the summer of 1750 he went forward with his expedition.[90]

The expedition, like those before it, was an utter failure. Llamas attempted the same tactic that Troncoso had employed with limited success in the first expedition against Santos, dividing his troops into two groups, one entering through the Tarma entrada and the other through Jauja. Santos withdrew to Eneno, allowing the jungle and small raiding parties to defeat his enemy. The hot humid conditions, difficult terrain, and lack of supplies, combined with

Montaña archers harassing the soldiers as they marched, eventually caused the expedition to retreat back to the highlands.[91] The 1750 expedition was the viceregal government's last attempt to quash the rebellion.

It is no coincidence that the cessation of expeditions against the Juan Santos rebels corresponds with the discovery of the Lima conspiracy and the outbreak of the Huarochirí rebellion, which Manso de Velasco blamed in large part on friars Calixto and Isidoro. In his 24 September 1750 report on the two disturbances in which he accused the two friars of treason, Manso de Velasco worried that, since the viceroyalty had no ability to produce arms and all its weapons had been committed to the frontiers of Jauja and Tarma, he had limited resources to combat rebellions closer to Lima. Though he was concerned that rebels in Huarochirí could join forces with Santos, he downplayed the rebel's capabilities. The viceroy instead emphasized that potential unrest in the highlands was a greater threat to the security of the viceroyalty than an actual rebellion in the Montaña. Indeed, as Santos himself seemed to recognize, the highlands' large population and mineral wealth were the economic engine of Spain's South American possessions. Though Manso de Velasco claimed victory in crushing the Huarochirí rebellion, he expressed fear that further unrest was fomenting among the indigenous population of Peru. Huarochirí in particular was, as Manso de Velasco called it, the vital "throat" of Peru, for it was not only a major source of grain for the barren coastal capital but a crossroads for commercial trade throughout the region.[92]

To emphasize the threat Huarochirí posed to Lima, the viceroy also included a map of the areas affected by rebellion in his report to the crown (figure 6). Like the letter, the map was intended to convince crown officials unfamiliar with Peru's geography that the viceroy was justified in ending expeditions to the jungle in order to take a more defensive posture to protect the capital. The map depicts the Andes as small bumps frequently trespassed by large valleys. Roads flow easily from each rebellious region into the viceregal capital. Even the name of the map, "Lima con sus contornos" (Lima and its outskirts), conveys this false sense of proximity. Though depicting the distances between regions accurately, it ignores the physical realities of Peruvian geography. Huarochirí, for example, is only approximately fifty miles from Lima, yet travel to Lima could take several weeks. The small bumps on the map, which evoke an image of rolling hills, are actually part of the second-largest mountain range in the world. Most roads, especially in the highlands, were little more than small trails that hugged sheer cliffs over deep gorges. In sending this stylized map, Manso de Velasco tried to create a sense of urgency of the potential threat that rebellion in the mountains posed to Lima.

After the Lima conspiracy and Huarochirí rebellion in August 1750, Manso de Velasco unofficially closed the Jauja and Tarma entradas. The viceroy never again ordered an expedition against Juan Santos, nor did he issue any

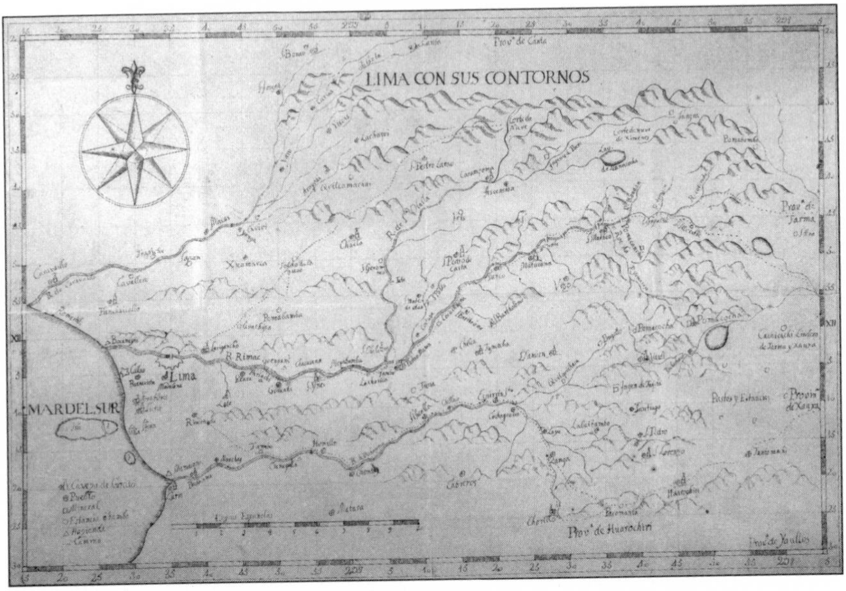

FIGURE 6. Manso de Velasco's map of the region around Lima, 1750. "Lima con sus contornos," ESPAÑA. MINISTERIO DE EDUCACIÓN, CULTURA Y DEPORTE, AGI, Mapas y Planos, Peru-Chile 33.

more licenses for missionaries to reenter the territory. Instead he opted for a policy of containment. He ordered that the three regular companies that José de Llamas had brought to Tarma and Jauja in 1745 (two of infantry and one of cavalry, approximately fifty men each) remain there indefinitely. These companies were to act as a barrier to further assaults by Juan Santos's rebels.

Manso de Velasco had decided to end offensive military actions against the rebels in the Montaña, but Juan Santos had not ceased his hostilities toward the Ocopa missions. As Amich so aptly stated, "The pretend Inca [Santos] seeing himself free of the whirlwind that threaten him with the entrance of the Spanish decided to take . . . Sonomoro."[93] Sonomoro was the Ocopa missionaries' last mission in the Jauja entrada and the only indigenous community in the Jauja and Tarma entradas that had refused to join Juan Santos. Its fortress had been built several decades earlier under Viceroy Castelfuerte and had been the model for the then-defunct fortress of Quimirí. Despite having access to 150 Spanish regulars as well as local militia, the local governor, perhaps under the viceroy's order, had garrisoned the fortress with only fourteen soldiers. The fortress was also poorly maintained and supplied. One missionary lamented "the little care that the subjects, in whom the Superior Government had entrusted [Sonomoro], had for this enterprise."[94] In

September, at the outset of the rainy season, Juan Santos began to cut off Sonomoro's lines of communication to and from the highlands. When the governor of Jauja became aware of these actions, he ordered an immediate withdrawal from the fortress. Before the order even arrived, the missionaries and soldiers had already realized that their position was indefensible and had begun to prepare to withdraw—just as Juan Santos's troops began to occupy the farms around the mission, forcing converts into the fortress itself and slowing down their efforts. Juan Santos laid siege for eighteen days.

Finally, on the 28 September, fearing they would be massacred just as Spanish troops had at Quimirí eight years earlier, twenty-three soldiers, three missionaries, and fifty-one converts slipped out of the fortress under the cover of darkness, taking a lesser-known path to Andamarca, the closest frontier village. Several converts stayed behind to fight a rearguard action. The converts who escaped were eventually taken to Ocopa, where they suffered severely from the high altitude and cold weather. Within a few years all of them died from diseases they had not been previously exposed to in the jungle.[95] Manso de Velasco justified to the crown the loss of Sonomoro by claiming that the fortress was poorly situated and that he maintained it only "because of the discomfort that it caused the missionaries to be without this shelter." He argued that, ultimately, maintaining a fort in this location was inadvisable and that if would "remain vulnerable to the same risks." The loss of Sonomoro, he argued, was strategically neutral, if not beneficial, for he no longer had to waste resources on an indefensible position.[96]

Despite Manso de Velasco's insistence that the loss of Sonomoro posed no strategic threat to the viceroyalty, in 1752 Juan Santos used the former mission as a staging ground for his boldest raid to date—the attack on the highland city of Andamarca. In late July 1752, Santos along with five hundred Montaña archers left Sonomoro to make the arduous journey up the eastern slope of the Andes. In early August they entered Andamarca and incarcerated the three missionaries present in the village.[97] According to many accounts, however, the inhabitants of Andamarca received Juan Santos with a hero's welcome. Historian Luis Miguel Glave argues that century-old commercial and cultural ties between Andamarca and the Montaña contributed to Santos's popularity among the people of Andamarca.[98] Juan Santos, nonetheless, stayed only a few days, probably because his archers refused to remain in the cold highlands for long. As Santos left, his men burned key buildings in the village, including the prison. A few locals saved the three missionaries from being incinerated in their jail cell, implying perhaps that at least some contingent of the city was still loyal to the missionaries, or that, caught between the two forces, they were willing to play both sides.[99]

In many ways Santos's raid on Andamarca was his movement's crowning triumph. Though Ocopa essentially controlled Andamarca (the crown had granted the missionaries the village's mita labor and Ocopa friars manned its parish), it was a fully incorporated part of the viceroyalty, not a loosely held frontier mission. It also was both physically and culturally clearly in the highlands, at an altitude above 10,000 feet, with Quechua-speaking inhabitants. Santos had effectively extended his rebellion out of the jungle into the highlands, the economic and demographic heart of Spanish Peru. Still, his inability to hold Andamarca demonstrated the limitations of his rebellion. Though Santos dreamed of a larger insurrection, he could never marshal widespread highland support.

Though Santos could not hold Andamarca, the raid shocked some provincial leaders, provoking them to extreme actions to counter the perceived danger of the rebellion spreading to the highlands. The governor of Jauja, Laureano José de Torres y Ayala, marqués de Casa-Torres, was so paranoid about the Santos rebellion spreading to his province that he had three highland Andeans hanged as spies after they were caught praising the exploits of Juan Santos. The executions were so summarily carried out that the audiencia later fined Casatorres 6,000 pesos for not consulting them before applying capital sentences. Manso de Velasco again downplayed the threat that Juan Santos posed to the viceroyalty in his correspondence to the crown. He argued that, although Santos would continue to raid along the frontier in order to steal tools to maintain his popularity, he would not pose any permanent threat to the highlands. Certainly this argument favored Manso de Velasco, who had to prove his effectiveness in keeping the peace in Peru to crown officials in Madrid, though Santos's inability to occupy Andamarca for any length of time certainly supports this argument. At the same time, the viceroy also used the continued threat of raids against the highland to justify his policy of containment, arguing that the crown needed to retain military forces on the frontier to protect against any future raids. Although he was confident that in a pitched battle the Spanish forces could easily defeat the rebels, any new campaign, he argued, would be fruitless since the montañeses would simply withdraw into the interior and wait until Spanish forces left, as they had continually done before. Manso de Velasco told the crown that the "sagest method" to conquer Juan Santos was "to introduce the missionaries into their old reductions . . . [and] restore the Indians to the faith," though he seemed unwilling to provide them with military protection to do so.[100]

Juan Santos's withdrawal from Andamarca marked the effective end of the rebellion. According to various reports, Santos died sometime after the Andamarca raid, though exactly when is not known. Manso de Velasco, in his official report of his government, described a gradual decline for the rebel leader. Frustrated by his inability to expand his rebellion outside of the Montaña, Santos became increasingly embittered and paranoid. Fearing that Gatica and his other principal generals would betray him, he eventually had them executed. The missionaries of Ocopa, on the other hand, claimed that two natives from Manoa told them in 1776 that Santos had died in the former mission of Metraro. When pressed for details about his death, they said they had witnessed him being swallowed by Hell in a cloud of smoke and fire.[101]

Over the next decade, the missionaries and viceregal government continually blamed each other for the loss of the missions. Manso de Velasco felt that, if the missionaries had done their job in converting the montañeses and placing their missions in more defensible locations, a military intervention would have been unnecessary. In 1753 the viceroy chided Ocopa's leadership regarding their new missions in Huánuco, stating, "This work has to come from the zeal of the missionaries and from their wisdom to locate the Indians in a place where they are less willing to return to the infidelity that they once professed, which decision will be in your hands."[102] The missionaries, on the other hand, vehemently blamed the viceroy in particular for failing to defeat Juan Santos. As one missionary accused, "Any man with average intelligence and average zeal could have in two or three years, at the most, destroyed the rebel but [only if he] listened to the missionaries [*Religiosos*], who are the ones that can speak [with authority] on this subject."[103]

Maintaining troops on the frontier was far costlier to the royal treasury than the missionaries' annual stipend had ever been. For the cost of maintaining two companies of infantry and one of cavalry, approximately 150 men, the royal treasury meted out 51,326 pesos annually, significantly more than the 6,000 pesos annually the viceregal officials had been ordered to pay Ocopa.[104] The financial burden bankrupted the royal treasury at Jauja, requiring that the viceroy transfer funds from elsewhere. Indeed, the Jauja treasury remained insolvent, due completely to the cost of maintaining troops in the region, until its dissolution in 1788.[105] Several royal ministers complained about the excess cost of maintaining the troops along the Jauja/Tarma frontier. In 1757 the fiscal of the Council of the Indies for Peru lamented this large expenditure and opined that the crown should send more missionaries to the region in the hope that they would be able to secure the frontier and thus cut costs.[106] Over time the cost of these troops began to add up, and in 1776 Manso de Velasco's successor, Manuel de Amat, complained that during his term of office the viceregal government had wasted almost 1,000,000 pesos on this unnecessary garrison of troops.[107] Amat even considered pulling the troops out, but ultimately he did not, because he feared that if the rebellion was somehow rekindled he would be removed from office as Villagarcía had been.[108]

The missionaries, of course, also complained about the defensive (they would say idle) nature of this force, whom they believed should be attempting to retake their lost missions. They "have not restored even one handful of dirt," lamented the guardian of Ocopa, Friar Joseph Ampuero. The guardian maintained that these troops lived in "notorious slothfulness" and that some were so inept that they did not even know how to fire their muskets. He was particularly bitter about the inactivity of these troops because Manso de Velasco had "not even given one *real* [a coin worth one eighth of a peso]" to protect their remaining missions in Huánuco.[109] Despite the comparatively enormous cost, Manso de Velasco decided that the eastern frontier of Peru would be better protected by military arms than by religious communities, and he was not alone in his belief among reformists (see chapter 4)

The Juan Santos Atahualpa rebellion represented a great triumph for the Asháninka and Yanesha nations, who would remain relatively unmolested for the rest of the colonial period. It also revealed serious tensions within the Bourbon reform process. Though in theory these reforms emanated from the king, it was his ministers in Madrid (Ensenada) and in Lima (Manso de Velasco) who interpreted and even created them in reaction to perceived events on the ground. In particular, they hoped to attenuate the power and influence of the regular clergy (foremost among them the Franciscans), who they perceived to be disloyal to the king, or at least to their regalist projects. Ocopa, therefore, presented a difficult case for these reformers. On the one hand, Ocopa's missionaries were pious peninsulars trying to evangelize Spanish America's vast borderlands. On the other, they were a substantially well funded nongovernmental (Franciscan) operation, whose distance from the metropolis gave them great autonomy. Furthermore, their popularity and successful lobbying at the court in Madrid made them even more difficult to control.

Initially, the Juan Santos Atahualpa rebellion did little to help reformist ministers reduce Ocopa's influence. The viceroys had, at least publicly, to continue to support the missionaries, for three reasons: the rebellion demonstrated the viceregal government's inability to protect its own frontiers; despite the rebellion and criticisms from reformers such as Juan and Ulloa, the missionaries still enjoyed an excellent reputation at court; and the Franciscans' appeal to his piety seemed partially to trump King Ferdinand's regalism. The turning point came when the former Ocopa missionary Friar Calixto, for whom Ocopa's representatives in Madrid had been advocating, was implicated in the Lima conspiracy. The connection, however tenuous, between Franciscans (and Ocopa specifically) and the conspiracy seems to have given Manso de Velasco the political cover he needed to end campaigns against the rebels and cede victory to Juan Santos, thereby depriving Ocopa of most of its missions. It is certainly possible that, even with a greater military force, the Spanish would never have been able to control the territories lost in the rebellion completely; however, by choosing to cordon off the region they negated any future rapprochement or negotiations with the rebel indigenous nations, which after Santos's death and the break-up of his alliance may have been more likely.

Even after hostilities with Juan Santos effectively ceased, the debates they spawned over the nature of Spanish power in the Montaña only increased as each side brought its case before authorities back in Spain. As chapter 3 demonstrates, the resulting ambiguities in the central government's positions reflected fundamental doubts and conflicts about the reform process during a crucial turning point.

Notes

1. As early as the 1770s, Ocopa's chronicler, Friar José Amich, in *Historia de las misiones del convento de Santa Rosa de Ocopa,* wrote extensively on the rebellion and its effects on the missionaries. Amich complained that the lack of crown support for missionaries allowed the rebellion to flourish. This not so subtle condemnation was strategically aimed at convincing the crown to maintain, if not increase, its financial and military support of the missionaries with the hope of retaking the lost missions even twenty years later. Amich's writings also attempted to deflect the blame for the rebellion, which crown officials had placed squarely on the Franciscan missionaries at Ocopa. Amich's sentiments were echoed, albeit less pointedly, by his contemporary Franciscan chronicler, Friar Fernando Rodríguez Tena (*Crónica de las misiones franciscanas del Perú, siglos XVII y XVIII,* vol. 2, also completed sometime in the 1770s). The emphasis of Franciscan historians on Juan Santos continued even until the 1920s, when Friar Bernardino Izaguirre dedicated several chapters of his multivolume work on Franciscan missions in eastern Peru (*Historia de las misiones franciscanas*) to the rebellion.

2. In the notes and introduction of historian José Loayza's 1942 document collection, *Juan Santos, el invencible,* he argued that the rebellion was a "precursor" to the Peruvian independence movement of the 1820s. Indigenismo intellectuals, such as Loayza, attempted to reconcile the creole-led independence movement with earlier attempts at indigenous autonomy, such as the Juan Santos Atahualpa rebellion, to create a unifying national identity in a republic where a creole elite ruled over the indigenous majority. Although most scholars reject this interpretation of Juan Santos as a proto-nationalist figure, the idea has remained popular in Peru and was reflected in journalist Mario Castro Arenas's 1973 *La rebelión de Juan Santos.*

3. The "Great Andean revolts" is a term used by historians to describe three nearly simultaneous uprisings: Tupac Amaru rebellion in the Cusco region of modern-day Peru (1780–82), Tomás Catari in Chayanta (1780–81), and Tupac Katari rebellion near La Paz (1780–82) in modern-day Bolivia. These rebellions shared similar causes, principally a reaction to economic pressures created by the Bourbon reforms. The rebels were aware of each other, and after the death of Tupac Amaru his followers fought alongside the Tupac Katari rebels. Steve J. Stern argues that the Great Andean revolts were part of larger consciousness of resistance that started with the Juan Santos Atahualpa rebellion; see Stern, "The Age of Andean Insurrection, 1742–1782: A Reappraisal," in Stern, *Resistance, Rebellion,* chap. 2. Certainly all these rebellions were caused in some part by the impositions of colonialism, but historical records do not seem to support the type of direct relationship between the Juan Santos Atahualpa rebellion and the later revolts that Stern insinuates.

4. These rebellions include the Lima conspiracy of 1750 and the Huarochirí rebellion, discussed later in the chapter.

5. Amich, *Historia de las misiones,* 167.

6. Friars Manuel Santos and Domingo García, Report to Commissary Father Friar José Gil Muñoz, Pichana, 2 June 1742, JSEI, 1–7. In the notes of his document collection of the Juan Santos Atahualpa rebellion, Loayza attempts to connect the activities of British privateers in the Pacific with the rebellion. Since Spain and Britain were still opposing com-

batants in the War of Jenkins Ear (subsumed into the War of Austrian Succession on the continent) until 1748, his evidence is circumstantial at best.

7. Amich, *Historia de las misiones,* 167. Amich's account is deeply flawed, containing an extreme bias toward the missionaries and having been written several decades after the rebellion (1770s), but his access to missionaries who had been around during the rebellion signifies that at the very least his account reflects the missionaries' general consensus about Juan Santos, which shaped their reaction to him.

8. José Patricio de Arbeiza y Elizonda and Manuel de Barrenechea, officers of the Royal Treasury, Report to the crown, Pasco, 14 March 1744, JSEI, 50–53.

9. Rodríguez Tena, *Crónica de las misiones franciscanas,* 337.

10. Joseph Gil Muñoz, commissar of the missions of Peru, Petition to the crown, 8 March 1741, Lima, AGI, Lima 808.

11. Amich, *Historia de las misiones,* 167–68.

12. Friars Manuel Santos and Domingo Garcia, Report to Commissar Father Friar José Gil Muñoz, 2 June 1742, Pichana, JSEI, 5–6.

13. Ibid., 4.

14. Santos-Graneros, "Anticolonialismo, mesianismo," 37.

15. Amich, *Historia de las misiones,* 167–70; Friars Manuel Santos and Domingo Gracia, Report to Commissary Father Friar José Gil Muñoz, 2 June 1742, Pichana, JSEI, 5–6.

16. See Stavig, *World of Túpac Amaru.*

17. Varese, *Salt of the Mountain,* 87–96.

18. Amich, *Historia de las misiones,* 169.

19. Ibid., 155–60.

20. Messianic millenarianism is a common theme in most belief systems. But given the area's recent Catholic evangelization, the idea that the Yompor Ror gave immortality, a less common messianic tradition, suggests that at least that aspect of this belief came from Christianity; Santos-Graneros, "Anticolonialismo, mesianismo," 37–38.

21. These nations included the Machiguengas, Piros, Shipibos, Conibos, and Cashibos; ibid.

22. Lay Friar Juan de San Antonio, Report to the crown, 28 February 1757, Lima, AGI, Lima 808; Joseph Antonio Manso de Velasco, "Relación que hizo de su Gobierno," BNE, Mss. 3108, f. 120r.

23. Friars Manuel Santos and Domingo Garcia, Report to Commissar Father Friar José Gil Muñoz, 2 June 1742, Pichana, JSEI, 5–7.

24. Baptismal record for the mission of Eneno, AGN, Sección Republicana, Ministerio de Hacienda, Libro 5, ff. 1–22.

25. Hyland, *Jesuit and the Incas,* 4–7, 32–38.

26. Lynch, *Bourbon Spain,* 158–60.

27. The correspondence regarding the funding and allocation of weapons is found in JSEI, 13–19.

28. Amich, *Historia de las misiones,* 168–69; a record of the war council formed by Milla and Troncoso is located in ARJ, Protocolos Notariales, Tomo 19, ff. 204r–206r, Santa Ana de Pampas, 7 August 1742, scribe Juan de Mesa Valera.

29. Amich, *Historia de las misiones,* 168–69; Villagarcía, Report to the king, 16 August 1744, Lima, JSEI, 55–69. A daily log of the Milla expedition is found in JSEI, 19–48.

30. Amich, *Historia de las misiones,* 174.

31. Ibid., 174–75.

32. Sebastián Eslava, Viceroy of New Granada, Report to the crown, 12 June 1744, Cartagena, JSEI, 54–55; Amich, *Historia de las misiones,* 175–76.

33. Amich, *Historia de las misiones,* 176–77.

34. Villagarcía, Relación de su gobierno, BNE, Mss. 3107, f. 21v; also found in Real Biblioteca, Real Palacio de Madrid, II/1349, f. 25v; and JSEI, 86.

35. See ARJ, Protocolos Notariales, Tomo 21, ff. 639–641, 8 June 1750, Santa Rosa de Ocopa, scribe Juan de Mesa Valera.

36. Causa contra Fray Domingo Garcia, 8 October 1745, ibid., 106–9.

37. Villagarcía, Correspondence with Manso de Velasco, 1745, RAH, 9-9-3 1699.

38. Villagarcía, Report to the crown, 28 August 1744, Lima, AGI, Lima 415; JSEI, 69–71.

39. Villagarcía, Report to the crown, 28 August 1744, Lima, AGI, Lima 415; JSEI, 69–71. During the Villagarcía's administration, the Ocopa friars should have been paid 60,000 pesos.

40. Amat, "Relación que hizo de su Gobierno," BNE, Mss. 3112, f. 188v.

41. Walker, *Shaky Colonialism,* 75–78.

42. Kuethe and Andrien, *Spanish Atlantic World*, 173.

43. Lynch, *Bourbon Spain*, 160.

44. For a good example of this type of language, see Ensenada, Correspondence with Manso de Velasco, 30 November 1748, Madrid, AGI, Lima 643.

45. Ensenada, Instructions to Viceroy Manso de Velasco, 21 December 1744, Madrid, JSEI, 74–76.

46. Amich, *Historia de las misiones*, 176–77; Ensenada, Report to the crown, 17 March 1747, Madrid, AGI, Lima 983. The beginning of this report, which was started in December 1744, is found in JSEI, 72–75.

47. Walker, "Upper Classes," 55; Pérez-Mallaína Bueno, *Retrato de una ciudad,* 54.

48. Walker, *Shaky Colonialism,* 117–18; Andrien, "Coming of Enlightened Reform," 183–85.

49. Burns, *Colonial Habits*, 48.

50. Manso de Velasco, *Relaciôn y documentos*, 263–64.

51. On Manso de Velasco's loan policies, see Walker, *Shaky Colonialism,* 123–28.

52. Ibid., 76–77, 102; Pérez-Mallaína Bueno, *Retrato de una ciudad*, 240–41.

53. Walker, *Shaky Colonialism*, 120–21.

54. Andrien, "Coming of Enlightened Reform," 190–91; Royal decree, 1 May 1747, ASFL, r. 2, I-2, n.1, doc. 38, ff. 202r–204r.

55. Royal decree, 1 May 1747, ASFL r. 2, I-2, n. 1, doc. 38, ff. 202r–204r.

56. Andrien, "Noticias Secretas," 175. The original title of the report written for the Spanish court was *Discurso y reflexiones políticas sobre el estado presente de los reinos del Perú; su gobierno, régimen particular de aquellos habitadores y abusos que se han introducido en uno y otro; Dase individual noticia de las causales de su origen y se proponen algunos medios para evitarlas.* In 1826, however, Englishmen David Barry published the report as *Noticias Secretas de América,* by which it is more commonly known.

57. Juan and Ulloa, *Discourse and Political Reflections*, 102.

58. Ibid., 166–67 (quote); Andrien, "Coming of Enlightened Reform," 185–86.

59. Andrien, "Noticias Secretas," 184–87.

60. Walker, *Shaky Colonialism,* 172–73; Nicolas de Salazar, Account of the Lima conspiracy, n.d., Lima, AGI, Lima 988; Manso de Velasco, Report to the crown, 24 September 1750, Lima, JSEI, 161–78 (originally AGI, Lima 988); a similar, more strongly worded version of this letter is found in AGI, Lima 417.

61. Spalding, *Huarochirí,* 274–78; Manso de Velasco, Report to the crown, 24 September 1750, Lima, AGI, Lima 417.

62. Manso de Velasco, Report to the crown, 24 September 1750, Lima, JSEI, 163. The issue of corrupt corregidores especially would haunt the Spanish colonial authorities as one of the major catalysts in the Túpac Amaru rebellion in Cuzco of 1780–82.

63. Ocopa's book of incorporations dates only to 1755, when Ocopa became a college of propaganda fide. If the friars kept official records of who served in their missions previous to this date, it has since been lost. See Heras, *Libro de Incorporaciones.*

64. Bernales Ballesteros, "Fray Calixto Tupac Inca," 6; Father Isidoro Cala y Ortega, Petition to the crown, 7 May 1751, Cádiz, AGI, Lima 988; Walker, *Shaky Colonialism,* 164–66; Calixto, Petition to the crown, CVU, Papeles Varios, Mss. Tomo 18, no. 25.

65. When and for how long is not known, but according to Joseph de San Antonio he spent at least a few years working in the Ocopa missions; Joseph de San Antonio, Petition to the crown, 2 May 1751, Madrid, AGI, Lima 541.

66. Cabildo de Indios of Lima, License for Fray Calixto, 30 October 1756, Lima, AGI, Lima 988.

67. O'Phelan Godoy, "'Ascender a al estado eclesiástico,'" 312.

68. Juan de San Antonio, Report to crown, 17 May 1751, Cádiz, AGI, Lima 988.

69. Mathías de Velasco, Summary of Joseph de San Antonio's petition to the crown, 28 June 1751, Madrid, AGI, Lima 541.

70. Joseph de San Antonio, Petition to the crown, 2 May 1751, Madrid, AGI, Lima 541.

71. Bernales Ballesteros, "Fray Calixto Tupac Inca," 6–7.

72. The full name is *Representación Verdadera y exclamación rendida y lamentable que toda la nación Indiana hace a la Majestad de Rey de las Españas y Emperador de la Indias El Señor Don Fernando VI pediendo los atienda y remedie, sacandolos del afrentoso viperio y oprobio en que están más de doscientos años* [hereafter cited as *Representación Verdadera*].

73. Manso de Velasco, Report to the crown, 15 January 1757, Lima, AGI, Lima 988.

74. *Representación Verdadera,* 16–17; Walker also paraphrases this in *Shaky Colonialism,* 165.

75. Walker, *Shaky Colonialism,* 164–65.

76. Estenssoro and Ramos, *Del paganismo a la santidad,* 36–47; Walker, *Shaky Colonialism,* 164–65.

77. O'Phalen Godoy, *La gran rebelión,* 47–63.

78. Manso de Velasco, Report to the crown, 24 September 1750, Lima, JSEI, 164.

79. Navarro, *Una denuncia profética,* 26–34.

80. A narration of this journey is found in Bernales Ballesteros, "Fray Calixto Tupac Inca," 6–8. As well as Calixto, see Letter to the Cabildo de Indios of Lima, 14 November 1751, Madrid, AGI, Lima 983; and Joseph de San Antonio, Petition to the crown, 2 May 1751, Madrid, AGI, Lima 541.

81. This frantic search is evident in Ensenada's letters to the Council of the Indies, 7, 8, 9, 10 May 1751, Madrid, AGI, Lima 988.

82. Bernales Ballesteros, "Fray Calixto Tupac Inca," 8. On Commissary-general Velasco's support, see Manso de Velasco, petition to the crown, 3 March 1751, Madrid, AGI, Lima 541.

83. Royal decree, 19 January 1751, Madrid, AGI, Lima 988.

84. Joseph de San Antonio, Petition to the crown, 2 May 1751, Madrid, AGI, Lima 541; see also Mathías de Velasco's response to San Antonio's petition, 28 June 1751, Madrid, AGI, Lima 541.

85. Manuel Maria, Petition to the archbishop of Lima, Lima, 9 September 1755, AAL, Sección San Francisco VIII–44, ff. 1v–2v.

86. Manso de Velasco, License for Friar Joseph de San Antonio to travel to Spain, 8 January 1747, Lima, AGI, Lima 541.

87. Amich, *Historia de las misiones,* 180.

88. The only other reference to this expedition by these four missionaries is in a letter written by Alonso Santa de Ortega to a Friar Juan de Jecla Santa, 30 May 1747, Lima, JSEI, 122–23.

89. Amich, *Historia de las misiones*, 180–81.

90. Manso de Velasco, Report to the crown, 20 August 1748, Lima, AGI, Lima 643; Manso de Velasco, Report to the crown, 20 April 1751, Lima, AGI, Lima 643.

91. Amich, *Historia de las misiones*, 182–83.

92. Manso de Velasco, Report to the crown, 24 September 1750, Lima, JSEI, 169–79.

93. Amich, *Historia de las misiones*, 183.

94. As expected, Amich decried the decrepit state of Sonomoro's fortress (*Historia de las misiones*, 183). But there are strong indications from AGI, Contaduría 1870 and 1873, that the fortress was indeed in disrepair. The quote is from a report of the journey of the twenty-seven missionaries, n.d., AGI, Lima 541.

95. Ocopa lies at 11,102 feet and temperatures range from 20°F to 65°F. The narrative of the fall of Sonomoro was constructed from accounts in four sources: Amich, *Historia de las misiones*, 183; Manso de Velasco, Report to the crown regarding the fall of Sonomoro, 20 November 1751, Lima, AGI, Lima 643; Juan de San Antonio, Report to the crown, 12 July 1752, Lima, AGI, Lima 541; and Report of the journey of the 27 missionaries, n.d., AGI, Lima 541.

96. Manso de Velasco, Report to the crown regarding the fall of Sonomoro, 20 November 1751, Lima, AGI, Lima 643.

97. Amich, *Historia de las misiones*, 184.

98. Glave, "El Apu Ynga," 28–68. Whereas Glave seems to localize pro-Santos sentiment to the region immediately around Andamarca and perhaps within the province of Jauja, Stern argues that the willingness of the people of Andamarca to join the rebellion demonstrates an anticolonial consciousness throughout the viceroyalty, one that periodically manifested itself in rebellions; see Stern, "Age of Andean Insurrection, 1742–1782: A Reprisal," in Stern, *Resistance, Rebellion*, chap. 2.

99. Amich, *Historia de las misiones*, 184; "Causa seguida contra Julián Auqui, Blas Ibarra y Casimiro Lamberto . . . por traidores a la Corona," 1752, AGN, Sección Real Audiencia, Causas Criminales, Leg. 15, C. 159; also found in AGI, Lima 988, Escribanía 527.

100. Manso de Velasco, Report to the crown, 4 January 1755, Lima, AGI, Lima 988; Manso de Velasco, "Relación que hizo de su Gobierno," BNE, Mss. 3108, ff. 113r–120v.

101. Lehnertz, "Land of the Infidels," 147–49. A draft of a royal decree dated 19 May 1767 written at Aranjuez (AGI, Lima 834, c. 65) has Santos being poisoned by his own people.

102. Manso de Velasco, Letter to Friar Juan de Antonio, 5 May 1753, Lima, AGI, Lima 808.

103. Friar Bernardino de San Antonio, Correspondence with Friar Mathías Velasco, 15 November 1756, Ocopa, AGI, Lima 808.

104. BNE, mss. 3113, ff. 24v–25r; RAH 9-3-3 1680, ff. 48v–49r; AGI, Contaduria 1870, 1873.

105. For a breakdown of the number of troops in Tarma and Jauja, see AGI, Contaduría 1870 and 1873, for the corresponding years 1745–55. For evidence after those dates, see RAH 9-3-3 1680, ff. 48v–49r.

106. Fiscal's report on the petition from Joseph de San Antonio, 28 February 1757, Madrid, AGI, Lima 808.

107. Amat, Relación de Govierno que dejó el Exmo. Señor Don Manuel de Amat, 1776, BNE, mss. 3112, f. 188r (also found in RAH 9-9-3 1704).

108. Amat, Relación que hizo de su gobierno, BNE, mss. 3112, f. 188v.

109. Friar Joseph Ampuero, guardian of Ocopa, Report, 5 January 1757, AGI, Lima 808.

Chapter 3
In the Aftermath of Rebellion

The Andamarca campaign in 1752 marked the end of hostilities between Juan Santos and Spanish forces in the Montaña. Nevertheless, Manso de Velasco's refusal to continue to pursue the rebels ignited debates between the viceroy and the Ocopa missionaries that raged over the next decade. In addition to continuing its campaigns against Juan Santos until the missionaries were restored to the Jauja and Tarma entradas, Ocopa wanted the viceregal government to deliver on the financial support promised by the crown. Viceroy Manso de Velasco, however, sought at every occasion to block the Ocopa missionaries' requests, delaying or simply refusing to follow orders from Madrid to aid them.

The conflict between the viceroy and the missionaries provides a window into fissures during the 1750s, not only between regular clergy and the Spanish government but within the crown bureaucracy itself. In 1714, King Philip V created the Ministry of the Indies (headed by the minister of state for the Indies), which handled many of the executive functions that the Council of the Indies had previously exercised. The new ministry, in theory, allowed the king and his ministers to enact reform more rapidly and efficiently. The move severely weakened the power of the Council, though it still retained its judicial authority and remained an important advisory body for the king on matters regarding Spain's overseas possessions.[1] The Council also tended to be more conservative than the Ministry, particularly on matters relating to the Church, and it attempted to retain the Habsburg model of administering the empire in partnership with the clergy. This traditional approach, of course, clashed with reformers' attempts to consolidate royal authority. For this reason, in 1753 the minister of the Indies, the marqués de la Ensenada, convinced the king to form a *junta particular de ministros* to circumvent the Council and force more radical anticlerical reforms. As a result of these meetings the crown received the Concordat of 1753, which gave it the *patronato universal* (universal patronage) over all the Spanish Church. This meant that for almost all secular Church offices within its empire the crown had the right of presentation, a process by which crown officials created a short list of possible candidates from which the Church could select one to fill a particular office. Previously the crown had this privilege only for selecting bishops. Though in practice the Concordat of 1753 changed little of the character of the Spanish secular clergy, it demonstrated the advance of regalist ministers within the court of Ferdinand VI.[2]

Within this context Ocopa presents an important case study. To some reformers the Ocopa missionaries were ideal clerics. They performed missionary services that helped to expand Spanish hegemony to a previously unincorporated hinterland and, according to the design of the Apostolic Institute, they were dependent on the crown for funding and manpower. To conservatives, they fulfilled the godly mission to convert the "infidels," which the pope had charged the crown with in its donation of the Americas to Spain. Even King Ferdinand, who until 1754 supported the more anticlerical factions within his government, seemed to see the missionaries as fulfilling his own moral commitments to God. For this reason, Ocopa had received generous concessions from Madrid, including the annual stipend and reimbursement for the travel costs of new missionaries. To Manso de Velasco, however, Ocopa seemed to pose a threat to royal authority. Because they were members of the regular clergy, the crown still had little direct authority over the actions of the Franciscan missionaries. Furthermore, the missionaries of Ocopa had proven their subversive tendencies by supporting the now-discredited Friar Calixto. From the perspective of Madrid, Ocopa appeared to be under the authority of the state, since the Franciscans remained dependent on the financial largesse of the crown, but the vast distances between Ocopa and Spain meant that the friars enjoyed relative autonomy within Peru. This left Manso de Velasco with a powerful, well-funded institution that he could not easily control.

Therefore, in the aftermath of the Juan Santos Atahualpa rebellion, the viceroy continued his attempts to neutralize the missionaries, even ignoring royal decrees supporting the missionaries when they impeded his efforts. Though crown officials in Madrid, even some more radical regalists, seemed convinced that Ocopa was aiding the reform and renovation of the empire in Peru, Manso de Velasco apparently judged the missionaries a threat to the regalist cause. The resulting tensions created by Ocopa between imperial and local interests, as well as conservative and radical forces, exemplify the complex political process that shaped the Bourbon reforms in Peru. What happened to Ocopa in the wake of the rebellion was a negotiation between the Franciscans and the numerous political factions at various levels within the Spanish bureaucracy. These clashes over Ocopa were certainly rooted in competing philosophical beliefs, but the geographic perspective of each minister also shaped his decisions regarding the missionaries. Though Ensenada did not openly oppose crown concessions to Ocopa, his hand-picked viceroy did so vigorously.[3] Therefore, for Ocopa to receive aid from the crown, the missionaries had to conform not only to the sometimes contested views of reformist ministers in Madrid but also to the regalist visions of the viceregal government in Peru.

Ocopa's Attempts to Regain Crown Support

In 1747, to counter the increasing intransigence of the viceregal government, the Ocopa missionaries decided to send one of their own to Madrid to solicit aid for their missionary efforts directly from the crown. The missionaries selected Friar Joseph de San Antonio, a native of Extremadura with seventeen years of missionary experience in both the Tarma and Jauja entradas.[4] Sometime between 1748 and 1750, San Antonio traveled to Spain armed with the necessary recommendations and licenses for such an undertaking, including a license to travel from Manso de Velasco that praised the missionaries' exploits in the Montaña. Though the viceroy seemed to mistrust Ocopa, he understood that its popularity at court made it difficult for him to criticize these missionaries openly. The viceroy may have also wanted to avoid drawing attention to his negligence in providing them with crown-mandated money and support.[5]

On 11 July 1750, San Antonio wrote the first of a string of petitions to the crown. These petitions, of which San Antonio would submit more than a dozen over the next decade, laid out the missionaries' plan for expansion throughout most of the eastern jungle of modern-day Peru. He hoped that the crown would not only help the missionaries grow their enterprise but also increase their autonomy from local viceregal officials, whom he argued were ignorant of how to govern the Montaña. To emphasize this point, he began his first petition, dated 11 July 1750, as well as most subsequent petitions, by recounting the history of the Ocopa missions, taking great pains to emphasize both the concessions in funds and manpower that the crown had promised as well as the failure of successive viceregal governments to fulfill them. He particularly emphasized that the viceregal government rarely paid the promised annual stipend of 6,000 pesos, lamenting that "all of these mentioned promises, sire, have not had effect for the most part, for they have delivered few payments, [and] have not satisfied them in total," although he did concede, perhaps to avoid a direct attack on the viceroy, that these failures were "without doubt due to the occurrences of wars and the increased costs associated with them." Therefore, "to remedy the damages" caused by this neglect, San Antonio pleaded that the crown grant four dispensations.[6]

The first two requests echoed the missionaries' previous petitions. San Antonio asked that the crown pay for a group of sixty peninsular friars to travel to Ocopa at a cost of nearly 4,500 pesos.[7] Ocopa had not received new missionaries from Spain for more than sixteen years, and only twelve missionaries remained in the community.[8] Later he requested an additional twelve to fourteen lay friars trained in medicine, blacksmithing, and other useful trades to serve in the distant missions, though he subsequently reduced that petition to ask for only eight.[9] Second, San Antonio pleaded for the restoration of the

TABLE 2. Payments to the Ocopa missionaries during Manso de Velasco's term of office as viceroy

Year	Amount (pesos)
1745	0
1746	0
1747	3000
1748	0
1749	2000
1750	1500
1751	0
1752	3000
1753	3000
1754	3000
1755	3000
1756	3000
1757	3000
1758	3000
1759	6000
1760	6000
1761	6000

Source: AGN, Caja Real, Jauja, 627–29; AGN, Ministero de Hacienda, Libros 794, 817; Francisco Davila y Thores, Petition in the name of the three conversions, 9 November 1748, Lima, AGI, Lima 541; Lehnertz, "Land of the Infidels," 316.

annual stipend of 6,000 pesos. Under Manso de Velasco the mission had received only three payments, each less than the mandated 6,000 pesos (table 2). As before, San Antonio requested not just that the annual payments resume but that the government give them the unpaid balance for every year since the decree was originally issued in 1718. By 1750 this amounted to 153,000 pesos.[10] Both of these requests had been repeated in multiple petitions over the past four decades (as detailed in chapter 1), and, though the crown had funded two groups of missionaries to travel from the peninsula to Ocopa in 1730 and 1737, the viceregal authorities had consistently refused to pay the annual stipend. Ocopa hoped that somehow the Council of the Indies could force the viceregal government to comply with what it believed was the king's will.

A third request asked the king to make a further investment in Franciscan missionary work in the viceroyalty of Peru. In the original text of the letter, San Antonio requested only that Santa Rosa de Ocopa be elevated to a college de propaganda fide.[11] Again, this was a request that the Apostolic Institute had been making since it had acquired Ocopa in 1725. Viceregal officials and the provincial Franciscan leadership in Lima had previously blocked this request by failing to provide the necessary recommendations for the petitions to go forward in the Council of the Indies. By obtaining the status of a college de propaganda fide, Ocopa would become independent of Franciscan provincial leadership in Lima and be directly subject within the Spanish Church only to the Franciscan commissary-general in Spain. Such independence, in theory, would free Ocopa from the types of local political intrigues and pressures that afflicted most Franciscan institutions in Peru, particularly in Lima, and allow the missionaries to focus on the work of evangelization. The separation would also make Ocopa more difficult for viceregal officials to criticize, since it would have disassociated Ocopa completely from the order in Lima, which many saw as corrupt.

In a note added to the back of the petition, however, San Antonio went beyond just calling for Ocopa's elevation and requested that the king approve and fund the erection of two such colleges in every one of the seven Franciscan provinces in the viceroyalty of Peru. The establishment of two colleges de propaganda fide in each Franciscan province had been one of the principal stipulations of the papal bulls that created the Apostolic Institute in 1686. By 1750, several of these colleges dotted the viceroyalties of New Spain and New Granada, but no such institution existed in the viceroyalty of Peru. Such an expansion would allow the Franciscans to extend their influence into most of the frontiers of the viceroyalty as well as cement the state's patronage of their evangelization efforts.[12] To show the widespread desire for these colleges, San Antonio included in the petition letters of support from many of the major spiritual and political leaders of the viceroyalty, including the audiencia of La Plata, the cabildo of Lima, and several archbishops.[13] The fiscal of the Council of the Indies for Peru, Manuel Pablo de Salcedo, who represented the interests of the crown to the Council, agreed that the construction of these colleges along with the elevation of Ocopa were essential to teach missionaries from Spain the necessary languages to preach to the "infidels" along the frontier. He even implied that such colleges would allow Franciscans to engage fully in missionary activities in the New World instead of "amusing themselves to other ends."[14] Fiscal Salcedo's remarks demonstrate that many royal officials, particularly the more conservative ones, saw the colleges de propaganda fide as the proper means of curtailing the excesses of the regular clergy. This opinion made it difficult for more hardline regalists to openly oppose these expansions, even though such policies would extend Franciscan influence in Peru.

San Antonio's fourth request asked that the crown redouble its efforts at retaking the missions lost to Juan Santos Atahualpa. Although the viceroy had not yet ordered an end to expeditions against the rebels when San Antonio had left Peru in 1748, by the late 1740s the missionaries must have suspected that he was not interested in restoring them to their former territories. Therefore, San Antonio, on behalf of the missionaries, presented the crown with their own plan for retaking the area lost to Juan Santos. This plan centered on controlling the salt deposits of the Cerro de la Sal. San Antonio argued that if they had a fort of fifty to sixty soldiers, along with several Spanish or mestizo settlers to support them, they could completely control this vital resource. This would give the missionaries the opportunity to evangelize the jungle Amerindians, who were constantly traveling to the deposits to collect salt. It would also deter any "gentile nations" from attacking the missionaries "for fear of Catholic arms prohibiting them from taking the fruit [the salt] that they so crave."[15] Since Cerro de la Sal was so deep in the jungle, however, he also suggested that the crown build two forts to protect the roads leading to it. He wrote that these fortifications should be placed at the passes in the Oxabamba and Chanchamayo river valleys (see figure 1), with bridges to allow for the easy passage of soldiers in case of a rebellion. The Chanchamayo River valley in particular, which was already under coca cultivation by Spaniards, mestizos, and highland Amerindians, he reasoned would be an ideal location for the first fort to serve as a staging ground for either spiritual or military expeditions into the Montaña.[16]

Convincing the government to go forward with the Chanchamayo plan, as it became known, remained an obsession for the Ocopa missionaries over the next few decades. Though some of the details changed, it would be included in almost every petition to the crown well into the 1770s, and it became the source of constant friction between Ocopa and the viceregal authorities. Even Fiscal Salcedo, who had readily supported San Antonio's other three proposals, equivocated with this fourth request. He recognized that the Juan Santos Atahualpa rebellion had shown that the missions were vulnerable and in need of military defense, and he had "no doubt of the certain zeal and truthfulness of this missionary [*religioso*], with his great practice, experience, and knowledge of those missions' locations, rivers, entrances and exits." But he did not believe he could recommend to the Council such a large expenditure of money and manpower without first consulting the viceroy.[17]

At the end of his petitions, San Antonio reminded the king of the numerous martyrs who had died in the establishment of the missions as further evidence of the need to retake them. He enumerated that forty-five friars, ten oblates, three tertiaries, and 254 other Christians had been martyred since evangelization began in the region in 1634 (even before the arrival of the Apostolic Institute). And surely countless others died that would "only be known on the day of Judgment." To make these deaths more real to the reader, San Antonio included a copy of what he called a map (*mapa*) originally created in 1737 that had been on display in the viceroy's offices (figure 7). Ostensibly, the map was a census of the Ocopa missions at their greatest extent before the rebellion, demonstrating the sheer magnitude of the accomplishment, but it also conveyed something more. The census data for each mission was placed around tableaus depicting the death of each martyr killed in that

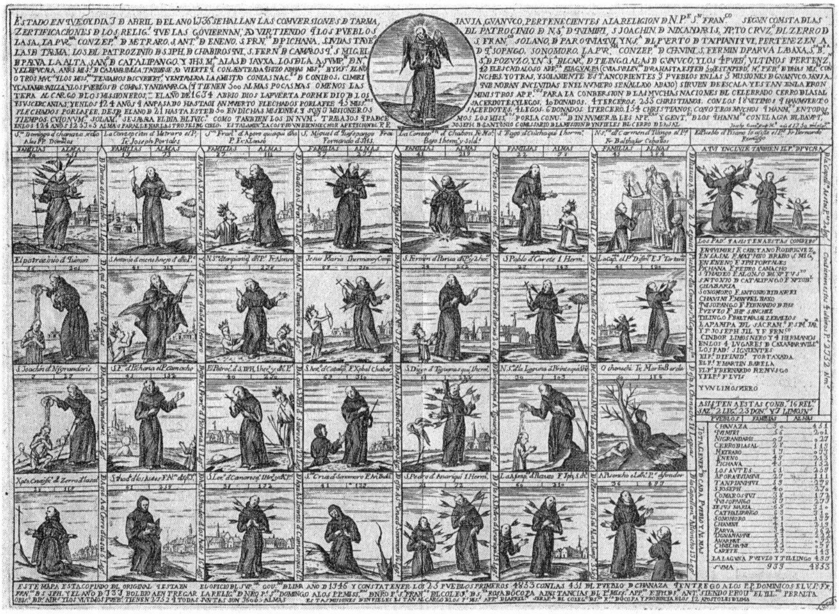

FIGURE 7. Martyrs' map, 1737. "Mapa de los Mártires de Santa Rosa de Ocopa" (copied 1746). ESPAÑA. MINISTERIO DE EDUCACIÓN, CULTURA Y DEPORTE, AGI, Mapas y Planos, Peru-Chile 32.

particular mission along with their names. Though the pictures were small, even a casual observer would note that most of the friars died from arrow wounds. Although the bow and arrow was the most common weapon of the jungle, this might also have been an allusion to the iconography of Saint Sebastian, who was similarly martyred by arrows.

The invocation of martyrdom has been a common literary trope throughout the history of Christianity, particularly in the baroque artwork of the seventeenth century. As the wars of religion during this period ravaged Europe, descriptions and depictions of martyrs were used to motivate faithful Catholics (and Protestants) to action. As historian Brad Gregory states, "Martyrs were the living embodiment of what they believed and practiced as members of religious communities." They personified the communities' commitment to their beliefs and "infused religious dispute with human urgency. Any compromise could unfold only 'over their dead bodies.'"[18] In sending the martyrs' map, Friar San Antonio was attempting to convince crown officials that the retaking of the missions would not just benefit expansion of the empire but would fulfill the moral imperative by not letting those Franciscan martyrs die in vain.

In many ways, the martyrs' map's stylistically baroque sentiment demonstrates Ocopa's philosophical rift with the reformists at court. Baroque art emerged from the Catholic counter-reformation of the seventeenth century to combat the austerity of Protestant religious reformers and demonstrate the power and majesty of the Church. Through sensual displays of the divine, baroque religious devotion attempted to create an atmosphere that was radically different from daily life. Church authorities encouraged individual devotees to concern themselves with the plight of their eternal soul rather than the state of the secular world. Spiritual purity, therefore, should be achieved through emotional displays of devotion.[19] Historian Charles Walker, in his work on the Lima earthquake and tsunami, argues that chaotic baroque sentimentality displayed in the processions and religious devotions after the earthquake deeply offended "enlightened" Bourbon ministers' logical, orderly sensibilities. Reformers, Manso de Velasco in particular, believed that these great and ostentatious displays of emotive religious fervor were disorderly and wasteful. They drained economic resources that could be used to promote the commercial renewal of the city. Religious devotions should, according to "enlightened" reformers, be simple, private, and logical.[20]

The martyrs' map was not intended to be logical. In fact, logic might dictate that so many missionaries' deaths proved that the Ocopa missions were not viable, as Manso de Velasco apparently believed. The map was intended to appeal to personal devotion and even outrage over the deaths of these saintly friars. In many ways it can be placed in contrast to Manso de Velasco's own map included in his 24 September 1750 report to the crown (see figure 6). Whereas the martyrs' map appealed to emotion, the viceroy's map attempted to demonstrate logically the threat that the rebels in Huarochirí and beyond posed to the viceregal capital. Ironically, though the two maps reflected differing philosophies, both formed part of more or less successful petitions, perhaps reflecting the deep schisms among officials over their clashing conceptualizations of governance.

Whether or not the religious overtones of the martyrs' map were the catalyst for garnering the Council of the Indies' support, they ultimately agreed with most of San Antonio's proposals. On 5 November 1750, the Council deliberated. In its summary of the decision it lambasted previous viceroys for their failure to give the Ocopa missionaries the promised financial aid and manpower mandated by the king since the establishment of the Apostolic Institute in Peru. The Council recommended that the king accede to all of San Antonio's requests but added that the creation of colleges de propaganda fide in other Franciscan provinces need be decided on a case-by-case basis. Most important, however, the Council asked the king to "personally charge" the viceroy with the task of retaking the lost missions, utilizing San Antonio's Chanchamayo plan. The councilors argued that it was the viceroy's duty to "correct with greatest severity the abuses" of the rebels with the "efficiency and promptness that is expected in such an important work." They even recommended that the viceroy offer freedom to criminals in exchange for colonizing the Cerro de la Sal.[21]

On 13 March 1751, the king issued a royal decree that closely followed the Council's recommendations. He even chided the viceroy for the "omission and lack of zeal with which until now you had treated this material," warning that he would "from this moment forward take the corresponding [actions] to remedy it" and would "punish whomever is involved in such culpable neglect prejudicial to the service of god and myself."[22] The wording of the decree regarding exactly how it was going to be implemented, however, was vague and easily ignored. For example, several months later in October a separate decree had to be issued to detail the exact amount of money the crown would pay for each missionary's travel expenses to Ocopa and from where crown officials would draw these monies.[23]

Clearly the decree backed San Antonio's Chanchamayo plan, though leaving how to launch expeditions and finance the plan up to the viceroy. In reality the crown had little choice in the matter. The viceroy was not only the supreme political authority in Peru but also its supreme military commander. Long experience in managing a vast empire had taught the monarchs of Spain not to micromanage such a distant and complicated operation. For this reason, royal decrees (*real cédulas*) had a long tradition in colonial law of being negotiable in a practice known as *arbitrio judicial* (judicial discretion). Distant colonial administrators, particularly at the highest levels (viceroys and audiencias), had frequently been given leeway in implementing such decrees or even sending them back for further review. Only when the crown issued a cédula with the words "*sin replica*" (without reply) would colonial authorities know that the decree was not negotiable. Even then implementation was not guaranteed, demonstrating the limits of governance over such long distances. Later in the eighteenth century, as a way of strengthening royal power, reformers did create new legal instruments, more binding than cédulas, attempting to end this type of noncompliance, but such practices were not put into effect until several decades later. Therefore, the decree's legal flexibility along with its vagueness allowed Manso de Velasco to delay its execution almost indefinitely. For the next three decades the 13 March 1751 decree would be a point of conflict between Ocopa and the viceroys of Peru.

In the meantime, encouraged by his success with the Council of the Indies, San Antonio continued to petition the crown. One month later he presented a second, longer list of requests. These included small increases in the number of lay friars allowed to travel to Ocopa as well as a heartfelt plea for Brother Calixto de San José Tupac Inka to receive a dispensation to become a lay friar (see chapter 2).[24] Three of these new requests aimed to maintain or even increase Ocopa's independence. One was a request to prohibit any friar who had served in Ocopa from joining any other Franciscan convent in Peru after his ten-year term as a missionary had ended, forcing him to return home to Spain at the crown's expense.[25] This request reflected a serious problem for Ocopa that was only intensifying as it began to bring ever-larger numbers of peninsular friars to Peru. The missionaries had always insisted on sending an experienced member of their community to escort each new group of friars so they could not take advantage of leadership opportunities created by the alternativa as they passed through New World cities before arriving at Ocopa.

They could not, however, stop missionaries from taking up these posts after they had completed their ten-year term of service. San Antonio worried that the eventual opportunities this created would attract the wrong type of friars to the missions, ones who were more concerned with advancing their careers than preaching the word of God in the far reaches of the Montaña.[26] San Antonio hoped to "close this door of even the remote hope that they could be motivated to pass to the Indies where they would serve for ten years in the missions and ascend with more ease to positions within the order than in the province from which they came."[27]

The Council of the Indies did not, however, agree. It pointed out that nowhere in Pope Innocent's bulls of 1686 that created the Apostolic Institute did it stipulate that missionaries had to return after their term had ended. Furthermore, the Council was probably not interested in shouldering the extra cost of transporting the missionaries back to Spain.[28] Not only did these missionaries refuse to actually serve in the jungle missions, spending their entire term of service at Ocopa, but they tended to be more interested in the political intrigues of the viceroyalty. In the 1780s the problem of ambitious friars continued to plague Ocopa and led to a vitriolic, even violent conflict in the college as a faction of these missionaries took power (see chapter 5). Such conflicts only gave cause for viceregal authorities to take control of Ocopa's enterprises.

The second new request was that the king order the archbishop of Lima to grant one of the older missionaries certain ecclesiastical privileges that were normally reserved for a bishop. These included the ability to preside over confirmations and give dispensations for marriages in cases of couples too closely related. This practice was common among frontier missions as a simple matter of convenience. Bishops would never travel so far from their episcopal seats, and such dispensations allowed the faithful in the margins of the Catholic world to receive the rites they believed necessary for their salvation. Practically, however, this gave the missionaries almost complete pastoral control over their missions and thus eliminated one of the few areas in which the secular clergy had power over Ocopa. San Antonio argued that this prefect, as they were to be called, should be from Ocopa to avoid any unforeseen conflicts. The Council of the Indies agreed, though it reserved the right in the future to select a non-Ocopa friar to the position.[29] Accordingly, the archbishop created the position of prefect of the missions and endowed it with the episcopal power requested by San Antonio, which an Ocopa missionary held continuously for the rest of the colonial period.

Third, San Antonio requested that the king put the Ocopa missions under his personal protection and create a "conservator judge" to serve as his witness to ensure that the "royal ministers in those kingdoms [the viceroyalty of Peru] foment and protect the missionaries and employ themselves in such a holy work and give aid for the happy achievement of said undertaking."[30] San Antonio hoped that, by having some sort of outside arbitrator charged with ensuring that the viceroy fulfill the royal decrees issued on Ocopa's behalf, they could avoid the "gravest inconveniences" previous neglect had created.[31] The request for a conservator judge demonstrates one of the core problems that Ocopa faced in its relationship with the crown. Although it could get Madrid to promise aid, it could not convince viceregal ministers, endowed with arbitrio judicial, to honor these promises. The Council, perhaps in a tacit admission of its own limitations, rejected this request, stating that the king has already issued all the decrees "the Council has deemed necessary."[32] Though pro-Ocopa ministers in Madrid could try to cajole the viceroy, unless they could convince the king (and at this point Ensenada) to remove Manso de Velasco from office there was little they could do to force the viceroy to help the missionaries.

Manso de Velasco's Continued Resistance

The 13 March 1751 royal decree arrived in Lima on 9 May of the next year.[33] At least for the moment, two of the clauses, the elevation of Ocopa to a college de propaganda fide and the transportation of sixty new missionaries to Ocopa, did not affect Manso de Velasco since arrangements for those concessions were still being handled in Spain. As for the order to retake the Ocopa missions from Juan Santos, the viceroy had already decided, as he had indicated in his report to the crown of 24 September 1750, on a policy of containment.[34] Nevertheless, Manso de Velasco could not completely ignore the decree's insistence that the treasury pay 6,000 pesos annually to Ocopa. The decree stipulated that the monies be disbursed "without the officers of the royal treasury or any other minister pretending to know how to distribute it, claiming it was my [the king's] will, [and] that the decision [on how to spend it] should be left to the missionaries or their leaders."[35] The viceroy, however, only partially obeyed the decree's provision to pay the stipend. He ordered the royal treasury in Jauja to pay the missionaries, but he reduced the payment by half to 3,000 pesos. He reasoned that since the missionaries had only one entrada (Huánuco) of the three for which they had originally been given the funding (they had lost Tarma and Jauja), 3,000 pesos was more than adequate for their needs (see table 2).[36]

The reduction of Ocopa's stipend may have been more than a matter of limiting clerical power; it also reflected another aspect of the Bourbon reforms—streamlining the colonial budget. Over three hundred years, Spain's American colonies had provided the crown with an immense source of revenue. Over time, however, a larger colonial bureaucracy, local corruption, tax evasion, and failing mineral production had all led to a decline in remittances to Spain. Reformers hoped that by cutting colonial budgets, more closely enforcing taxation, and promoting colonial industry and commerce, the crown could recover and even augment colonial revenues. Therefore, colonial ministers were under extreme pressure to increase their remittances to Spain. The pressure to remit money back to Spain was so intense that, despite the devastation of the earthquake in Lima, Manso de Velasco had to devise a method of keeping the funds flowing to the metropole. Within two years after the earthquake, the viceroy had already remitted 115,000 pesos back to Spain.[37] This was impressive, considering that taxable commerce on the sale of luxury goods in Lima had almost completely disappeared in the years immediately after the disaster. Additionally, Manso de Velasco, who as well as being viceroy was the superintendent of the royal treasury, was able to balance Lima's budget for nearly a decade after the earthquake. As figure 8 details, between 1746 and 1755 he matched income to expenditures almost exactly, with the exception of 1750.

Balancing the ledger, even in times of decreased revenues, was not an unusual practice for colonial treasuries. Usually when in deficit viceregal authorities just borrowed money. After the earthquake, however, viceregal treasury officials in Lima resorted to a subtler method to balance their ledgers. Total expenditures were increasing (to rebuild the city), but so was income from the account entry *extraordinario de la Real Hacienda*, an account that normally contained miscellaneous entries. In fact, the increases and decreases in these two accounts match up closely. Both total expenditures and extraordinario saw increases in 1746, 1747, 1748, 1751, and 1752 and decreases in 1749, 1750, 1753, and 1754. The two accounts increased and decreased in similar intervals, as the two-year moving averages for total expenditures and extraordinario indicate. The viceroy drew upon tax revenues from neighboring treasury districts and placed them in Lima's multipurpose account entry, extraordinario, to pay for the reconstruction of Lima.[38] In a letter to Ensenada dated shortly after the earthquake, Manso de Velasco admitted using profits from the taxes on mercury production in Huancavelica to rebuild Lima's most vital government buildings, such as the viceregal palace, the chambers of the audiencia, and the fortress at Callao. In later letters he indicated that in 1747

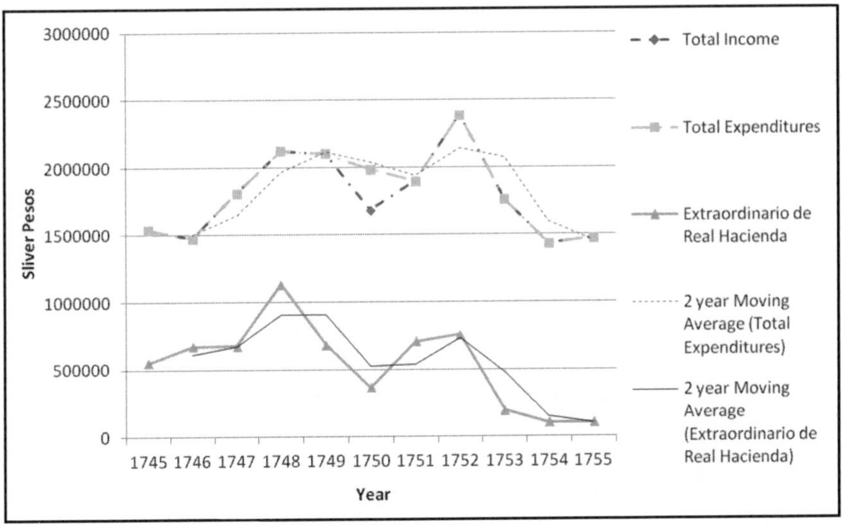

FIGURE 8. Finances after the Lima earthquake and tsunami of 1746. Data from TePaske, Klein, and Brown, *Royal Treasuries*, 362–67.

he had diverted 176,911 pesos from neighboring areas, using this and other sources of income to rebuild public buildings in the capital.[39] In truth, the viceroy probably used these sources of income more than he was willing to admit publicly. From before the earthquake, 1745, to its highest point, 1748, extraordinario saw a 105 percent increase. In 1748 the extraordinario account held 1,131,508 pesos, 53 percent of the city of Lima's total income.

By 1751, when Manso de Velasco decided to end campaigns against Juan Santos and reduce the friars' funding, the city's financial income had greatly improved. Manso de Velasco depended less on outside sources of income as his city began to recover. As figure 8 indicates, in 1751 extraordinario accounted for only 37 percent of the city's total income—down from 53 percent in 1748—and in 1752 it was only 32 percent, less than pre-earthquake levels. Furthermore, at the same time that the city's tax income rose, the viceroy completed most of the government's major rebuilding projects. By 1750, as figure 9 demonstrates, most of the work for rebuilding the viceregal palace, the royal mint, and the fortress at Callao had been completed. The final large reconstruction project for the crown, the rebuilding of the Lima cathedral, did not start in earnest until after 1754, because the viceroy had been reluctant to assume responsibility for this task, believing that it should fall to the *vecinos* (prominent citizens) of the city and the Church.[40]

In fact, except for the reconstruction of government buildings, the crown felt little obligation to rebuild any part of the city. Likewise, the care of the

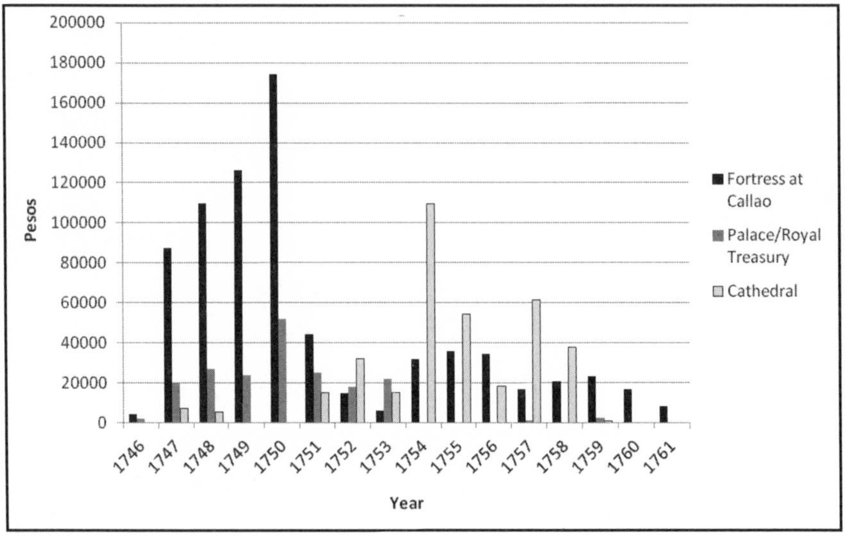

FIGURE 9. Government expenditures for the rebuilding of Lima. Data from Pérez-Mallaína Bueno, *Retrato de una ciudad en crisis,* 123.

thousands of limeños injured in the earthquake was left completely to the Church. Traditionally, the Catholic Church had been colonial Latin America's principal healthcare provider, but in the wake of the tremendously destructive earthquake and tsunami the ecclesiastical hospitals struggled to cope. During the reconstruction of Lima, the viceroy allocated only 27,998 pesos for the maintenance of hospitals in the city, as compared to the approximately 1.3 million pesos he spent on the reconstruction of government buildings. Even the burying of the dead was left to a secular religious brotherhood, the Hermandad de la Caridad. As historian Pablo Pérez-Mallaína Bueno so aptly stated, in the minds of Bourbon officials "charity was not a matter of state."[41]

Despite the costs of rebuilding Lima, then, Manso de Velasco had found ways to continue and even increase remittances back to Spain. His superior, Ensenada, made it clear that even the rebuilding of the city of Lima was less important than increasing revenue to Spain. As early as 1748, Ensenada pressured Manso de Velasco to increase the flow of money from Lima to help Spain conclude the War of Austrian Succession. Ensenada chastised Manso de Velasco for spending too much on the rebuilding of the viceregal capital. He instructed the viceroy to use only the 176,911 pesos that he had admitted taking from outside sources in 1747 on the reconstruction of government buildings, though, as the volume of cash flowing through the extraordinario account suggests, the viceroy used far more outside funds than his superior had conceded.[42] Ensenada was perhaps willing to ignore Manso de Velasco's insubordination, since during his tenure of office (1745–61) he sent approximately 3.5 million pesos back to Spain in the form of remittances. In the fifteen years before his administration, previous viceroys of Peru had sent a little less than 1.5 million pesos in total. Of the 3.5 million pesos Manso de Velasco remitted to the metropolis, 2.5 million were sent between 1748 and 1752—the years during which he decided to limit funding to Ocopa. Still, had the viceroy continued to fund fully the Ocopa missionaries' annual 6,000-peso stipend during his final ten years as viceroy, remittances to Spain would have been reduced by less than 1 percent, suggesting that cutting Ocopa funds was not simply for the purpose of increasing remittances.

While Manso de Velasco worked to streamline royal treasury expenditures so that he could remit more money to Spain, he was also filling his own pockets. Like many others before him, Manso de Velasco hoped to profit financially from his government post in the Americas. On his initial voyage to South America to become governor of Chile in 1737, his personal baggage contained boxes of clothing, jewels, and other valuables listed for "personal use," including 150 pounds of tobacco. Manso de Velasco hoped to sell these luxury goods for an inflated price in Chile. To pay for these goods, the new governor had borrowed nearly 15,000 pesos, clearly confident of a profit. By the time he left his office as governor of Chile in 1745, he had done little more than pay off his initial debts.[43] But as viceroy of Peru he had access to wealth much greater than anything found in Chile. Manso de Velasco's annual salary as viceroy was 30,000 silver escudos (approximately 31,000 silver pesos). Exactly how much went to maintain his household remains unstudied. But upon arriving in Lima, Manso de Velasco worked quickly to set up a web of subordinates in key government positions in Lima, such as corregidores and treasury officials, to help advance his other business ventures.[44] He also maintained close ties with *consulado* (trade guild) members in both Lima and Cádiz. He would ultimately send back a total of 490,500 pesos for his own personal estate.[45]

Shortly after Manso de Velasco's decision to reduce funding to the Ocopa missionaries by half (in defiance of the 13 March 1751 decree), the missionaries appealed to the viceroy to reconsider his actions. Perhaps to assuage the politically powerful friars and to garner support for his controversial decision, one day after his initial decision the viceroy agreed to take the matter before the audiencia of Lima.[46] By 1752, after seven years as viceroy, Manso de Velasco had surrounded himself with many like-minded government officials, several of whom were members of the audiencia. Not surprisingly, on 24 April the audiencia confirmed Manso de Velasco's decision to cut Ocopa's funding.[47] That same day Ocopa's representative in Lima, Juan de San Antonio, lamented that the viceroy and the audiencia were "determined to ignore" his demands for full payment but took comfort in the fact that "his royal highness commanded the reverend father missionaries to inform him yearly on the state of the missions, and the use of said 6,000 pesos."[48]

Once word of the reduction in funding reached Madrid several months later, Joseph de San Antonio heeded his spiritual brother's suggestion and informed the king of the viceroy's decision. On 23 September 1752, San Antonio begged the king to order the viceroy (once again) to pay the full payment of 6,000 pesos annually.[49] In response, on 7 October the king wrote to Manso de Velasco, "I command you that you give attention to this subject [the missions of Ocopa], commendable as it is, and of great interest to the service of God and myself." The king ordered him to pay the full 6,000 pesos "without delay," writing, "I want to have proper and prompt fulfillment of what has been ordered in these decrees [of 13 and 26 March 1751] so that the missions receive the necessary aid. This is my will."[50]

This type of language was uncharacteristically direct when compared to the officious and flowery rhetoric that dominated eighteenth-century bureaucratic correspondence. The personal attention of Ferdinand VI, who generally remained aloof from matters of state and left the day-to-day affairs to Ensenada, is also noteworthy. Perhaps Ferdinand, despite Ensenada and his faction's attempts to reduce the power of the regular clergy, felt that the case of Ocopa was somehow different. Although the king perhaps could accept attacks on the more corrupt regular houses of Lima or Quito, he could not oppose such notable pious work the delaying or preventing of which might imperil his immortal soul. Despite the king's demands, however, Manso de Velasco continued to ignore calls to restore full funding to Ocopa. As a result, in 1757 San Antonio once again attempted to get Ocopa's funding restored. He accused Manso de Velasco and the rest of the viceregal ministers of "disobedience" because they "pretend to have knowledge" of "his majesty's royal will."[51] Fiscal Salcedo agreed, stating that the viceroy's logic for not funding the missionaries was "twisted" and "not credible," but he also said, perhaps in recognition of the Council's weakness, that they had tried to force Manso de Velasco several times to obey, but since he still refused to restore the funding there was nothing more they could do.[52] Despite a reissuing of the royal decree in 1755, Manso de Velasco did not restore Ocopa's full funding until 1759, perhaps because he sensed a change in his political fortunes in the wake of the downfall of his patron, Ensenada.[53]

Manso de Velasco further thwarted the Ocopa missionaries from receiving funds promised in the 13 March 1751 royal decree by failing to pay the travel costs for new missionaries coming to Peru. On 23 March, a few days after the initial decree, the crown specified that it would provide 21,900 pesos to transport sixty-seven missionaries (sixty full friars, including San Antonio himself, and six lay friars) but stipulated that the money be paid upon their arrival in Lima from the city's own *mesadas eclesiásticas* account (a tax levied on clergy upon taking office).[54] This stipulation that money come from Lima's treasury worried San Antonio. He complained to the crown that "experience has taught the supplicant and his companions that in thirty-two years the treasury of Lima has not paid the balance of the stipend designated by his majesty for the missions to the infidels, which I fear will now happen if the corresponding expenses are not paid in every port and royal treasury until they arrive at Santa Rosa de Ocopa."[55] Both Fiscal Salcedo and the Council of the Indies agreed with San Antonio, but the resulting royal decree of 16 October did nothing to rectify the problem.[56]

Because the number of missionaries headed for Ocopa was so large, San Antonio decided to have them travel in two groups, one by way of Cartagena and the other through Buenos Aires. In 1752 the first group of twenty-seven missionaries left Cádiz, passing from Cartagena to Lima. When they arrived in Lima, the viceroy honored the royal decree and paid the first half of the promised funds, 15,684 pesos. The second group, numbering forty-four missionaries, left a year later. Unfortunately, as their ship entered the Rio de la Plata estuary it ran aground and, though none of the missionaries were killed, they lost all of their supplies and documents. The group's bad fortune continued to plague them when they arrived in Lima absolutely penniless and the viceroy refused to pay them the rest of the promised funds, arguing that the first group of missionaries had completely emptied the mesadas eclesiasticas account. The missionaries, of course, complained to the crown. In an attempt to silence them, the viceroy made a token payment of 2,350 pesos—quite short of the 14,937 pesos the treasury still owed. The missionaries did not receive the balance of their compensation until after Manso de Velasco left office.[57]

Calixto's Final Deportation and the Viceroy's Fall from Favor

Manso de Velasco also renewed his attacks against Friar Calixto. The newly elevated lay friar had humiliated the viceroy when he had secretly traveled to Madrid with the *Representación Verdadera*, which flatly condemned the administration of the viceroyalty. In 1753 after taking vows in Valencia, Friar Calixto petitioned the king to allow him to return to Peru and serve in the missions the Apostolic Institute was creating in the high jungle region north of Cusco.[58] With the help of commissary-general and former Ocopa missionary Friar Mathías Velasco, Calixto secured not only license from the crown to return to Peru but funding for the voyage as well.[59] Nevertheless, Calixto feared that the viceroy would try to arrest him when he arrived in Lima since he had made the journey to Spain illegally. To assuage his fears, the crown ordered the viceroy and the archbishop of Lima to let Calixto pass unmolested through the viceregal capital.[60]

Upon returning to Peru, Calixto may have gone to Cuzco for a time, as he had told the crown, but by 1756 he was in Lima in residence at the city's principal monastery, San Francisco de Jesús. There, according to Manso de Velasco, Calixto enjoyed a significant following among the brothers of the monastery, and in October 1756 he began hosting secret meetings in his cell, sometimes lasting all day, with a small group of prominent indigenous leaders and businessmen. On 15 January 1757 the viceroy dispatched a blistering report to the crown, drawing parallels between these meetings and the Lima conspiracy of seven years earlier. He still blamed Calixto and his companion, Friar Isidoro de Cala, for inciting the unrest in 1750 by disseminating the *Representación,* which, among other things, advocated allowing natives to receive holy orders as well as serve in government offices. The viceroy complained that Calixto did not understand "the inconveniences nor the consequences of this universal permission, which the nature and condition of the Indians will not allow" and, further, that this secret cabal espoused exactly the same ideals, which taught the natives "to hate the Spanish nation" and had instilled a desire to "throw off their yoke of domination." The viceroy even complained that the group believed he had been too harsh in executing the traitorous Lima conspirators for their crimes. To stem the potential threat the viceroy believed these meetings posed, he ordered audiencia judge Pedro Bravo de Rivero to incarcerate Calixto while they searched his cell for condemning evidence. The viceroy admitted that the search turned up no new evidence, but it did produce two letters which, according to Manso de Velasco, demonstrated Calixto's animosity toward the Spanish as well as his evil intentions. One letter, from the Cabildo de Indios of Lima, complaining about American natives' inability to receive priestly orders, and another from one Felipe Tancuri detailed the suffering of the natives of Mexico. Nonetheless, the search did not produce enough evidence to convict Calixto of treason. Manso de Velasco therefore condemned him for illegally meeting with an indigenous assembly, which according to colonial law had to be attended by a crown representative, though no other suspected member of this supposed cabal was ever arrested or even investigated.[61]

The viceroy's condemnation of Calixto's activities was enough to cause concern among crown officials in Madrid. Therefore, when the viceroy asked the crown for permission to deport Calixto back to Spain, both crown and Franciscan officials in Madrid agreed. While Calixto waited for his deportation from Peru, the viceroy placed him under house arrest and banned him from any communication with indigenous groups. In January 1759, Calixto sailed from Callao. The viceroy insisted that he be placed on a ship bound for Cádiz by way of Cape Horn, probably to minimize any risk of him escaping during a land journey through the Andes to Cartagena or Buenos Aires. The ship, however, was waylaid in Chile for almost a year until the viceroy personally ordered it to set sail, warning that under no circumstance could Calixto stay in the Americas. Manso de Velasco also requested that, upon arrival in Spain, Calixto be sent to an "austere" monastery in Castile (not Valencia, where he took his vows), remain prohibited from any communication with anyone back in Peru or elsewhere, and be banned from living in any community in a port city to ensure that the lay friar could never return.[62] Both the crown and the order again acceded to the viceroy's request, and when Calixto arrived on 16 September 1760 in Cádiz he was escorted in "secure custody" from the port to the remote monastery of San Francisco del Monte near the landlocked Andalusian village of Adamuz, where he resided until 1765, when he disappeared from the historical record.[63]

Calixto's second run-in with the viceroy certainly only reinforced to Manso de Velasco the danger that the regular orders, and perhaps specifically Ocopa, posed to the control of the viceroyalty. Calixto was certainly a provocateur whose activities, even in earlier times, may have appeared subversive to colonial officials. Manso de Velasco's determination in pursuing the friar, however, demonstrated not only a personal concern about Calixto's growing influence but a symptom of a growing uneasiness among more regalist crown officials as they began to suspect that the Church was no longer a partner in the maintenance of a harmonious social and racial colonial hierarchy. Ocopa's association with Calixto helped to keep the missions at the center of these debates.

At almost every opportunity between 1750 and 1761, Manso de Velasco attempted to use the full power of his office to block or retard the expansion of the Ocopa missions as well as other projects of the Apostolic Institute. In 1756 he denied a request that would give the Ocopa missionaries access to labor from the mita of twenty-three Indians from the frontier villages of Panao and Acomayo. In 1717 the crown had already given the missionaries mita rights to the labor of one hundred men in the frontier villages of Chinchao and Pillao. The missionaries used these men mainly as soldiers to protect their expanding missions in the only entrada they had left, Huánuco. Not only did the viceroy reject their proposal for more mita labor but insisted that they report yearly on how they were using utilizing the labor from the mita workers they already had.[64] The viceroy further attenuated Ocopa's missionary activity by ignoring its request to exempt from secularization the highland parish servicing the villages of Comas and Andamarca, which Ocopa controlled. Andamarca was of particular interest, not only as the site of Juan Santos's last raid but as an important staging ground for any future attempt to reenter the entrada of Jauja. The viceroy argued that only the king could grant such an exemption, but he never passed the request on to Madrid. The parish passed into the hands of a secular priest in November 1755.[65] The viceroy also personally blocked the Apostolic Institute from expanding missions into Tarija (in modern-day Bolivia), even though the local audiencia of Charcas had already approved the Franciscan takeover of the region. Instead he gave the area over to the Jesuits.[66]

The most divisive issue between the Ocopa missionaries and the viceroy continued to be his intransigence over the continuation of campaigns against Juan Santos. Manso de Velasco followed a policy of containment until the end of his term of office. In an attempt to force Manso de Velasco's hand, however, the missionaries devised other ways to reach the missions of the Tarma entrada. In 1753 they asked the viceregal government for more troops to protect their remaining missions in the Huánuco entrada. The missionaries were using these men, mostly militia, to launch expeditions to explore areas near their old Tarma missions in the Pampas de Sacramento. They justified reentering the former missions by claiming that "the motive for said enterprise is the continuous pleading of those apostates in repeated messages that they have been sending to the college [Ocopa] offering to restore their mission villages if they were given missionaries to govern them and soldiers to defend them."[67]

The viceroy tried to limit the number of troops he sent to the Huánuco entrada so that the missionaries would not have enough to expand into the Pampas.[68] Possibly he feared that if the missionaries once again got into an armed conflict with Juan Santos he would have to respond with force to avoid criticism from Madrid. To stop the missionaries from inciting further violence, the viceroy issued an order on 2 June 1755 that barred the Ocopa missionaries from entering "infidel lands," with the caveat that it was just "for now."[69] The Ocopa missionaries, of course, vehemently objected, pointing out that the crown had paid for the transport of peninsular friars to come to Peru just for this purpose. The newly elected guardian of Ocopa, Friar Joseph Ampuero, personally traveled to Lima with a petition signed by the community to press the viceroy to rescind his order. Even before Ampuero arrived in Lima, however, Manso de Velasco had reversed his decision.[70] Perhaps he realized that barring the missionaries not only from retaking their Santos-occupied missions but from sending any new expeditions elsewhere in the jungle was politically untenable.

In rescinding the order, however, the viceroy added a clause that deeply offended the missionaries; he stated that in any future expeditions they should "use convenient precautions and not disrupt the peace of those providences with the insults experienced nearby [in the Tarma and Jauja missions]."[71] Ampuero lashed out at the viceroy, saying that such a clause, which essentially blamed the missionaries for the Juan Santos Atahualpa rebellion, impinged on "the honor of the sacred religion [the Franciscan order] and its children [the friars] who have striven to conserve the holy desire to convert."[72] Like Juan and Ulloa, Manso de Velasco saw Ocopa's frontier missions as a liability to the stability of the empire. Unable to persuade the viceroy to launch new campaigns against Juan Santos, the missionaries pressed the Council of the Indies through their representative, Joseph de San Antonio, who had just returned to Madrid from escorting the new missionaries to Ocopa. Once again San Antonio pleaded that the Council force Manso de Velasco to launch new campaigns to recuperate Ocopa's lost missions, calling the viceroy's efforts up to this point "useless." Although the Council heartily agreed and convinced the king to issue a new decree, they were impotent to make the viceroy comply. Even in reissuing this order, just as in the royal decree of 13 March 1751, they left implementation to the discretion of the viceroy.[73] The missionaries fumed about their treatment, so much so that the fiscal of the Council of the Indies noted that "these friars demonstrate little satisfaction in the conduct of the Viceroy regarding these missions."[74]

By the late 1750s, Manso de Velasco's political position in the Spanish bureaucracy had begun to weaken with the fall of his patron, the marqués de la Ensenada, in 1754. Ensenada's radical reform agenda, not just in religious matters, deeply upset the more conservative factions in the Spanish government. His fall began with the death of his partner, José de Carvajal y Lancaster, in April 1754. Many ministers within the more radical factions of the government did not trust Ensenada's ambitions, and without Carvajal to check his power they began to abandon him. Eventually two pro-British ministers, Fernando de Silva Mendoza y Toledo, duke of Huéscar, and Ricardo Wall, convinced the king that Ensenada had been secretly trying to start another war with Britain over the cutting of logwood in Central America. On 21 July 1754, Ensenada was placed under house arrest and eventually exiled to Granada. The king replaced him as minister of the Indies with the conservative president of the Council of the Indies, Julián de Arriaga.[75] Though Ensenada's removal did not mean the end of Manso de Velasco's tenure as viceroy, it certainly limited his freedom to ignore direct requests from Madrid. The viceroy still continued to try to undermine Ocopa, but he could not ignore all demands from Madrid to aid them. On 24 June 1758, the viceroy finally relented and restored Ocopa's annual funding of 6,000 pesos, but in most other issues, including the retaking of the lost missions, he remained unmoved.[76]

The State of the Missions in the Wake of Juan Santos and Viceroy Manso de Velasco

The 1750s were not a complete disaster for the Ocopa missions. The missionaries began expanding into the Huánuco entrada as well as opening a new one at Cajamarquilla. Most significant, the 13 March 1751 royal decree also elevated Ocopa to a college de propaganda fide. Though official recognition of its elevation was delayed because the royal decree was lost in the shipwreck in the Rio de la Plata estuary in 1754, few challenged Ocopa's new status.[77] In reality the day-to-day function of the College of Ocopa changed very little with its elevation. Experienced friars still instructed new missionaries in indigenous languages to prepare them for the college's new entradas. Though control of the Ocopa missions passed from the temporary position of commissary of the missions to the guardian of Ocopa, in practice this change meant very little. In theory, this new status allowed Ocopa to be completely autonomous of Franciscan leadership in Lima, but Ocopa had long since ignored the province.[78] Formally at least, between the elevation and the creation of the position of prefect, the college was almost completely independent of any sort of Church leadership in Peru.

With the arrival of sixty-six new missionaries from Spain, the college also had the manpower to capitalize on its most recent territorial expansions. Just as San Antonio had feared, however, many of these friars sought missionary service in the New World in the hope that once there they could obtain leadership positions created by the alternativa.[79] According to San Antonio, these ambitions made many of the new missionaries "incompatible" with the type of evangelization they would need in the jungle.[80] Both Manso de Velasco and his successor Amat complained about these missionaries, whom the crown had paid to preach to the "infidels" and not to fulfill their ambitions for advancement.[81] In order to force these office-seeking missionaries to go out to the Montaña, as early as 1751 San Antonio tried to ban them from preaching locally around Ocopa so as to remove any excuse to stay in the sierra.[82] Unfortunately for the Ocopa leadership, many missionaries continued to stay at the college for as much of their ten-year term as possible, leaving only after they had completed their service and taking up posts throughout the viceroyalty.

By the end of the 1750s the proximal mass exodus of all the missionaries who had come earlier in the decade had caused Ocopa to confront another shortage in manpower. Not all the friars were being wooed away by alternativa opportunities. The Ocopa leadership had sent eighteen missionaries to found a new college de propaganda fide in Tarija. Though the viceroy later blocked this project, the missionaries did not return to Ocopa. Others, who actually had ventured out into the missions, died of diseases. In 1757, San Antonio once again asked the crown to send over new missionaries. Perhaps in a fit of zeal he requested four groups of fifty to sixty friars, two groups for Ocopa, one for the new missions in Huánuco and Cajamarquilla entradas, and another for the "reconquest" of the Tarma and Jauja entradas. Another group would be sent to Tarija (news had not yet arrived in Madrid of the viceroy ending the endeavor) and another to start a new college in Chile.[83] Confused by such a large request, the Council of the Indies asked the commissary-general, Friar Mathías Velasco, to clarify the order's request. Velasco reduced the request to just one group of fifty to sixty missionaries for Ocopa, with perhaps a smaller group for Chile in a separate request.[84] The Council, however, ultimately rejected even the commissary-general's more moderate proposal, stating that "for now there are not sufficient motives for His Majesty to concede the request of this friar."[85] This rejection left the Ocopa leadership in a difficult position. By 1762, when the first group of new missionaries' ten-year term expired, thirty-seven had already left Ocopa and twelve had died. Of those who remained, one had gone insane and another suffered from what the missionaries labeled "hypochondria," which was perhaps severe depression. Many remaining missionaries were old and infirm, and within two years four more died.[86]

In 1761 the newly crowned King Charles III ordered a report on all the religious institutions in the archdiocese of Lima. Friar Joseph de San Antonio responded on Ocopa's behalf in 1764. The friar began his report with a lamentation of the fallen state of the Ocopa missions. He complained that only ten missionaries remained, and two of those were too sick to work.[87] He argued that they needed at least sixty new missionaries, as well as the support of arms and soldiers to protect them, just to occupy the missions they currently had. He still bemoaned the loss of the Tarma and Jauja entradas, whose continued abandonment he, of course, blamed on the "indifference of His Majesty's ministers." Though most throughout the viceroyalty believed Juan Santos to no longer be a threat, he warned that "the lack of corresponding punishment" would allow Santos to gain more followers and arms.[88] To support San Antonio's dire assessment of the state of the Ocopa missions, Friar Joseph Gil, commissary-general for the order in Peru, stated that "there are few [missionaries in Ocopa] who are capable of work in the Montaña, some due to their old age, others because they are too ill," and that Ocopa and its missions would be in complete ruin "without anyone who can replace those members of the college who have died."[89]

San Antonio's 1764 report lambasted Peru's ministers, but it also marked a shift in the Ocopa missionaries' rhetoric to accommodate the reformist ministers surrounding King Charles. In describing the Pampas de Sacramento, for example, San Antonio claimed that it was a "very rich region, with abundant gold, which we know from the many Indians already baptized. . . . We have seen them pull out of the rivers' sand banks large nuggets and flakes of gold, but the gold of greatest quality, in which the missionaries are most interested, is the souls redeemed with the blood of Jesus."[90] Although the friars still touted evangelization as their goal, appeals from San Antonio and those who followed began to emphasize the commercial potential of expanding their missionary enterprise. The missionaries had used such rhetoric in a limited fashion before this time (e.g., exploiting the salt deposits), but more often they had resorted to an appeal to the officials' duty to God, as exemplified by the martyrs' map. After the 1750s, suggestions that the crown use the missions to strengthen colonial commerce became the centerpiece of Ocopa's lobbying to the government. These appeals helped missionaries' petitions on two geographic scales: At the imperial level, missionaries could further win over officials in Madrid, not only by touting the missions' spiritual potential, allowing the king to fulfill his mandate to evangelize the Americas, but by emphasizing the Peruvian jungle's commercial potential to help reinvigorate the empire. At a regional level, this aided viceregal officials in seeing Ocopa not as a deficit on their ledger but as a potential way of increasing their remittances back to Spain. Furthermore, the development of local commerce would give space for regional and local officials to benefit from any corruption that would inevitably occur.

These promises helped to improve relations between the missionaries and viceregal officials, but ultimately they came at a cost. The increasing closeness with the local officials provided increased benefits, generally in the form of compliance with the concessions the crown had already promised to Ocopa. But viceregal officials expected something in return. When the missionaries were unable to offer something, and sometimes even when they did, viceregal officials began to demand more and more control over the missions. Ultimately, the conflicts with Manso de Velasco had made Ocopa a more politically savvy institution, but in doing so they had planted the seeds of later conflicts. The friars had realized that to survive in the political climate of reform they needed to align their spiritual goals more closely with the temporal vision of viceregal officials. Which, however, would take precedent, the spiritual or the material? The guardian of Ocopa best summed up this quandary in a letter to Manso de Velasco in 1756: "The main object of our [missionaries] coming from the Kingdom of Spain . . . [is] to serve both majesties, the divine in the conversion of the souls of the infidels and the human in the greatest increase of his vassals and domains."[91]

Notes

1. Burkholder, *Biographical Dictionary*, xi.

2. Lynch, *Bourbon Spain*, 187–88.

3. Whether this dissonance within the regalist ranks was planned remains unknown, though such a conscious collusion on this particular issue seems unlikely.

4. Heras, *Libro de Incoporaciones,* 35.

5. Manso de Velasco, License for Friar Joseph de San Antonio to travel to Spain, 8 January 1747, Lima, AGI, Lima 541.

6. San Antonio, Petition to the crown, 11 June 1750, Madrid, JSEI, 142–44.

7. Ibid., 144. The total cost is listed in a royal decree, Buen Retiro, 26 March 1751, AGI, Arribadas, 591.

8. Heras, *Libro de Incoporaciones,* 29–31.

9. Mathías de Velasco, Report regarding Fr. Joseph de San Antonio's petition to crown, 29 June 1751, Madrid, AGI, Lima 541. The reduction to eight lay friars is noted in a royal degree dated 26 October 1751, AGI, Arribadas 538, where the missionaries had been given six but were granted two more for a total of eight.

10. San Antonio, Petition to the crown, 11 June 1750, Madrid, JSEI, 144–46. A list of payments showing Manso de Velasco's refusal to pay missionaries before 1752 is located in AGI, Lima 1607. A royal decree mandating that the viceroy distribute the back pay was finally issued 20 February 1761 at the palace of Bien Retiro (AGI, Lima 1606). The amount the crown should have paid is located in Diego de Chaves, mayor of Lima, Testimony in support of Ocopa, 19 December 1748, Lima, AGI, Lima 541.

11. San Antonio, Petition to the crown, 11 June 1750, Madrid, JSEI, 145–46.

12. This note is left out of the published version of this letter in JSEI, 131–59, but can be found in San Antonio, Petition to the crown, 11 June 1750, Madrid, Lima 541 and 1607.

13. The original letters are found in AGI, Lima 541.

14. Fiscal's report regarding San Antonio's 11 July 1750 petition, 11 September 1750, Madrid, AGI, Lima 541.

15. San Antonio, Petition to the crown, 11 June 1750, Madrid, JSEI, 146–47.

16. Ibid., 147. The plan also called for a reinforcement of the fortress at Sonomoro, which had already fallen to Juan Santos in 1749. It seems word of its capture had not arrived in Madrid.

17. Fiscal's report regarding San Antonio's 11 July 1750 petition, 11 September 1750, Madrid, AGI, Lima 541.

18. Gregory, *Salvation at Stake*, 6–7.

19. Walker, *Shaky Colonialism*, 15.

20. Ibid., 14–18, though the concept is a reoccurring theme throughout the book.

21. Consulta regarding San Antonio's 11 July 1750 petition, 5 November 1750, Madrid, AGI, Lima 1607.

22. Royal decree regarding the missionaries of Ocopa, 11 March 1751, Buen Retiro, AGI, Lima 542.

23. Royal decree regarding the transportation of 60 missionaries to Ocopa, 26 October 1751, San Lorenzo de El Escorial, AGI, Lima 542.

24. San Antonio, Petition to the crown, 2 May 1751, Madrid, AGI, Lima 541.

25. Ibid.; Mathías Velasco, comments on San Antonio's petitions, 28 June 1751, Madrid, AGI, Lima 541.

26. San Antonio, Petition to the crown, 2 May 1751, Madrid, AGI, Lima 541.

27. Fiscal's comments on San Antonio's petition, 29 June 1751, Madrid, AGI, Lima 541.

28. Ibid; see note on the back of the fiscal's comments.

29. San Antonio, Petition to the crown, 2 May 1751, Madrid, AGI, Lima 541; Fiscal's comments on San Antonio's petition, 29 June 1751, Madrid, AGI, Lima 541.

30. Mathías Velasco, Comments on San Antonio's petitions, 28 June 1751, Madrid, AGI, Lima 541.

31. San Antonio, Petition to the crown, 2 May 1751, Madrid, AGI, Lima 541.

32. Fiscal's comments on San Antonio's petition, 29 June 1751, Madrid, AGI, Lima 541.

33. The arrival was recorded in ledger notes for the royal treasure of Jauja, AGN, Caja Real, Jauja, 627, Libro de Cuentas, Contador, 1751–52.

34. Manso de Velasco, Report to the crown, 24 September 1750, Lima, AGI, Lima, 169–79.

35. Royal decree regarding the missionaries of Ocopa, 11 March 1751, Buen Retiro, AGI, Lima 542.

36. Manso de Velasco, "Relacion que hizo de su Gobierno," BNE, mss. 3108, f. 70vr.

37. Manso de Velasco, Letter to Ensenada, 30 March 1748, Lima, AGI, Lima 643.

38. Cuentas de caja de Lima, 1748–53, Contaduría 1771, AGI.

39. Pérez-Mallaína Bueno, *Retrato de una ciudad*, 118–19.

40. Ibid., 151–52.
41. Ibid., 124–26.
42. Ibid., 120–21.
43. Latasa Vassallo, "Negociar en red," 470–73.
44. It is unclear whether these practices were actually illegal, but his remittance back to Spain through his merchant connections was; ibid., 490–92.
45. Ibid., 477–87.
46. Salcedo, Fiscal's report, 4 November 1754, Madrid, AGI, Lima 541; Real Acuerdo, 24 April 1742, Lima, AGI, Lima 808.
47. Real Acuerdo, 24 April 1752, Lima AGI, Lima 808; Tribunal de Cuentas, 22 September 1751, Lima, AGI, Lima 808.
48. Juan de San Antonio, Petition to the crown, 24 April 1752, Lima, AGI, Lima 542.
49. Joseph de San Antonio, Petition to the crown, 23 September 1752, Madrid, AGI, Lima 541.
50. Ferdinand VI, Letter to Manso de Velasco, 7 October 1752, Buen Retiro, AGI, Lima 1607.
51. San Antonio, Petition to the crown, 14 September 1757, Madrid, AGI, Lima 542.
52. Fiscal's report regarding San Antonio's 14 September 1757 petition, 1 October 1757, Madrid, AGI, Lima 542.
53. The 1755 decree is noted in a petition to the crown from San Antonio, 14 September 1757, Madrid, AGI, Lima 542.
54. Previously the missionaries had collected the funds at every city with a royal treasury they passed though on their way to Peru. Royal decree about funding travel for the missionaries of Ocopa, 26 March 1751, Buen Retiro, AGI, Lima 808.
55. San Antonio, Petition to the crown, 9 May 1951, Madrid, AGI, Lima 541.
56. Note at the end of San Antonio's petition to the crown, 9 May 1951, Madrid, AGI, Lima 541; Royal decree, 16 October 1751, AGI, Lima 808.
57. Petition of syndic-general of Ocopa, n.d., AGI, Lima 808; Friar Julian de Arriaga, secretary of the Indies, Letter to the Manso de Velasco, 19 March 1758, Madrid, AGI, Lima 1607.
58. Calixto, Petition to the crown, 27 June 1753, Madrid, AGI, Lima 541.
59. Summary of the Council's decision, 12 July 1753, Madrid, AGI, Lima 988; Mathías Velasco, Petition to the crown, 15 January 1753, Madrid, AGI, Lima 988.
60. Royal decree, 10 July 1753, AGI, Lima 988.
61. This account is based on two reports Manso de Velasco wrote on 15 January 1757, Lima, AGI, Lima 988. Both basically narrate the same events, and one is probably an earlier draft of the other.
62. Ibid; Order of deportation for Friar Calixto, 22 November 1757, Madrid, AGI, Lima 988; Manso de Velasco, Letter to Julian de Arriaga, minister of the Indies, 30 January 1759, Lima, AGI, Lima 988; Manso de Velasco, 1 August 1760, Lima, AGI, Lima 988; Mathías de Velasco, Order, 9 December 1760, Madrid, AGI, Lima 988; Bernales Ballesteros, "Fray Calixto Tupac Inca," 12–13.
63. Friar Antonio Juan de Molina, Franciscan commissary-general of the Indies [replaced Mathías de Velasco], Order, 12 December 1760, Madrid, AGI, Lima 988; Bernales Ballesteros, "Fray Calixto Tupac Inca," 12–13. Mostly likely Calixto died in or around 1765 since his last correspondence complained about his failing health. Unfortunately, the San Francisco de Monte monastery was destroyed in the Spanish civil war.
64. Order of the Real Acuerdo, 13 September 1756, Lima, AGI, Lima 808.
65. Juan de San Antonio, Petition, 11 November 1755, Lima, AGI, Lima 1596; Joseph de San Antonio, Petition, n.d., AGI, Lima 1596; Pedro Gonzáles Agüeros, Petition, 1781, Lima, AAL, Sección San Francisco, XI–19, ff. 1r–2v.

66. Mathías de Velasco, Petition to the crown, 6 September 1759, Madrid, Lima 808, Cuaderno 34.

67. San Antonio, Petition to the crown, 6 September 1759, Madrid, AGI, Lima 808.

68. Manso de Velasco, Letter to General Juan Ignacio, corregidor of Huánuco, 5 June 1755, Lima, AGI, Lima 808; Manso de Velasco, Letter to Friar Juan de Antonio, 5 May 1753, Lima, AGI, Lima 808; Manso de Velasco, Letter to General Juan Ignacio, 3 August 1753, Lima, AGI, Lima 808; Manso de Velasco, Letter to General Juan Ignacio, 20 November 1753, Lima, AGI, Lima 808.

69. Fray Joseph Ampuero, Letter to Manso de Velasco, 4 October 1756, Lima, AGI, Lima 808.

70. Ibid.; Friar Juan de San Antonio, Letter to Manso de Velasco, 10 April 1756, Lima, AGI, Lima 808; Friar Bernardino de Mathías, Report, 15 November 1756, Lima, AGI, Lima 808.

71. Ampuero, Letter to Manso de Velasco, 30 November 1756, Lima, AGI, Lima 808.

72. Ibid.

73. San Antonio, Petition to the crown, 12 February 1757, Madrid, AGI, Lima 808; a note of the Council's decision and action are at the end of the copy of the petition.

74. Fiscal's report on San Antonio's petition, 28 February 1757, Madrid, AGI, Lima 808.

75. Lynch, *Bourbon Spain,* 182–90.

76. Treasurer's report, 24 April 1759, Cuentas de Caja 1758–59, Jauja, AGN, Caja Real 629.

77. The minister-general of the Franciscan order instructed the provincial in Lima to treat Ocopa as a college de propaganda fide, 31 March 1751, Madrid, AGI, Lima 542; Ampuero, Report to the crown, 5 January 1757, Ocopa, AGI, Lima 808.

78. Ampuero, Report to the crown, 5 January 1757, Ocopa, AGI, Lima 808.

79. San Antonio, petition to the crown, 2 May 1751, Madrid, AGI, Lima 541; Mathías Velasco, comments on San Antonio's petitions, 28 June 1751, Madrid, AGI, Lima 541.

80. Fiscal's report on San Antonio's petition, 8 May 1764, Madrid, AGI, Lima 634.

81. Manso de Velasco, "Relación que hizo de su Gobierno," BNE, mss. 3108, f. 52v; Amat, Relación que hizo de su Gobierno, RAH 9-9-3 1704, 85.

82. Mathías de Velasco, Commentary on San Antonio's petition, 28 June 1751, Madrid, AGI, 541. The request was rejected by the Council because the Innocence bulls commanded the Apostolic Institute to preach to both the faithful and "infidels"; see Fiscal's report, 29 June 1751, Madrid, AGI, Lima 541.

83. San Antonio, Petition to the crown, 12 February 1757, Madrid, AGI, Lima 808.

84. Mathías de Velasco, Petition to the crown, 6 September 1759, Madrid, AGI, Lima 808.

85. Fiscal's comments on San Antonio's petition, 20 April 1760, Madrid, AGI, Lima 808; Council's decision, 18 August 1760, Madrid, AGI, Lima 808.

86. Heras, *Libro de Incorporaciones,* 31–42. The missionary with "hypochondria" died a year later.

87. It is unclear whether this is just in Ocopa or throughout all of their mission stations. San Antonio, Report on Ocopa, 7 April 1764, Madrid, AGI, Lima 834.

88. Ibid.

89. Friar Manuel Gil, commissary-general of Peru, Report on the state of the Franciscan missions in Peru, 7 September 1764, Madrid, AGI, Lima 834.

90. San Antonio, Report on Ocopa, 7 April 1764, Madrid, AGI, Lima 834.

91. Joseph Ampuero, Letter to Manso de Velasco, 4 October 1756, Lima, AGI, Lima 808.

Chapter 4
"To Serve Both Majesties," 1759–1784

The ascension of Charles III (1759–88) to the throne represented a significant change in Ocopa's fortunes. With the fall of the "Jesuit party" (Ensenada, Carvajal, and Rávago) and Charles' more pro-Franciscan sentiments, the Franciscan order began to eclipse the Society of Jesus and became predominant among the regular clergy. Although reformists at all levels of the Spanish bureaucracy continued to push for a stronger centralized government, the Ocopa friars were able to avoid the most crippling anticlerical reforms. This was due, in part, to their status as peninsulars, whom reformers believed were more loyal to the crown, but probably also because of the missionaries' new lobbying strategy of making their activities more palatable to the rising political discourses. The missions were able to sell themselves as not just about saving souls but also about contributing to the coordinated attempt by the Bourbon administrators to solidify the crown's presence on the Spanish American frontier and exploit these regions for commercial gain more effectively. This adroit manipulation of Ocopa's image also improved the friars' relations with viceregal authorities, leading to a rapid growth of missionary opportunities and access to funding for Ocopa.

Furthermore, the Ocopa college had matured as an institution. Not only did its leadership change their lobbying strategies, but they seemed more willing to cut their losses. True, they never lost the desire to reenter the Jauja and Tarma frontiers. But they were able to shift their attention to other regions, which promised a rich "spiritual harvest" of indigenous converts. As for the new indigenous nations living within the Ocopa missions, their responses were varied. Those groups with previous exposure to missionaries tended to accommodate the Ocopa friars; those with little or no experience with Europeans, like the montañeses of the Tarma and Jauja entradas, violently resisted the impositions of the rigid mission regime.

Therefore, although the winds of change throughout the empire brought on by Charles's more reformist government invariably shaped Ocopa's fate, it was still dependent on groups on the ground. Within the Spanish bureaucracy, for example, the interpretations of Bourbon reforms depended on a particular minister's geographic perspective just as much as his personal beliefs or political ambitions. Many bureaucrats in Madrid saw the missionaries as a net benefit to the empire as a whole, but some viceroys and reformists in Peru, such as Manso de Velasco, had seen them only as a threat to viceregal power. Fortunately for the missionaries during the period 1761–84, Ocopa benefited from a series of viceroys who, though regalists in many regards, interpreted Ocopa as an asset to the reformist movement as a whole. At least initially, therefore, Ocopa was able to maintain its autonomy while benefiting from the largesse of the state, utilizing this period to expand its missionary activities to the fullest extent possible without sacrificing its independence.

Charles III and the Rebirth of Ocopa

On 27 August 1758, Queen Barbara of Spain died, leaving King Ferdinand VI in a deep, crippling depression. Like his father, Ferdinand suffered from mental instability almost his entire life and consequently never recovered from the grief of his wife's passing. He spent the next year secluded in the Castle Villaviciosa de Odén wandering unshaven, unwashed, refusing to change his clothes. This caused a crisis within the government and for an entire year it was completely paralyzed, unable to make decisions without the king's authorization. Mercifully, Ferdinand joined his wife just a year later on 10 August 1759.[1]

Ferdinand was succeeded by his half-brother Charles, the duke of Parma and king of Sicily. Influenced by the propaganda perpetuated by his ministers, many historians have succumbed to the temptation to characterize King Charles III as Spain's greatest "enlightened monarch," who over his almost three-decade reign guided the Spanish bureaucracy to a more efficient, regalist state. Charles was certainly interested in reform, yet he himself seemed to have little personal interest in Enlightenment philosophies, directing much of his energies toward his greatest passion, hunting, which he did twice daily. Instead, Charles brought something to the institution of the crown that it had lacked for several years: stability. Already experienced as an administrator, Charles was able to focus the energies of talented reform-minded ministers. These ministers attempted to neutralize traditionalist factions in Spain and its empire, emphasizing their "rational," "enlightened" form of governance. More than anything, however, Charles was a royal absolutist, believing in the supremacy of the crown in all state matters. Once he made a decision, he was not easily swayed, even by his own ministers.[2] Charles was, however, also a deeply religious man with a particular fondness for the Franciscan order. He was a member of the Franciscan third order and selected a Franciscan, Friar Joaquín de Eleta, as his confessor. Consequently, while he worked to bring the regular clergy under the power of the state, the Franciscan order enjoyed a privileged position in the eyes of the monarch, who attempted not to destroy it but to coopt and control it.

Two years after coming to the throne in 1761, Charles recalled Manso de Velasco, who by then was seventy-three years old and had served as viceroy for sixteen years. He replaced him with Manuel de Amat y Junyent Planella Aymerich y Santa Pau, the fourth son of a Catalonian aristocrat. Amat, like Manso de Velasco, was a soldier by training and had seen combat in Europe. His previous post had been as governor of Chile, so he was also a seasoned colonial administrator.[3] Amat was not particularly religious, and he was deeply committed to regalist concepts. He called the royal patronage "one of the most precious and resplendent jewels that adorns [the] crown and that every day [we] discover a deeper appreciation [for it]."[4] The beginning of Amat's term of office nevertheless signaled a reprieve for Ocopa from the neglect of the previous administrations. This was possibly for two reasons: Amat, especially at first, lacked the personal animosities that Castelfuerte or Manso de Velasco had harbored against the clergy. Though he would enact reforms with a soldiers' obedience, Amat seemed to, at least publicly, maintain good relations with higher clerical offices, particularly with the archbishop of Lima. Second, in religious matters Amat seems to have submitted himself to Charles's inclination toward the Franciscans and adhered more closely than his predecessor to decrees emanating from Madrid regarding Ocopa.[5]

Shortly after taking office Amat met with Ocopa's leadership. He seemed impressed with their missionary zeal and promised that he would retake the territory lost in the Juan Santos Atahualpa rebellion, so that "not one handful of dirt" would remain in rebel hands. He informed them, however, that Spain's recent entry into war (the Seven Years' War, 1756–63) made it impossible for him to undertake another military expedition at that time. As a consolation to the missionaries, he finally paid 14,986 pesos promised by the royal decree of 1751 for the travel costs of the group of missionaries who came to Ocopa in 1752 that his predecessor had refused to reimburse (see chapter 3).[6]

In this more pro-Franciscan climate the missionaries were finally able to secure a steady source of income from the crown. In 1759, Manso de Velasco, sensing an impending shift in power, had already restored Ocopa's annual stipend of 6,000 pesos. Furthermore, San Antonio's constant petitioning for the restoration of not just the annual stipend but all the money they should have received since they were initially granted the crown funding back in 1718 finally bore fruit. On 2 February 1761, the king issued a decree granting the missionaries an additional 4,000 pesos per year for the unpaid balance, for a total of 10,000 annually.[7] Unlike his predecessors, Amat immediately ordered that the extra money be paid as soon as the decree arrived in Lima in December 1763.[8] By 1773, the College of Ocopa was receiving the largest such stipend in the viceroyalty. This was almost six times greater than the next largest recipient, without even counting the extra 4,000 pesos for back pay-

Table 3. Annual crown contributions to Franciscan institutions

Institution	Annual payment (pesos)
College of Ocopa	6,000*
Monastery of Huánuco	75
Monastery of Huancavelica	264
Monastery of Huamanga	264
Observant Monastery of Cusco	690
Recollect Monastery of Cusco	900
Monastery of Urquillos	207
Recollect Monastery of Urubamba	543
Observant Monastery of Arequipa	168
Recollect Monastery of Arequipa	115.5
Observant Monastery of Arica	164
Monastery of La Paz	133
Monastery of Oruro	178.5
College of Tarija	270
Observant Monastery of Cochabamba	345
Recollect Monastery of Cochabamba	240
Observant Monastery of La Plata	1,005
Recollect Monastery of La Plata	360
Observant Monastery of Potosí	780
Monastery of Mizque	240
Monastery of San Francisco Puqsi	54.5
Total	**12,996.5**

Source: "Plan de las contribuciones anuales, y limosnas que se deven hacer a los conventos de San Francisco en este Reino del Perú," 8 July 1773, Lima, RAH 9-9-3 1680, f. 55rv.

*This number does not reflect the additional 4,000 pesos given to Ocopa every year for the royal treasury's unpaid balance.

ments (table 3). Ocopa's 6,000-peso stipend constituted nearly half of all crown contribution to the Franciscans in the viceroyalty.

Furthermore, payments during Amat's administration proved to be more consistent than ever before. Over nearly his entire administration (1761–76), the funds for Ocopa were paid from the royal treasury at Jauja without fail each 31 December (table 4).

After Amat left office, payments were less consistent, but usually the Franciscans always received some money each year from the crown. These inconsistencies in payments largely reflected a lack of funds in the account from which the money was drawn, *vacantes ecclesiásticas* (an account funded by the salaries of church offices that had no current occupant), rather than the viceroy deliberately withholding funds as Castelfuerte, Villagarcía, and Manso de Velasco had done.[9] The exception was between 1784 and 1786, when money was withheld from Ocopa for the Elizalde expedition (see chapter 5).

TABLE 4. Royal treasury payments to Ocopa, 1762–1786

Year	Amount (pesos)
1762	6,000
1763	no data*
1764	10,000
1765	10,000
1766	10,000
1767	10,000
1768	10,000
1769	10,000
1770	10,000
1771	10,000
1772	10,000
1773	10,000
1774	10,000
1775	10,000
1776	5,109
1777	7,836
1778	7,054
1779	8,270
1780	10,000
1781	6,087
1782	13,913
1783	no data
1784	7,000
1785	2,590
1786	8,847

Source: AGN, Sección Republicano, Ministero de Hacienda, Libros 817, 840, 845, 866 (for years 1762–66); AGN, Sección Colonial, Caja Real, Jauja 629–38 (for years 1767–84); and Pasco 1182,1184 (for years 1785–86).

*The treasury records for 1763 are missing, but it seems likely that the full amount was paid.

By the 1760s, Ocopa also began to have other significant sources of income. After several decades in the Mantaro Valley, local elites in the regions around Ocopa began to donate to the college. Many of these donations came in the form of bequests from the wills of local elites, generally in exchange for prayers for the departed's soul in purgatory. As the college's reputation for spiritual devotion began to spread, these mortmain donations became a significant source of wealth for Ocopa.[10] Notary records from Jauja indicate that the missionaries owned at least one large farm (the *estancia* of Runatullo near Comas), which boasted 188 cows, 2,455 sheep, a large, fully furnished house, a chapel, and several other minor buildings. Notary entries also record other landholdings and livestock throughout the Mantaro Valley, all the result of the "alms" received by the college from private donors. In 1770, for example, the missionaries rented out no less than ten thousand sheep to Colonel Bonifacio de Torres y Esquibel for a period of nine years. Such vast material wealth did not, however, come without strings. Many of these properties had liens on them, which the missionaries were forced to pay before the properties could be sold. The estancia of Runatullo, for example, was 659 pesos in debt, compelling the missionaries to rent out the property.[11]

The bequest of Teresa Apolaya typifies the difficulty of assessing the value of these mortmain donations. Before her death in 1729, Apolaya, wife of Benito Troncoso, one of the local governors who fought Juan Santos, donated the entirety of her dowry of 10,000 pesos to the missionaries of Ocopa for the "construction of the church of the College of Santa Rosa de Ocopa" and for the maintenance of the missions. Husbands in colonial Spanish America managed their wives' dowries, but the money remained the wives', and they were free to donate it to whomever they liked upon their deaths or retain it if their husbands died before them. Payment of Apolaya's bequest, however, did not begin until 1750, twenty-one years after her death. With interest the dowry was then worth 16,542 pesos, for her husband had invested it in livestock as well as loaned it to other people. Because it was tied up in investments, Troncoso was required to pay the bequest in small annual sums.[12]

Despite the missionaries' mendicant vows of poverty, they themselves engaged in many forms of business transactions. Though they would certainly welcome donations as a lump sum of hard currency, guarantees of long-term rental income and loan payments provided a level of financial security the missionaries had lacked in the early years. Therefore, like many monastic institutions in the Hispanic world, they actively engaged in lending money. The notary records for Jauja contain contracts for several loans, some for thousands of pesos. Generally, the interests on these loans were low, about 5 percent annually, typical of ecclesiastic loans. Lending at low interest rates allowed the missionaries to avoid the appearance of engaging in the sin of usury, which was prohibited by Catholic doctrine. Indeed, merchant loans could be as much as 20–30 percent.

The missionaries themselves did not directly handle the day-to-day business of their properties and loans, instead relying on a designated agent (*síndico*), generally a prominent member of the local elite. From all available records it appears these agents were not paid but received preferential treatment when renting property or taking out loans from the missionaries. Both Benito Troncoso and Bonifacio de Torres served as agents for Ocopa.[13] Since the crown specified that its annual stipend went only to funding missionary work in the field, it seems that most of Ocopa's income from private donors went to building the college itself. By the late eighteenth century the college boasted a large church, a library, and a large cloister where the missionaries lived and trained for work in the Montaña (figures 10, 11).

FIGURE 10. College of Santa Rosa de Ocopa, façade, 2011. Though the building in the foreground dates from the early twentieth century, construction on the church and cloisters behind began in the mid-eighteenth century. Photo by author.

While support for Ocopa was growing locally, it also became better represented in Madrid. Previously, the college had to either send a missionary to court at great cost to argue for further crown support or rely on agents in Spain to do so. In 1762, Ocopa established a permanent *apoderado* (representative) at court in Spain. This friar, though resident at court, remained a member of the community and was empowered to petition on Ocopa's behalf. The apoderado generally was a missionary with many years of service in the field who had demonstrated his loyalty to the college. Naturally the first missionary to hold this office was Friar Joseph de San Antonio, who for the previous two decades had advocated for Ocopa as well as supervising the ferrying of missionaries to Peru from Spain. By order of Viceroy Amat in 1763, 500 pesos were set aside from Ocopa's 10,000-peso stipend for the apoderado's maintenance and use in Madrid. The apoderado used these funds for his own food and lodging, as well as to produce printed tracts to recruit new missionaries for Ocopa from the colleges de propaganda fide in Spain.[14]

Thanks to San Antonio's efforts in 1764, after a thirteen-year gap the crown finally granted Ocopa funds for the transport of new missionaries to Peru. Although he had requested seventy missionaries, he was granted forty-

FIGURE 11. Santa Rosa de Ocopa from above, 2015. Though the three cloisters in the back (in the foreground) were added later, the one just to the right of the church, the cloister of the "portero," dates from the mid-eighteenth century. The original hospicio can be seen on the far right of the photo. Photo by author.

eight and initially was able to recruit only thirty-seven. Two years later, when he presented the list that was supposed to contain the names of the remaining eleven friars, it contained twenty-eight names. After an intercession by the Franciscan commissary-general of the Indies, the crown eventually relented and gave him funds and passports for the additional missionaries. In general, the reign of Charles III saw proportionately the largest influx of missionaries to Ocopa from Spain. Of the 302 missionaries to come over during its 115-year history (1709–1824), 128 came during this thirty-seven-year period. Furthermore, more missionaries during this period completed their ten-year term (*decenio*) at Ocopa: 83 percent as opposed to only 38 percent before 1761, and 57 percent after 1788, with an average of 60 percent during the entire 115-year period (table 5). The groups also came in closer intervals, with four groups arriving during the 1761–88 period, an average of more than one group every ten years, thereby assuring a steady source of manpower for Ocopa's missions. Both the increase in numbers of missionaries and percentage of completion are most likely explained by the presence of a permanent apoderado in Spain. San Antonio and his successors, apart from their duties petitioning at court, could take time to visit colleges and monasteries throughout Spain to find more and better candidates for missionary service. In such circumstances, secure in both financial and human resources, the mis-

Table 5. Status of peninsular missionaries who traveled to Ocopa at the end of their service, 1730–1820

Year	**Left for Ocopa**	**Arrived at Ocopa**	**Completed *decenio***	**Died before end of *decenio***	**Left before end of *decenio***	**Percentage of missionaries who completed *decenio***
1730	12	10	4	4	3	33%
1737	30	19	9	1	6	30%
1751	32	28	16	5	11*	50%
1752	55	52	20	9	25*	36%
Total 1730–61	**129**	**109**	**49**	**19**	**45**	**38%**
1767	37	37	32	2	3	86%
1769	28	25	20	2	2	71%
1778	22	22	17	5	0	77%
1784	45	44	41	3	1	91%
Total 1761–88	**132**	**128**	**110**	**12**	**6**	**83%**
1796	9	9	7	1	1	78%
1802–4	43	42	32	5	2	74%
1818	14	14	0	0	14	0%
1820	2	no data	no data	no data	no data	0%
Total 1788–20	**68**	**65**	**39**	**6**	**17**	**57%**
Total 1730–1820	**329**	**302**	**198**	**37**	**68**	**60%**

Source: Lehnertz, "Lands of the Infidels," 399; Heras, *Libro de Incorporaciones,* 19–85; AGI, Arribadas 538, 591.

*Thirty missionaries from these groups were sent to found other colleges de propaganda fide, most to Tarija (Bolivia). When Manso de Velasco blocked the Franciscans from building a college at Tarija, however, the missionaries did not return to Ocopa and incorporated into the local province.

sionaries began the process of rebuilding their missionary program to its former glory before the Juan Santos rebellion.

The missionaries also benefited from the leadership of a new, active guardian. This new prelate shared the same vocational name as Ocopa's founder, Friar Francisco de San Joseph. Born Francisco Antonio Josef de Mora Fernández in 1721 in the Castilian village of Manzanares, La Mancha, "San Joseph II" was most likely part of the local hidalgo class. At age sixteen he took the habit of a Franciscan at a college near Cartagena, and later he was ordained a priest in the diocese of Cuenca. In 1751, San Antonio recruited San Joseph. After arriving in Peru in 1752, he distinguished himself as an able missionary and was part of the first expedition to the Manoa region. His biographer claimed that he was known as *el Apóstol de las Montañas del Perú* (the Apostle of the Peruvian jungle) but admitted that he was "vulgarly" known as *el quatro ojos* (four eyes), probably because he wore spectacles.[15]

After his election to the guardianship in 1767, San Joseph II enacted a series of reforms aimed at controlling missionaries under his charge more effectively as well as improving the college's reputation for diligence and obedience, which had been tarnished during the turbulent 1740s and '50s. He stated that though he found the missionaries to be "very able and zealous . . . there has occurred very grave scandals and disturbances [that have] discredited them and [been] a detriment to the conversions." San Joseph's reforms ostensibly attempted to improve relations between the missionaries and the natives living within the mission stations. He extolled the missionaries to treat the montañeses "with love and pity, and never with opprobrium." They should never "cane or whip" the converts but let local leaders mete out punishments, for this has caused "very grave scandals," perhaps in reference to the whipping of Mateo de Assia, which some viceregal officials cited as the cause of the Santos rebellion (see chapter 2). Other reforms included not borrowing money from the natives or trying to collect debts personally, not changing community rules established by previous missionaries, as well as prohibiting the missionaries from letting women serve them directly. Most important, San Joseph II tried to order an end to unauthorized expeditions. Previously, missionaries periodically had left their stations, guided by their mission's converts, to find other nearby (and sometimes not so nearby) indigenous populations. The practice was indeed part of their mandate to seek out new converts, but it led to the chaotic expansion of the college's missions before 1767. San Joseph, therefore, prohibited missionaries from leaving their assigned stations without permission from the guardian. The practice continued, but expeditions became more centrally organized by the Ocopa leadership.[16]

What effect San Joseph II's reforms had on the Ocopa missionary effort is debatable. Ocopa continued to enjoy an excellent reputation, particularly in Spain, but the expansion of its missions after 1767 cannot be characterized as orderly. With this reform, however, San Joseph established the preeminence of the guardian of Ocopa over not just the communal life of the college but the pastoral affairs of all of its dependent missions. Over the next few decades, San Joseph II was frequently cited as an exemplary missionary and guardian, and his reforms as the ideal for mission life, sometimes by both sides in a disagreement over a particular policy. And as Ocopa saw a renewed expansion starting in the 1760s, such disagreements proliferated.

One of those conflicts came from within the order itself. In 1765 the Franciscan commissary-general for Peru, Friar Bernardo de Peon y Valdes began, as one Ocopa missionary described it, "[to] lead missionaries to blood and fire, recklessly trampling on the powers of the colleges."[17] The position of commissary-general of Peru at times served as mediator between local Franciscan provinces and the commissary-general of the Indies in Spain. Ocopa's position as a college de propaganda fide, however, left it in a nebulous position within the Franciscan hierarchy. The missionaries argued that Ocopa's status meant they were not subject to Peon's leadership, just as they had argued against the provincial minister's interference a generation earlier. They complained that Peon was trying to micromanage Ocopa, overriding the guardian's decisions and controlling which missionaries could leave Ocopa for expeditions into the jungle. The commissary-general of the Indies agreed, and Peon was forced to lessen his involvement.[18]

Peon was, however, successful in forcing the missionaries to allow architect, mathematician, and cartographer Friar José Amich to enter their ranks as an inspector (*visitador*) of the missions. Amich was originally from Barcelona, where it appears he studied mathematics. Before taking vows as a Franciscan in 1750, he had been involved in the initial planning for the rebuilding of the Real Felipe fortress in Callao after the 1746 earthquake.[19] Two separate royal decrees in 1747 and 1761 demanded that the missionaries bring a cartographer with them on any new expedition. The missionaries welcomed the manpower, but they balked at Amich's assignment to inspect the missions—and Peon persisted. Amich even led an expedition out of Pozuzu in 1765. Perhaps because the other missionaries saw him as an interloper, Amich spent only a few years as a member of the college.[20] After returning to Lima in 1769 he drew some of the most detailed maps of the Ocopa missions (e.g., figure 1) and wrote a detailed chronicle of their history. Ironically, because of his chronicles Amich came to be one of the names most closely associated with Ocopa.[21]

The Missionaries Advance

In the wake of the Juan Santos Atahualpa rebellion, the missionaries of Ocopa were left with only two small missions in the Huánuco entrada, Pozuzo and Tillingo. The missionaries had hoped that these could be a staging point for expansion east into the Pampas de Sacramento, but by the 1750s, after several failed attempts, this appeared increasingly unlikely. For example, one expedition in 1757 failed after five Yanesha escorts died at the hands of a group of unseen archers. Ultimately, fears that the Yanesha converts would join the Juan Santos rebels motivated an almost complete abandonment of the two communities. In 1753 the frontier governor of Huánuco moved three hundred inhabitants from Pozuzo and Tillingo farther north to a mission station abandoned in the seventeen century called Cuchero. The governor left only one hundred inhabitants in Pozuzo, those at risk of fleeing the mission (presumably to join Juan Santos). Tillingo was completely abandoned. Unfortunately, the journey took the Montaña-born Yaneshas over the high mountain pass of Tambonuevo, resulting in many deaths. More died once they arrived at Cuchero. The valley was not large enough to support agricultural production sufficient to feed the population, nor could it support growing coca to trade for food. The Yaneshas were forced to work in nearby haciendas to survive. Within a few years "all but a few died," and most of those who survived made their way back to Pozuzo. The missionaries also constructed a new village in the highlands above Pozuzo named Santa Cruz de Muña, which was populated by highland Andean settlers, giving the friars a place they could escape if Pozuzo were ever attacked.[22]

By the 1750s, however, the focus of Ocopa's missionary activity had shifted much farther north (see figure 12). Because the Juan Santos rebels blocked the missionaries from the Tarma and Jauja frontiers, the missionaries had to look elsewhere to expand their evangelization efforts. In 1752 the guardian of Ocopa persuaded Franciscan provincial leaders in Lima to cede to the Ocopa missionaries the high jungle region known as Cajamarquilla. The Cajamarquilla missions lay more than 120 miles (200 km) linear distance from their northernmost entrada of Huánuco. Along the most likely path from Ocopa the journey was more than 500 miles (850 km) and took several weeks. To facilitate working in the far-off region the missionaries established a base of operations in a hospicio in the highland village of Huaylillas in the sierra of Ancash. Friars from the Franciscan Province of the Twelve Apostles based in Lima had previously evangelized Cajamarquilla, and it already boasted at least four mission communities, each with several hundred inhabitants from the Cholón and Hibito nations. The Cajamarquilla missions proved to be the most stable missionary zone Ocopa would administer during the colonial period. From 1753 to 1824, little changed in the native population. The missions had already suffered a wave of epidemics in the 1690s, and the region regularly saw immigration from the highlands. Additionally, the missions had been established for almost seventy years, and the montañeses seem to have already adjusted to mission life.[23]

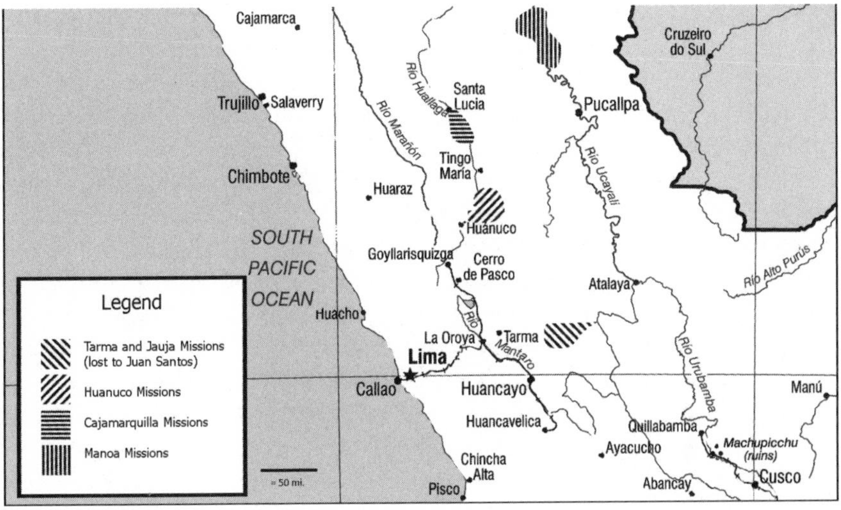

FIGURE 12. Ocopa's missionary zones in Peru. Map courtesy of William G. Silva. Reproduced with artist's permission.

Ultimately Cajamarquilla was just a launching point for expeditions farther into the jungle. Almost as soon as Ocopa took control there, the friars began organizing expeditions deeper into the Amazon basin, utilizing large numbers of Cholónes and Hibitos as guides and porters. The missionaries' goal lay some 150 miles east of Cajamarquilla along the banks of the Ucayali River. The Ucayali is one of the largest rivers in the Amazon basin and at its confluence with the Marañón River forms the great river itself. At 994 miles (1,601 km) in length and at places more than three-quarters of a mile (1,200 m) wide, it was home to one of the largest human populations in the Amazon. The right to evangelize in the region had been hotly contested by the Franciscans and the Jesuits during the seventeenth century as each attempted to send expeditions to the nations along its banks. Neither group, however, was able to maintain a permanent presence.

During the 1750s the Ocopa missionaries had similar luck. Between 1753 and 1760 the missionaries in Cajamarquilla organized four expeditions, three of which ended without encountering any significant population centers. The exception was in 1757, when an unusually large expedition composed of nearly three hundred Cholónes from Cajamarquilla and five friars encountered a village of Setebos along the Manoa River, one of the Ucayali's many tributaries. Unfortunately, someone in the retinue set fire to some of the Setebos' huts, resulting in a violent skirmish. One friar and thirteen natives died, but the expedition was able to take three children captive. The oldest child was baptized, adopting the Christian name Ana Rosa. She became the missionaries' guide and translator for most of the future expeditions into the region.[24]

Capturing children was a common tactic used in Latin America. Indeed, the practice dated back to Columbus and included such famous (or perhaps infamous) names as Doña Marina (La Malinche), Hernán Cortés's translator and later paramour. Several years before Francisco Pizarro confronted Atahualpa at Cajamarca in 1532, he captured several young boys and brought them into the Spanish-speaking world to later serve as translators. Pizarro's choice of youths was intentional. The Europeans believed, probably correctly, that youths would be more susceptible to acculturation, thus making them more loyal. These captives served as what later historians would call go-betweens, individuals who were intermediaries for Europeans in the Americas. Go-betweens were usually translators and often advocated for Europeans, thereby helping to extend foreign hegemony. As Alida Metcalf has argued, however, that despite European attempts at acculturation go-betweens, even youth-captive ones, still occupied a liminal cultural and political space between European and indigenous interests and, though rarely revealed, had their own agendas.[25]

The friars of Ocopa, though more skilled in languages than most frontier missionaries, had in the past relied on translators. It seems, however, that they had not used the youth-capture method, because there is no recorded mention of it. Most likely the intense trading between highlands and the areas where they had previously labored made finding competent translators or even learning the local languages more manageable. The Manoa missions' distance from more hispanicized areas presented a more difficult challenge. Most of the peoples in the region spoke Panoan languages, quite distinct from the mostly Arawak languages the missionaries had encountered previously. Indeed, Ana Rosa is the only such youth-captive go-between that the Ocopa missionaries mentioned by name. Frequent references to Ana Rosa in Ocopa's correspondence certainly reflect her value as a go-between. Her linguistic assistance also may have contributed to the missionaries' rapid acquisition of the "Setteba" tongue. Anecdotal evidence suggests that within a decade the missionaries were speaking it with at least some degree of competency.[26] The friars still struggled with Yanesha (an Arawak language) even fifty years after their first contact.[27]

Ana Rosa's prominence in Ocopa's correspondence was also probably a function of her propaganda value. Her exposure to Catholicism and Hispanic culture was relatively short; she spent only three years with the missionaries (1757–60) before returning to her natal culture, and yet she remained committed to them at least well into the 1790s. The missionaries most likely sought to underscore this loyalty as a way of demonstrating their ability to bring "infidels" to the faith, even a member of the supposed weaker and more carnal gender.[28] Like most go-betweens, however, Ana Rosa's true motivations remain unknown. They certainly went beyond just simple devotion to the missionaries and their cause.

In May 1760, guided by Ana Rosa, the missionaries reentered the Ucayali flood plain. There they encountered a local Setebo cacique, Runcato, who took the missionaries to his village, where they built the first chapel in the region. They renamed the settlement San Francisco de Manoa. Manoa (which became synonymous with the missionary zone in the upper Ucayali) served as a base of operations for missionaries along the great river. Runcato's acceptance of the missionaries may have been strategic.[29] The Setebos were engaged in a prolonged conflict over resources with the neighboring Shipibo nation. Both groups spoke roughly the same Panoan language, which they shared with another group, the Conibos, suggesting that they had been part of the same ethnic group at some point in the past.[30] The Shipibos and Conibos had had periodic interactions with both the Franciscans and the Jesuits during the seventeenth century. Both orders had even established missions within their territories. All, however, were short-lived and ended violently.[31] The missionaries tended to agree that like the Asháninkas and Yaneshas, the Setebos', Shipibos', and Conibos' principal interest in Europeans was to obtain tools for farming. It was possibly with this motivation in mind that Runcato had invited the missionaries into his community despite their disastrous encounter with the Setebos in 1757. Perhaps Runcato hoped that the increased food production could help them in their conflicts against the Shipibos, or that the tools could also be used as weapons of war.[32]

From their base at Manoa, by 1764 the missionaries had begun to evangelize the more populous Shipibos and Conibos. Despite the conflict between these groups, by 1765 the missionaries had built three ethnically diverse mission stations, San Francisco de Manoa, Santo Domingo de Pischquí, and San Miguel de los Conibos—all three reportedly populated by approximately eight hundred individuals. The missionaries had even begun to venture farther up river (south), where they commenced evangelization efforts to the Piro nation (an Arawak-speaking group) as well. In 1765 these expeditions nearly stretched Ocopa's manpower to its breaking point, for many of the friars who had come to the college in 1751–52 had completed their ten-year term of service. So Ocopa asked for and received fifteen new missionaries, eight from the college de propaganda fide at Chillán in Chile as well as seven from the Franciscan province in Lima, including, as noted earlier, Ocopa's future chronicler, José Amich. As the new friars began to arrive, however, the Manoa missions exploded into full rebellion against Ocopa.[33]

The Manoa Rebellion and Rescue Mission

Sometime before October 1766, the cacique Runcato, who had helped the missionaries establish a presence in the Ucayali basin, withdrew with a large group of his supporters from the Manoa mission station to the old location of their village at Yapa-atí. On 8 October, two missionaries along with montañeses from Cajamarquilla left from Manoa to attempt to reestablish relations with Runcato and his band. Though they were initially greeted with gifts of food, as dusk fell Runcato's men attacked them, beating the party to death with clubs, starting with the missionaries and then eventually killing sixteen of their native escort. When word of the outbreak of the rebellion finally reached the highlands in early 1767, San Joseph II along with the commissary of the missions, Friar Manuel Gil, began organizing a relief expedition. The full extent of what had happen had not become clear yet, and it seems that the experienced San Joseph hoped to save the situation, probably through negotiation, since he decided to bring few soldiers. Certainly the thought that most of the missionaries in Manoa were relatively new weighed heavily on Ocopa's leaders. After some discussion the leaders agreed that the fastest, safest route to Manoa was not the direct overland path through Cajamarquilla but down the Ucayali itself from Port Mayro near Cuchero in the Huánuco missions. Amich desperately tried to join the expedition after completing his inspection of Cajamarquilla, but he arrived too late at the Huánuco missions to catch their departure. The missionaries did not seem willing to wait for him. On 10 June 1767, the relief party set out, led by Gil and San Joseph, with one other missionary, two Andalusian sailors, and eleven frontier militiamen.[34]

The expedition started in disaster. After Amerindian allies had spotted "infidels" near Port Mayro, the expedition leaders decided to embark farther upriver in a tributary of the Ucayali. Port Mayro, however, had been selected because it was the closest port below the rapids. The second day into the journey, while trying to navigate "a hidden crag," the largest of their canoes flipped, taking with it most of the expedition's supplies and many of the steel tools they had brought to negotiate for peace. The capsizing of the canoe delayed the trip several days as they attempted to salvage the supplies. Despite the loss of vital foodstuffs, the missionaries were resolved to continue. Before arriving in Conibo territory, the farthest upriver of the nations missionized in the Manoa entrada, they had to pass through Cashibo territory. The Cashibos had a reputation for being hostile to Europeans. When the expedition first encountered them, the Cashibos approached the missionaries armed, in what seemed to the expedition as an aggressive posture. The missionaries asked them what they wanted and they responded that they desired tools. Hoping to placate the Cashibos, the expedition gave them some machetes, but when the group did not disperse the militiamen pitilessly fired a volley into the crowd, killing "four or five men." The expedition proceeded down the river.

Upon arriving in Conibo territory on 6 August, they were met by a man in a small canoe. They asked him about the missionaries who had been stationed there, and he responded that they had left to go help the Piros, who had no food because the flooded river had washed away all of their fields. Like all rivers in the Amazon basin, the Ucayali flooded every year, but generally in a predictable manner. Flooding at the wrong time of year or a higher than expected flood could spell disaster for the people who lived along its banks. San Joseph was nonetheless suspicious and began to speak to the other Conibos they encountered. He found their stories to be "notably inconsistent" and the next day, as more and more Conibos gathered near their camp, the expedition leaders decided to leave immediately. After telling the Conibos that they would wait there for five days (the time it took for a message to reach Piro territory and for the other missionaries to return), they slipped out of their camp under cover of darkness. Careful not to paddle, they traveled only by the pull of the current until they had gotten out of earshot of the Conibos, then stroked "with all determination and strength." The missionaries who were supposedly with the Piros were never heard from again.

Later that day, as they followed the flow of the river, the expedition found their way blocked by "more than thirty" Conibo canoes with more natives on the shore. In response they beached their canoes, believing they could more easily defend themselves on land. San Joseph, however, recognized several in the group as Setebos from Manoa. When the missionaries asked the Setebos what they were doing there, they responded that they had come to visit the Conibos. When asked about the whereabouts of the other missionaries, one of them responded that he did not know anything about them. The response made the missionaries "highly suspicious." San Joseph finally recognized a Setebo cacique among them named Curiqui-barí. The cacique warned the friars that the Conibos with them "are agreed to kill you, because all the other Fathers and white men [*viracochas*] that they had received [into their villages] have died." Curiqui-barí advised that they give them steel tools in the hopes that the Conibos would be placated. The missionaries promptly surrendered their goods, but only after the crowd agreed to put down their arms.

The next morning San Joseph pressed Curiqui-barí for more answers regarding the fate of the other missionaries. Only at this point did the extent of the massacre that had taken place in the Manoa missions become apparent to the expedition leaders. First, San Joseph invited the cacique to join them in the relief of Manoa. Curiqui-barí responded that they could not because they had no food. When the friar pressed the cacique again for help to relieve Manoa, he finally revealed that they could not go to Manoa or any of the other missions because the Shipibos had killed all the missionaries and would kill them too. He promised, however, that he would negotiate safe passage from them back up the river through Conibo territory. San Joseph II then asked about the whereabouts of Ana Rosa, who, as he found out, was only a few miles away.

When Ana Rosa arrived, the missionaries heard the entire tale. After Runcato had killed the two missionaries who had come to parley with him, he convinced the Shipibos, who had traditionally been enemies of the Setebos, to eliminate the remaining missionaries in Manoa and Santo Domingo de Pischquí. Two missionaries escaped to Conibo territory, but after waiting fifteen days they decided to return to Manoa. As they were traveling downriver, the Conibos accompanying them beat them to death in midstream and dumped their bodies into the brown waters of the Ucayali. In all, Setebo, Shipibo, and Conibo warriors killed sixteen missionaries (seven full friars, four lay friars, and five oblates), five Spaniards (including the frontier governor, Antonio Thomati), and as many as twenty-seven Cholónes and Hibitos from Cajamarquilla. When San Joseph asked Ana Rosa why she and the other Setebos had fled Manoa, she revealingly answered that they feared reprisal from the missionaries for the deaths of their brothers. Perhaps the Setebos' fears were based on the events of the 1757 expedition, when the missionaries had arrived with three hundred Cholón warriors and almost burned down one of their villages.

After speaking with Ana Rosa, the expedition decided not to continue to Manoa. The Christian Setebos in the group begged San Joseph to stay, but the missionary made his excuses. He did ask whether they would be safe and, according to the missionaries' own accounts, they assured him that they would. Even if he had wanted to take them, the expedition's lack of supplies made that impossible. Good to his word, Curiqui-barí escorted the expedition through Conibo territory, and the missionaries gave him and his people the rest of the steel tools they were carrying. Once again, as they passed through Cashibo territory they were harried by arrow fire, but they arrived relatively unharmed in the Huánuco missions on 10 September 1767. It would be another two decades before the Ocopa missionaries again entered the Ucayali River valley.[35]

The exact cause of the Manoa rebellion may never be known, but the existing accounts of the rescue mission leave some revealing clues. The missionaries almost unanimously blamed the uprising on "severe ingratitude." Amich, who had just missed being on the rescue party but was certainly present for its return, penned an intensely racist diatribe in which he exclaimed that "even the fiercest animals can be beneficially domesticated, and remain grateful and loyal," suggesting that the Setebos were not only subhuman but more base than wild animals.[36] The missionaries, however, seemed to ignore, perhaps for propagandist reasons, clear evidence of interpersonal and even systemic problems with the Manoa missions, some of which were of their own making.

First, it seems clear that Runcato had initially felt obligated to help the missionaries, whether it was to obtain steel tools to gain advantage over his Shipibo enemy neighbors or because the large expedition of 1757 had shown the missionaries to be powerful allies, or both. Possibly, after a while, Runcato realized that the cost of the alliance outweighed its benefits and therefore attempted to distance himself from the missionaries. Then when two missionaries arrived at the village with sixteen men, he felt obligated to respond with lethal force. Furthermore, fears of reprisal by the missionaries, as expressed even by the devoted Ana Rosa, could have caused other groups to act aggressively. Evidence of these fears seems to be confirmed by the general desire of all of the groups involved to deny knowledge of the events. Also, the story of the deaths of the two friars at the hands of the Conibos, who died as they were trying to return to Manoa to find out what had happened, suggests an intense anxiety over the possibility of revenge.

Second, there seems to have been systemic agricultural failures resulting in famine. In the rescue expedition's account of their journey down the Ucayali, there are continual references to an utter and complete lack of food. The Conibos themselves suggested the mechanism: the unseasonal or unexpectedly high flooding the Ucayali river system. Jungle agriculture was already a poor, precarious enterprise; such a shock to production would have had an immediate and detrimental impact on the population, especially those concentrated in mission stations. Although the famine may not have been the catalyst for the rebellion, the net effect of this climatological disaster certainly intensified it.

Ironically, though more missionaries died in the Manoa rebellion than in the Juan Santos Atahualpa rebellion (sixteen as compared to only seven), the Ocopa missionaries made less of a public outcry than they had in the 1750s. There are several possible explanations. Ocopa had been in the region only a short time and such setbacks had been common in the early expansion of their other entradas. They also now had other missions on which to focus their energies, unlike after the Santos rebellion, when twenty-one of twenty-three missions were destroyed. So they simply redirected their efforts elsewhere. Furthermore, they may have felt that they had a less compelling argument to make to the government. The Ucayali flood plain had less strategic importance to the crown. It was quite distant from colonial strongholds in the highlands, and none of the combatants were highland Andeans, so making the case to the crown for a military intervention would have been more difficult. Finally, the missionaries could not complain to the crown that they had not received the aid they had been promised. By the late 1760s, funds were flooding into the college. Therefore, now that missionaries could not lay guilt on viceregal government, they had to be careful that the burden of blame would not be placed on themselves. With the loss of Manoa, Ocopa had to find new fields of labor from which to "harvest souls for conversion," if only to justify the massive expenditures the crown had invested in their institution. Fortunately for the missionaries, events in Madrid and elsewhere were helping them realize their mandate.

The Fall of the Jesuits

In January 1767 the crown sent sealed orders to all magistrates in the Spanish empire with instructions that they be opened at midnight on 2 April. When colonial officials unsealed the documents, they discovered orders to immediately round up and expel all Jesuits from Spanish territories. Just a decade earlier the Society of Jesus had been the most powerful and favored regular clerics in the Spanish empire. Ferdinand VI's partiality for the Society combined with the advocacy of the "Jesuit party" meant that the Society had enjoyed a privileged position at court and in the empire. Furthermore, the Society was not opposed outright to reform. Through the Jesuit party, the Society had spearheaded policies throughout the empire that limited the power of the regular clergy, though many of these policies, such as the secularization of indigenous parishes, negatively affected other regular institutions more than the Jesuits.

After the death of Carvajal and the fall of Ensenada, however, the Jesuit star began to dim. With the ascent of Charles III this decline became more rapid. Charles loathed the Jesuits, whose special devotion to the papacy clashed with his own royal absolutism. The king was not alone in his hatred of the Society. Jesuit power in almost every corner of the Spanish empire had spawned local jealousies and conflicts. The king's distaste for the Society allowed these attacks to grow. When riots broke out in Madrid on 23 March 1766, official inquiries almost immediately blamed the Jesuits. They were scapegoats for unpopular reformist policies such as new antivagrancy laws and high bread prices, which were the true catalysts of the uprising. The crown had to preserve its reputation, and implicating the Jesuits was a convenient solution. Not only could the crown save face, but it could rid itself of an institution which, by that point, it feared and mistrusted. The Jesuits had to go.[37]

Although the crown hoped the expulsion would be a warning to the regular clergy not to flout royal authority, the distribution of Jesuit wealth afterward greatly benefited the regular orders. The Franciscans were one of the largest recipients of Jesuit holdings. Almost immediately, Ocopa received two new missionary zones previously under Jesuit care. Only four months after the expulsion of the Jesuits, at the insistence of the bishop of Trujillo the viceroy ceded Ocopa their missions of Lamas, which lay in the high jungle 135 miles (216 km) north of Cajamarquilla. Lamas was located in a liminal area at the edge of Spanish colonial hegemony, and its proximity to more

FIGURE 13. Map indicating distance between the Archipelago of Chiloé, Chillán, Lima, and Ocopa. Map by author.

established cities meant that, although the region had a native population, it also contained large numbers of Spanish and mestizo migrants from the highlands. The native inhabitants of the region lived in three communities around Lamas, and the migrants dominated the city proper.

Within a few days of the missionaries' arrival, however, the local vecinos, probably all immigrants, asked the Ocopa friars to leave, stating that the region was no longer a missionary zone but a parish that required a secular priest, not missionaries. Amich strongly insinuated that the reason for the request was so that the local citizens could continue in their "vice," against which the missionaries had begun to preach. He implicated the local governor in particular, who he claimed openly cohabitated with a woman that was not his wife. A few months later the local citizens repeated their request, this time it seems more forcefully. According to Amich, the Spanish and mestizo immigrants feared being reduced into the strict mission life and becoming "subjects [of the missionaries] like converted Indians." Perhaps with the memory of the massacre in Manoa fresh in their minds, Ocopa acceded to their request and the town was handed over to the secular clergy.[38]

The other territory ceded to Ocopa after the expulsion of the Jesuits was the Chiloé Archipelago, dominated by the Isle of Gran Chiloé, located in southern Chile nearly 2,100 miles (3,300 km) from Lima (figure 13). Though the assignment of Ocopa to this region seems illogical, since Chile boasted numerous regular institutions much closer to the island, including a Franciscan college de propaganda fide in Chillán only 420 miles (670 km) away, the pairing was consistent with shipping patterns in eighteenth-century South America. Most ships leaving ports in Chile went north to the viceregal capital; only vessels en route to Europe via Cape Horn passed by the islands, and most of these ships originated from Lima's port, Callao. Indeed, the College of Chillán had attempted to establish a missionary presence on the islands even before the expulsion but found it difficult to find transport in Chile and had been forced to travel to Lima to find passage. Therefore, shortly after the Jesuits left in 1770, the crown decided to turn the island over to Ocopa.

Despite the relative ease of finding transport, the great distance between Ocopa and Chiloé was a burden on the college.[39] Manning and supplying religious activities on the islands was expensive, difficult to coordinate, and generally took years to execute. Chiloé was also a different experience for the missionaries. Most of its pueblos were not burgeoning mission stations but essentially full-fledged parishes, inhabited mostly by creoles and mestizos. Over the decades the college would send expeditions to the native Chono and Huiliche nations, but they met with little success. Compared to their entradas in the jungles of Peru, which had small, unstable populations, Chiloé was a much larger affair. In a census reported in 1788, Chiloé had eighty-one pueblos with a combined population of 23,216 spread mainly over Gran Chiloé itself but also over twenty-four others islands in the archipelago. To tend to such a vast population, the crown stipulated that the college send fifteen ordained friars. Ocopa was obligated to pay for the maintenance of these friars out of its own coffers until 1784, when the crown granted Ocopa the same stipend that the Jesuits had received, 250 pesos per full friar, totaling 3,750 pesos, per year. There was ambiguity, however, regarding whether the treasury in Lima or Chile would pay the missionaries' stipend, and it is unclear when or how much the missionaries were compensated for their services in Chiloé.[40] Though the Chiloé enterprise provided great prestige for the college, anecdotal evidence suggests that missionaries found service on the cold southern islands even less desirable than in the sweltering Peruvian jungles. There was even one suggestion that service in Chiloé was a punishment for unruly missionaries.[41] Perhaps some missionaries saw the routine labors of a parish priest as less romantic than forging out into the jungle to find new nations of "infidels" to convert.

The largesse of the crown in doling out former Jesuit possessions to Ocopa did have limits. Less than a year after the expulsion, Friar Manuel Gil Muñoz, commissary of missions in Peru, on Ocopa's behalf petitioned the crown to move the community of Ocopa, with its title of college de propaganda fide, to the former Jesuit college in Lima. Gil argued that the cold climate of the sierras was bad for the novice, old, and sick missionaries' health. Lima, he reasoned, would also be more convenient for newcomers because after their long journey from Spain they would not have to climb immediately into the Andes. They would be more comfortable and willing to receive instruction. He also suggested that perhaps they keep Ocopa as a way station to their missions in Huánuco, subject to the guardian who would be stationed in Lima. If the Jesuit college was unavailable, he added, perhaps they could just build a new college in Lima with the "numerous alms" they were receiving from private donors. The commissary-general of the order in Spain, Friar Manuel de la Vega, who ultimately presented the petition before the crown, also added that the missionaries could, as part of their training, preach to the vice-ridden people of Lima.[42]

As was standard practice, the Council of the Indies asked for the opinions of the religious and government officials in Lima regarding the move. The archbishop of Lima, Diego de Parada, disagreed. He rejected Gil's argument that Ocopa was a cold, unhealthy region, arguing that the locale had "good air" and the Mantaro Valley provided ample foodstuffs for their needs. Other communities, he pointed out, lived in similar climes without complaint. He added that Ocopa also was receiving financial support from local elites in the Mantaro Valley and that such a move would put these sources of revenue into jeopardy. Parada was most concerned, though, about having yet another regular community in Lima. The Franciscans already had three religious houses, and he feared that the alms a fourth institution required would bankrupt the faithful.[43] Viceroy Amat echoed the archbishop's opinion about having a fourth Franciscan institution in Lima and pointed out that the king was trying to limit the number of regular houses in the city, not increase them. He scathingly added:

> I am amazed that in a time when the Jesuits have been removed from their missions or conversions of infidels, these friars [*religiosos*], who aspire to take their place and cultivate those fields for the Church, try to retreat from the frontiers and take shelter and rest in this capital, from where many who inhabit it should leave to initiate that sacred conquest—especially when the Institute of Apostolic Missionaries profess that they are principally for frontier missions [*misiones vivas*].

Amat further complained that the crown did not pay Ocopa 10,000 pesos a year to be in Lima, but for the propagation of the faith in the far reaches of the empire. Instead of focusing their energies on building a new college, the Ocopa missionaries should use their vast wealth to reclaim the territory lost to Juan Santos.[44] Amat's and Parada's negative views of the missionaries' proposed move to Lima had the predictable consequence of the crown denying the missionaries request, on 6 July 1773.[45]

In 1774 the missionaries tried again to move to Lima, with the same consequences. Again the archbishop disagreed with the move, which almost guaranteed that the request would be denied by the Council.[46] Between March and May 1774, however, the missionaries apparently reformulated their plan. In this new plan, instead of taking over the Jesuit college or building a new facility, they would move into the Guadalupe seminary that the Franciscan province maintained in the outskirts of the city. The current faculty and students at Guadalupe would then move to the order's large monastery, Francisco de Jesús, in the city center. With this new adjustment to the plan, Viceroy Amat reversed his opinion and threw his support behind the missionaries. He admitted that the city had a "superfluity of regular houses," but since the missionaries would be constructing no new buildings they would not be in breach of crown policy. Guadalupe, he contended, was supposed to be a seminary but was essentially a siphon for the city's alms, and the students would be better supervised in the large monastery. Amat's only stipulation was to restrict missionaries from collecting alms in the city, saying that they should be forced to support themselves on the crown's stipend.[47]

Ultimately the community decided not to move to Lima. When the new proposal to move from Ocopa to Guadalupe arrived in Madrid in March 1776, Commissary-general Vega expressed reservations about the transfer, even though he had supported the initial plan, which did not involve taking Guadalupe away from the province. Though he did not mention Vega specifically, one of the Ocopa missionaries insinuated that the reversal of the order's position was due to the influence of provincial leaders in Lima, who did not want to lose control of Guadalupe. But Vega argued that a college de propaganda fide in the viceregal capital would inevitably lose its independence. These colleges by design were chartered to be free of regional influence, he reasoned, so as to maximize their ability to carry out missions to the borderlands. He feared that if the community was so close to viceregal authorities and Franciscan provincial leaders, it would struggle to maintain its autonomy. He cited similar problems with colleges de propaganda fide in Cali and Popayán.[48]

Ocopa versus the "New Method"

Church reform under Charles III did not end with the expulsion of the Jesuits, and increasingly the crown turned its attention toward securing its American frontiers. Particularly with the rise of the British as the dominant Atlantic power after the Seven Years' War, the Spanish crown looked to strengthen its borders against the incursions of competing imperial interests.

The slow progress of missionary work frustrated colonial officials, who had poured tens of thousands of pesos into frontier missionary enterprises such as Ocopa. At the heart of their criticism was the method the missionaries used to convert the frontier native populations. Reformers heavily criticized the missionaries' creation of separate communal societies that were dependent on the missionaries culturally, politically, and economically. This dependency was certainly at odds with the emerging tenets of liberal philosophy such as personal liberty, private property, and rewards for individual labor. From these debates regarding the frontier during the early eighteenth century, colonial administrators and political theorists alike developed "the new method of spiritual government," which sought to incorporate frontier indigenous populations more fully into colonial society.[49] The key aspect of this method was hispanicization through trade. As indigenous groups interacted economically with colonial populations, proponents argued, they would begin to adopt Hispanic cultural values including Christianity. The appeal of this system to the crown was obvious, because it would no longer have to invest in frontier missions while reaping the taxes the new commerce would produce.[50]

The crown first tested the "new method" in the Mexican frontier of Nueva Santander in 1749. The viceroy of Mexico selected José de Escandón, a soldier and successful businessman, to lead the expedition. Between 1749 and 1753, Escandón oversaw the settlement of six thousand colonists in twenty towns. Although he allowed Franciscans to accompany the settlers, he stripped them of any jurisdiction over the indigenous population and forced the friars to build their missions next to the new Spanish towns rather than in isolated locations as they had traditionally operated. The friars also served as parish priests to the towns in addition to their duties to convert the native populations. Escandón also obligated colonists and friars alike to pay the natives wages and prohibited natives from living on Franciscan lands. From the state's perspective, the plan was an astounding success; the more sedentary indigenous nations submitted to the new regime, and other groups fled. Though the native population was significantly reduced, from 13,000 in 1749 to around 2,000 in 1821, the area had been effectively hispanicized.[51]

In other more remote areas of the northern Mexican hinterland, particularly where there were already established missions, reformers struggled to enact the "new method." Apart from having to contend with the political and economic power of the missionaries already in the region, the biggest barrier to using the "new method" was simply a lack of settlers. Nuevo Santander had been adjacent to large hispanicized population centers that had been more or less eager to expand. Therefore, when the new inspector general of Mexico, José Bernardo de Gálvez y Gallardo, attempted to revitalize the missions in northern Mexico, out of practicality he abandoned many of the methods used in Nuevo Santander.

Probably the starkest example of the failure of the "new method" in Mexico was in Alta California. The California missions had been Gálvez's brainchild as a way of solidifying Spain's claim to the region, particularly against the Russians, who were moving south from Alaska. Gálvez quickly realized that a military-led expedition to Alta California was impossible, for he did not have enough soldiers in the region. In 1769, he turned the venture almost completely over to the college de propaganda fide of San Fernando in Mexico City. The result was that by 1800, although there were only four small municipalities in California, there were eighteen missions with a population of 18,000 natives. Gálvez's successors had no successes in wresting power in California from the Franciscans either. In 1772, when Gálvez's successor tried to limit Franciscan control to only pastoral matters, "only to say mass and preach," the friars threatened to simply abandon their missions, causing the government to retract the order. When Gálvez left Mexico to become minister of the Indies in 1776, he organized the northern regions of the viceroyalty of Mexico into the *comandancia general* of the Interior Provinces of New Spain. Gálvez urged the creation of this semiautonomous entity, in part, as a continued attempt to gain control of Mexico's northern frontier from the regular clergy. Its first commander, Teodoro Francisco de Croix Heuchin, once again ordered that the "new method" be implemented in Alta California near Santa Barbara, but the missionaries again successfully refused to comply.[52]

The Ocopa missionaries also took part in one "new method" expedition, in the Vitoc valley during the 1780s. Before the Juan Santos Atahualpa rebellion, Vitoc had been the site of intense coca cultivation, but it was abandoned when rebels raided several of the plantations. Though just south of Quimirí, the valley had never been under Ocopa's control, and crown officials made it clear that the expedition was not an attempt to reoccupy the lost Ocopa missions. As in Nueva Santander, the expedition relied on colonists to build commercial enterprises, in this case coca plantations, aimed at integrating the local montañeses into Hispanic society. The crown also built three forts to assure pacification and hoped that these could be launching points for a reoccupation of the Chanchamayo River valley. One Ocopa missionary accompanied the eighty colonists, but it seems that the expedition facilitated few conversions. The Vitoc valley had not been inhabited by any significant native population. In fact, its inhabitants before Juan Santos had been mostly settlers from the highland. The move was thus more a reoccupation of a buffer zone lost during the rebellion than a test of the "new method."[53]

Indeed, at almost the same time as the Ocopa missionaries were involved in the repopulation of Vitoc, they were also using the "old method" farther south in the high jungle near Huanta (in the modern-day Peruvian department of Ayacucho) to evangelize the Simarivas nation. In 1781, two Ocopa missionaries entered the region, baptized ninety individuals, and founded a mission along the Apurimac River.[54] A royal decree dated 25 June 1783 even seems to have granted Ocopa extra funding for the Huanta missions, but viceregal officials ignored the request.[55] According to the missionaries, the Huanta missions eventually floundered because of a lack of state funding.[56]

The "new method" was a manifestation of the reformist ideas that permeated discourses on government in the Spanish Atlantic during the late eighteenth century. Though the method, as executed by José de Escandón in Mexico, was not viable in the distant outposts of most of Spain's vast border regions, the ideas behind it—such as the emphasis on commerce rather than evangelization, the use of colonists as a mode of hispanicizing frontier populations, and the overall ceding of administrative control over these regions from regular orders to the government and military—lived on. Government officials were eager to implement them, as the situation and the willingness of the regular clergy to submit to these changes permitted. Furthermore, as the Bourbon reforms began to intensify, even the regular clergy, whether out of true belief in the new philosophy or because of political expediency, began to adopt them as well. Predictably these ideas created divisions within religious communities, as some members tried to ride the wave of reform while others resisted it. Ocopa was no exception.

Notes

1. Lynch, *Bourbon Spain,* 194–95.
2. Ibid., 247–68.
3. Rodriquez Casado and Perez Embid, "Estudio Preliminar," in Amat y Junient, *Memoria de gobierno*, xxiii–xxxvi.
4. Amat y Junient, *Memoria de gobierno*, 21.
5. Quiñones Tinoco, "Los funcionarios de Dios," 169–71.
6. Amat, Report to the crown, 16 August 1763, Lima, AGI, Lima 1607.
7. Royal decree, 20 February 1762, Madrid, AGI, Lima 1606.
8. Amat's acceptance of the decree was noted in the treasury's ledger notes, AGN, Sección Republicana, Ministerio de Hacienda, Libro 840.
9. On the failure to make a full payment from 1776–79 because of a lack funds in *vacantes ecclesiásticas*, see AGN, Sección Colonial, Caja Real, Jauja, 632–35.
10. Records of some these donations are in ARJ, Protocolos Notariales, Tomo 18, f. 327rv; Tomo 19, ff. 8rv, 57v–58v; Tomo 20, ff. 626r–627v; Tomo 21, ff. 636r–641r; and Tomo 25, ff. 167rv, 671r.
11. Regarding the estancia of Runatullo, see Torres [agent for Ocopa], Rental agreement to Francisco Lazo, 31 January 1750, Concepción, ARJ, Protocolos Notariales, Tomo 21, ff. 537r–540r (scribe, Juan de Mesa Valera). Other properties, see Torres, Sale of fields in Ayllo Yavios, Atique, Maraguata to Joseph Gabriel Astocuri, 4 March 1756, Huancayo, ARJ, Protocolos Notariales, Tomo 25, ff. 700r–704r (scribe, Manuel de Marticorena Gutierrez); Renting 10,000 sheep to Torres, 4 April1770, Jauja, ARJ, Protocolos Notariales, Tomo 25, 249v–253r (scribe, Manuel de Marticorena Gutierrez).

12. Troncoso acting on behalf of Teresa Apolaya, donation of 10,000 pesos, 7 August 1741, Huancayo, ARJ, Protocolos Notariales, Tomo 19, f. 8rv (scribe, Juan de Mesa Valera); and 8 June 1750, Ocopa, ARJ, Protocolos Notariales, Tomo 21, ff. 639–641 (scribe, Juan de Mesa Valera).

13. Such loan agreements are found in ARJ, Protocolos Notariales, Tomo 23, ff. 13v–14v; Tomo 24, ff. 131v–133r; and Tomo 25, ff. 231r, 311r–312v, 442rv. Preferential treatment for agents noted in a loan to Torres for 3,880 pesos, 6 reales, ARJ, Protocolos Notariales, Tomo 25, f. 231r (scribe, Manuel de Marticorena Gutierrez).

14. Friar Francisco Álvarez de Villanueva, Petition to the crown, Madrid, n.d., AGI, Lima 1607; Amat, Report to the crown, 1 July 1763, Lima, AGI, Lima 1607; Lehnertz, "Lands of the Infidels," 315.

15. Friar Martin de Martin, "Vida Exemplar del Siervo del señor y venerable Padre Francisco de San Joseph, llamado vulgarmente el quatro ojos, Predicador Apostólico Guardián y Vice Comissario de la conversión del Colegio de Santa Rosa de Ocopa en el Reyno del Peru," AL-MRREE, LEB-12-14, Caja 94. Martin never completed the manuscript, which literally ends mid-sentence.

16. Instructions from Friar Francisco de San Joseph to all the missionaries of Ocopa, 3 December 1768, AL-MRREE, LEB-12-4, Caja 94, ff. 110r–111r; Chapter proceeding 1767, AO, Libro de Elecciones, ff. 11r–20v.

17. Friar Manuel Gil Múñoz, Letter to the commissary-general of the Indies, 2 April 1765, Ocopa, AGI, Lima 834.

18. Friar Placido de Pinedo, commissary-general of the Indies, Report to the crown, 8 March 1767, Madrid, AGI, Lima 834.

19. Heras's introduction, Amich, *Historia de las misiones,* 14–16.

20. Royal decree, 14 June 1773, Madrid, AGI, Lima 1612; Friar Josef de Garmendia, commissary-general of Peru, Report to the crown, 4 March 1774, Lima, AGI, Lima 1612; Juan Maria de Gálvez, the intendant of Tarma, Report to viceroy, 18 April 1786, Tarma, AGI, Lima 763; Gálvez, Report to viceroy, 10 May 1788, Tarma, AGI, Lima 687.

21. Heras's introduction, Amich, *Historia de las misiones,* 14–16; Heras, *Libro de Incorporaciones,* 44.

22. Amich, *Historia de las misiones,* 187–88; Lehnertz, "Lands of the Infidels," 173–98.

23. Lehnertz, "Lands of the Infidels," 221–33, 394.

24. Ibid., 246–48; Amich, *Historia de las misiones,* 192–200; Friar Juan Perez de Santa Rosa, Letter to Friar Juan de San Antonio, 28 September 1756, San Buenaventura de Pizano, Cajamarquilla, AGI, Lima 808.

25. Metcalf, *Go-Betweens,* 1–16; see also Greenblatt, *Marvelous Possessions,* on which Metcalf draws in theorizing about the go-betweens.

26. San Joseph II shows his command of the language in Amich, *Historia de las misiones,* 220–27.

27. The missionaries' evolving understanding of Yanesha is discussed in Pozuzu's confession manual, AL-MRREE, LEB-12-4, Caja 94, ff. 33v–55r.

28. Fr. Narciso Girbal, Diario desde los pueblos de La Laguna con los gentiles Paños, Setebos o Manoas, y Conibos, 1791, La Laguna, AGI, Lima 703, ff. 28–65.

29. Izaguirre, *Historia de las misiones franciscanas,* vol. 2, 209.

30. In fact, demographic collapse in the nineteenth and twentieth centuries forced the Shipibos and Conibos to merge into one distinct ethnic group. The Setebos no longer seem to exist as a separate ethnic identity and may have been subsumed into the Shipibo-Conibo nation.

31. Lehnertz, "Lands of the Infidels," 246–48.

32. Indications of the importance of these tools can be seen in Amich, *Historia de las misiones,* 200–227.

33. Lehnertz, "Lands of the Infidels," 248–49; Amich, *Historia de las misiones,* 200–219.

34. Amich, *Historia de las misiones,* 220–21; Friar Gil Muñoz, commissary of missions, Report to the crown, n.d., Lima, AGI, Lima 882. The following expedition narrative is drawn from Amich, *Historia de las misiones,* 221–26.

35. As well as Amich, see Lehnertz, "Lands of the Infidels," 249; and Friar Gil Muñoz, commissary of missions, Report to the crown, n.d., Lima, AGI, Lima 882.

36. Amich, *Historia de las misiones,* 215.

37. Lynch, *Bourbon Spain,* 261–69, 280–86; Kuethe and Andrien, *Spanish Atlantic World,* 260–70.

38. Amich, *Historia de las misiones,* 231–33; Francisco Javier, bishop of Trujillo, Letter to Viceroy Amat with fiscal's comments, 15 July 1768 and 22 August 1768, Trujillo, AGN, Superior Gobierno, GO-BI4, Leg 123, Cua. 92.

39. Amich, *Historia de las misiones,* 234–38. Amich's chronicle abruptly stops in 1770 and was finished by two nineteenth-century Ocopa missionaries, friars Fernando Pallarés and Vicente Calvo.

40. Francisco Machado, Report about the Ocopa, 23 December 1777, Madrid, AGI, Lima 1606; Friar Pedro González Agueros, Report on the state of the Ocopa missions, 25 February 1787, Madrid, AGI, Lima 1607; Lorenzo de Osoz, accountant-general of Lima, Report, n.d. [but after June 1784], Lima, AGI, Lima 1606.

41. Friar Christobal Gomez, Letter to the Bishop of Trujillo, 5 December 1788, Hualillas, AL-MRREE, LEB-11-39, ff. 21r–22r.

42. Friar Manuel Gil Muñoz, Petition, 4 March 1768, Lima, AGI, Lima 882; Friar Manuel de la Vega, commissary-general of the Indies, Petition, 17 February 1769, Madrid, AGI, Lima 882.

43. Diego de Parada, archbishop of Lima, Report to the crown, 15 October 1770, Lima, AGI, Lima 882.

44. Amat, Report to the crown, 13 May 1770, Lima, AGI, Lima 882 (punctuation added for clarity).

45. Royal order, 6 July 1773, Madrid, AGI, Lima 882.

46. Parada, Report to the crown, 7 March 1774, Lima, AGI, Lima 882.

47. Amat, Report to the crown, 12 May 1776, Lima, AGI, Lima 882.

48. Vega, Petition to the crown, 4 March 1776, Madrid, AGI, Lima 882; Friar Francisco Álvarez de Villanueva, Petition to the crown, 28 March 1781, Madrid, AGI, Lima 808.

49. This idea seems to have emerged from a series of reforms in Mexico and Spain; see Weber, *Bárbaros,* 309n95.

50. Ibid., 102–4.

51. Ibid., 105–7.

52. Ibid., 122–23.

53. Gálvez, Report to the crown, 7 March 1786, Tarma, AGI, Lima 685, no. 4, ff. 260r–263v; Diary of the expedition to Vitoc, 1765, AGI, Lima 685, no. 4, ff. 223r–226v; Teodoro de Croix, Viceroy of Peru, Report to the crown, 31 March 1789, Lima, AGI, Lima 685, no. 4, ff. 216–22.

54. Juan González de la Reguera, archbishop of Lima, Report on the missions of Huanta, draft, 1787, Lima, AAL, Sección San Francisco, IX-27, 1787.

55. Pedro de Gallarrenta, accountant-general, Report of the missions of Huanta, 14 September 1787, Lima, AGI, Lima 1606.

56. A *diario* of an expedition to the region in 1782 is found in AGI, Lima 808 (dated 18 June 1782). On the missions floundering, see Deliberations of the Council of the Indies (*Consulta*), 13 February 1788, Madrid, AGI, Lima 1607.

Chapter 5
The Bullet and the Bayonet

For almost three decades since ascension of the more regalist monarch, Charles III, Ocopa's fortunes avoided the trend of most regular religious institutions, but it could not last. Ocopa could not receive such massive amounts of state funding without giving up at least some of its coveted autonomy. Although some crown interventions in frontier missions in northern Mexico and elsewhere had floundered, Bourbon administrators' desire for reform in the borderlands not only remained but intensified. They worried about external threats such as the British, who were quickly proving themselves the preeminent power in the Atlantic. In the Peruvian Amazon, crown ministers strove to remain vigilant toward Britain's closest ally, the Portuguese, who were beginning to push farther and farther up the Amazon River. Given Ocopa's power in Peru and influence at court, however, the possibility of local officials gaining control over the college's vast enterprise still seemed unlikely. Change had to come from within Ocopa itself.

What Ocopa's leadership could not stop was the philosophical changes in the empire, and ultimately within its own ranks. As an institution, the college had repelled attempts by the viceregal government to curtail its autonomy during and in the aftermath of the Juan Santos Atahualpa rebellion. In the 1780s, however, new missionaries, later called the Aragonese faction, saw opportunity in giving up some of this autonomy. Over the previous two decades, though Ocopa had maintained its primary focus on evangelization in the missions, it had also, at least rhetorically, justified the crown's large expenditures on its missionary enterprise by arguing that the work indeed advanced reformist causes. That work was carried out mostly by supposedly more loyal peninsular Spaniards who were helping to secure Spain's vast frontiers. The Aragonese faction, however, sought to further this justification in order to garner more support from Madrid and, perhaps more important, at the viceregal level, not just rhetorically but in practice. Going with the changing times, they began to emphasize the "new method" of evangelization through commerce while allowing crown officials more direct control over their frontier missionary enterprise. It is unclear whether this was out of a sincere belief that such changes were indeed beneficial to their primary goal of evangelization or simply a recognition of and submission to the realities of increased crown control. Such changes were, however, certainly indicative of larger trends within the viceroyalty as the Bourbon reforms reached their climax in Peru during the 1780s. Whatever was behind their motivations, their goals and close relationship with viceregal officials inevitably led them to conflict with their more conservative brothers in the college.

Divisions in Ocopa

The fissures among some of the Ocopa missionaries began to show during the late 1770s as the college considered its next expeditions into the jungle and, ultimately, the direction of its missionary efforts. The members of the college divided over two plans. One was the Chanchamayo plan. The plan originated with the apoderado Friar Joseph de San Antonio in the 1750s, and successive generations of Ocopa missionaries argued for its implementation, modifying it only slightly over the years. The plan required the crown to build a fortress on the Chanchamayo River as a launching point for expeditions into the old Tarma entrada. Ultimately the goal was to retake control of the salt deposits at the Cerro de la Sal. The hope was that if the missionaries controlled this vital resource, local Amerindian nations would not dare attack the new missions for fear of losing access to the salt. The plan's supporters also argued that the Chanchamayo plan fulfilled the royal decree of 13 March 1751, which called for the recapture of the territory lost to Juan Santos Atahualpa. The plan incorporated, rhetorically at least, some aspects of the "new method." The missionaries hoped to attract colonists to the area with offers of reduced taxes and free land and argued that these new settlements could bring in up to 150,000 pesos a year in agricultural production. Clearly, however, the missionaries believed that the main purpose of the colonists and the control of the salt mines was not advancing commerce but solidifying their hold on the region and recovering the souls lost to Juan Santos's heresies.[1] The plan's supporters included most of Ocopa's future leadership, including Friar Pedro González Agueros, who became guardian in 1780, and Mauricio Gallardo, elected guardian in 1783.[2]

Detractors saw this plan as a repeat of the failed responses to the Juan Santos Atahualpa rebellion rather than a vindication. As one Franciscan leader so concisely stated, retaking the lost missions "by [way of] Tarma is almost impossible, as was experienced during the governments of the Marques of Villagarcia and the Count of Superunda [Manso de Velasco], whose attempts we saw frustrated."[3] This dissenting Aragonese faction was in fact led by a Castilian, Friar Francisco Álvarez de Villanueva.[4] Álvarez de Villanueva, from the perspective of Ocopa's leadership, had been a problematic missionary since his recruitment in Spain. He had been enlisted in Spain for duty in Ocopa by its former guardian, Joseph Ampuero, in 1768. As he passed through Chile en route to Ocopa, however, he was retained by an army captain to be his chaplain. Álvarez de Villanueva later claimed that he did this under the direction of Ampuero.[5] Nevertheless, his securing of the post of chaplain was the type of move that Ocopa's leadership had been railing against for decades—missionaries who used the funds granted to the college for free passage to the Americas only to abandon the community for better, less rigorous positions elsewhere in the Americas. Within the year, Álvarez de Villanueva moved to Lima with his patron, where the captain died, and he finally incorporated into Ocopa in 1770.[6]

Despite Álvarez de Villanueva's early decision to stay in Chile, or perhaps because of it, he was able to ingratiate himself with several important Ocopa leaders during the early 1770s, including ex-guardian Friar Francisco de San Joseph and acting guardian Friar Antonio Cavallero.[7] Within a month, Álvarez de Villanueva returned to Lima as Ocopa's procurator. He was probably an ideal candidate to advocate for the college, having most likely made many contacts during his time as a chaplain in the viceregal capital. In 1775 he returned to Spain as the apoderado for Ocopa in order to collect a new group of missionaries. According to González Agueros, he did so without any official permission from Ocopa's leadership. Álvarez de Villanueva later produced a license to go to Spain, but it empowered him only to collect new missionaries, not to represent the college at court as other apoderados had done. Either faction, however, could do little to stop or support Álvarez de Villanueva's work, since war with Britain between 1779 and 1783 made sending a new representative to Spain impossible.[8]

Once in Spain, Álvarez de Villanueva did more than just collect new missionaries. He began to bombard the crown with proposals. He sent so many that the Franciscan commissary-general of the Indies griped that the Council of the Indies "suffered the annoyance of his quarrelsome ideas, reproving him [for] a few projects, which were judged [to be] impossible."[9] One proposal that received attention from the Council requested that the entire college move from Ocopa to the Franciscan monastery of Huánuco. Álvarez de Villanueva argued that, because most of Ocopa's missions were now far to the north, Huánuco was a more logical base of operations for the community. Also, the more temperate climate in Huánuco would prepare new missionaries better for the heat of the jungle. Ocopa's then-guardian Pedro Gonzáles Agueros countered these arguments by pointing out that Álvarez de Villanueva did not have the authority to negotiate relocation. He added that the monastery at Huánuco was too small for the large community, and that Ocopa's cold climate was the most effective motivation for new missionaries to leave the college for evangelization in the torrid jungle.

Gonzáles Agueros was in many ways Álvarez de Villanueva's opposite. Incorporated into Ocopa just a year before Álvarez de Villanueva, Gonzáles Agueros had spent much of his early career in the Montaña, where he was involved in several expeditions. He would later publish many of his experiences in the 1780s and 90s as a tool to recruit more missionaries. From his writings it is obvious that he saw Álvarez de Villanueva as a dilettante. The Council ultimately did not approve the move to Huánuco and the proposal eventually died, but Álvarez de Villanueva's push to focus northward toward the missions of Huánuco, Cajamarquilla, and ultimately Manoa did not.[10]

In 1777, Álvarez de Villanueva suggested an alternative to the Chanchamayo plan. He felt that the crown would waste its resources helping the missionaries regain a region that had already rejected them. Instead, he proposed investing in building a road from the mission of Pozuzu to the port of Mayro, along the Pozuzu River. From Mayro boats could navigate all the way to the Ucayali, connecting the Huánuco missions to then-defunct Manoa missions (which had also rejected the missionaries) and ultimately the rest of the Amazon basin. In contrast to advocates of the Chanchamayo plan, Álvarez de Villanueva went to great lengths to emphasize the commercial benefit of the enterprise as well. The new port, he claimed, would be an entrepôt for Amazonian products, and he listed no less than twenty-two potential trade goods including "gold, sugar, chocolate, cinnamon, Jesuit's bark [for making quinine], rice, beans, yucca, [and] yams."[11]

Not only would the port help commerce, it would also further Spain's strategic goals by solidifying its claims over the upper Amazon basin against the Portuguese. Overall command of the expedition would be given to the governor of Tarma, Jose Josef Abella Fuertes, with missionaries accompanying to establish a mission once the port was built. The expedition would use the troops guarding the Tarma and Jauja frontier, committed to the Chanchamayo plan, supplemented by "delinquents" who would forge a path and construct two bridges. Just as in the Chanchamayo plan, colonists would be required to help secure the area. According to Álvarez de Villanueva, in 1768, Manuel Gil, commissary of the missions of Peru, had suggested a similar plan, which viceregal officials had approved, but it did not come to fruition because of a lack of funding.[12] The Mayro plan apparently gained wide support in Madrid and Peru, with the governor of Tarma as a particularly vocal advocate. The plan's popularity was no doubt a result of the fact that Álvarez de Villanueva's arguments followed closely those espoused by many merchants and government officials throughout the empire.[13]

On 30 April 1779, Viceroy Manuel de Guirior and the audiencia of Lima considered both plans but decided initially to fund the Chanchamayo plan since its goal, the retaking of the missions lost to Juan Santos Atahualpa, was more in keeping with the 13 March 1751 royal decree and therefore more in line with the will of the monarch.[14] On 13 July a small expedition left the frontier fortress of Palca for the Chanchamayo River valley. The expedition consisted of eighty soldiers and a small contingent of Ocopa friars led by the ex-guardian, Francisco de San Joseph. Overall command of the expedition was given to Francisco de Robles, but his second-in-command, Josef Patricio Barrantes, led this initial foray. It took them three weeks, to 3 September, to cut a path 36.4 miles (58.8 km) through the high jungle to the confluence of the Chanchamayo and Ocsabamba rivers.[15] On 14 September, San Joseph sent a letter to the viceroy stating that they had built a chapel with a large wooden cross in front of it and were preparing to build fortifications, but that they had had little contact with the native population.

Only seven days later, however, the governor of Tarma, Abella Fuertes, whom Álvarez de Villanueva had suggested as commander of the Mayro expedition and who was one of its most vocal advocates, drafted an alarming missive to the viceroy regarding the status of the Chanchamayo expedition. According to his sources, on the seventeenth a "numerous" contingent of montañeses had erected a cross on an island in the middle of the Chanchamayo and declared that they already had a cross and did not need another. They promised that if the expedition did not leave they would take Spanish soldiers captive and "slit the priests' throats." Abella Fuertes continued by saying that the montañeses blew horns and sang songs at night to intimidate the soldiers and by day brandished European firearms, including the cannons the Juan Santos rebels had captured from Quimirí three decades earlier. To emphasize the Amerindians' capacity to use these weapons, he added that many of them spoke Spanish, suggesting that Europeans and mestizos escaping colonial justice had "gone native" and were now aiding the Montaña nations. Without more men and arms, which the governor contended he did not have, the expedition would soon be overrun.

Abella Fuertes concluded that the expedition must withdraw from Chanchamayo.[16] To add more weight to his opinion, and because the commander of the expedition refused to do so, the governor formed a council of war, which consisted of his own coterie of clientele. The council, of course, came to the same conclusions, adding that there were no montañeses in the area left to convert except "apostates" who mixed in with the "mestizos, blacks, and even Spaniards [still there since] the time of the uprising [Juan Santos Atahualpa rebellion] whose anger is principally against the missionaries whom they murder." The fiscal of the audiencia of Lima concurred completely with Abella Fuertes and urged the viceregal government to order the troops withdrawn.[17]

It seems clear, however, that Abella Fuertes had an agenda. Though not impossible, it is unlikely that he was well informed about the status of the expedition, given that he was in Tarma, several days' journey away. Most likely he saw some sort of personal benefit for himself in the expedition failing. This attitude probably had to do with wanting the Mayro expedition to go forward. Álvarez de Villanueva had suggested his name for commanding it, and he probably saw the commercial opportunity in being the first to open a path between the Mantaro Valley and a navigable port that could lead to the

Amazon. This in many ways contrasts with the relationship previous governors had had with Ocopa's leadership. Many had built strong relationships with the college, not only entrusting them with their prayers and alms but also taking advantage of the college's growing wealth to secure loans from them (see chapter 4). Perhaps Abella Fuertes's attitude is further evidence of the diffusion of regalist sentiments among the lowest levels of the Spanish bureaucracy. Or perhaps Abella Fuertes bet that the more politically sensitive Álvarez de Villanueva would soon be on the ascendancy at Ocopa.

It was not until three weeks later that Francisco de San Joseph and the rest of the expedition realized that Abella Fuertes was trying to undermine their efforts. San Joseph fired back with a letter to the commander of the expedition, Francisco de Robles, who it seems was still back in Tarma. The missionary included with his missive the testimonies of the acting field commander, Barrantes, Robles's second-in-command, along with those of the company's engineer, Alejandro de Arana, and the company sergeant, Silvestre Carbajal. All three men's accounts refuted the dire picture of the expedition that Abella Fuertes had painted. Indeed, for the most part the missionaries had little contact with the indigenous population, either peaceful or violent. On 17 September a group of montañeses had been spotted on the other side of the river, but communication was impossible, according to ex-guardian San Joseph, over the din of the rushing water. For some reason the montañeses fired one arrow at the leading friar, but it fell short. Weeks later the montañeses reappeared on the other bank brandishing machetes and axes, chopping down a few trees to show that they were real, and even erected a wood cross, but they made no other verbal threat to kill the priests. The montañeses clearly did not have firearms or cannon. In fact, the only injury sustained was on the night of 18 October, when montañeses tried to shoot arrows over the river. They again missed, but when the Spanish picket tried to return fire with a volley in the darkness they accidently aimed toward their own encampment and injured one man in the leg. Furthermore, Sergeant Carbajal, who had considerable experience along the frontier, confirmed that the group across the river indeed consisted only of Asháninkas and Yaneshas and was not mixed with Europeans, mestizos, or Africans as Abella Fuertes had claimed.[18] Even before San Joseph penned his letter, and over the urgings of the fiscal, the viceroy and audiencia had decided to leave the question of whether the expedition should withdraw from its position along the Chanchamayo up to the commander in the field, Barrantes.[19]

It was not, ultimately, the possibility of violence against the Chanchamayo expedition that most concerned the viceregal government but its lack of results. Despite the occasional sighting, it seems the Asháninkas' and Yaneshas' strategy for dealing with the missionaries was simply to ignore them. As Viceroy Guirior's successor, Augustin Jaurequi, wrote in frustration: "The fort was constructed in an incorrect manner, and since my entrance into this viceroyalty I have only seen these reports: that there has been no advancement of conversions, despite the immense expense on the Tarma and Jauja companies; that the soldiers . . . lack discipline; that the Chanchamayo expedition has produced no useful advancement, and the pathways that the missionary fathers have opened up are very defective." Jaurequi quickly concluded that indeed the Mayro plan seemed more "useful" for the "advancement of conversions" and attempted to convince the guardian of Ocopa, then Gonzáles Agueros, to support it, "but the guardian and his faction were determined to impede this enterprise."[20]

Gonzáles Agueros refused not only to help pay for the expedition but also to release troops from Chanchamayo to help with Mayro. In response to Gonzáles Agueros's intransigence in 1783, the viceroy sent his own expedition to Mayro. Led by a young captain, Francisco Elizalde, the expedition's goal was simply to gauge whether construction of a road from Pozuzu to Mayro was even possible. After a two-month expedition Elizalde concluded that it was, and Jaurequi ordered that construction begin. The Elizalde expedition enraged Ocopa's leadership, especially since the viceroy, unable to get funding from Ocopa directly, simply discounted the 4,099-peso cost of the expedition from its annual stipend.[21] Then, in 1784, the Mayro plan floundered with Jaurequi's recall and subsequent death.[22] The Chanchamayo mission did not survive either. That year the newly appointed intendant of Tarma, Juan Maria Gálvez (no apparent relation to the minister of the Indies, José de Gálvez), ordered the site demolished and burned, presumably under the orders of the new viceroy of Peru, Teodoro de Croix.[23]

Though the Chanchamayo/Mayro conflict ended in stalemate, it was only the first battle in a larger war between Ocopa's leadership (Gonzáles Agueros and Gallardo) and Álvarez de Villanueva and his supporters. In many ways the conflict underlined the ideological divide between the two factions. The more traditionalist faction wanted to reclaim former glories with minimal state involvement; the other tried forging into a new region under the auspices of the crown and employing its commercial and political goals. The conflict also demonstrated the tension between the choices and personal interactions of the historical actors in reaction to the larger philosophical changes taking place within the Spanish empire. Many leaders within the order and the Church blamed the discord solely on Álvarez de Villanueva. One commissary-general of the Indies stated, "Frankly hell has not spit out an equal monster, nor instrument perfectly suited [to the destruction of the College] as Friar Francisco Álvarez de Villanueva."[24] Even the archbishop of Lima faulted Álvarez: "It is inexplicable the pain that the ruin of the College of Ocopa causes me; most of the missionaries [*Religiosos*] are not only seduced but have been miserably penetrated by the venom of this very unhappy Álvarez."[25]

During the Gálvez period, however, Peru endured a radical and often violent transformation. These changes undoubtedly influenced Álvarez de Villanueva and subsequent viceregal officials with whom he interacted, as different factions within the Spanish empire vied for predominance, interpreting and reinventing regalism to their own ends.

Building Tensions

The ascension of José de Gálvez to the post of minister of the Indies in 1776 marked the start of a period of sweeping reform throughout the Spanish empire. Gálvez, who had previously been the inspector general of Mexico, attacked the reform process with a tenacity not yet seen among the Spanish bureaucracy. He completely pushed aside the traditional approach of consulting with colonial elites, which had continued, albeit in a more limited form, during the earlier Bourbon period, ramming through reforms as he saw necessary. The result, at least in the short term, was an impressive array of reforms and programs which, however, enflamed bitter resentment among the creole elites.[26]

Peru became a particular focus for Gálvez. Until the seventeenth century the viceroyalty had been the jewel of the Spanish empire, but its failing mining sector had long since left it in decline. Bourbon reformers hoped to invigorate the region and thus increase its remittances back to Spain. To do this José de Gálvez dispatched one of his former aides, Antonio de Areche, to Peru as inspector general. Areche oversaw a series of aggressive reforms aimed at increasing government revenue and centralizing authority to the crown. He set up mechanisms to increase both tax rates and collection enforcement. In 1778 the viceroyalty was divided in half, creating the new viceroyalty of Rio de la Plata with its capital in Buenos Aires. Areche also attempted to remove as many American-born creoles from political office as possible. Creoles, reformers reasoned, had less of a vested interest in the overall goals of the Spanish crown, wanting instead to grow rich off local corruption, thereby denying the crown central control and vital revenue. In his previous post as inspector general of Mexico, Gálvez had struggled to work with creole leaders, and he had created policies to replace them with peninsular Spaniards. The naturally doctrinaire Areche pursued this policy doggedly. He even had the viceroy of Peru, Guirior, removed from office in part for being too friendly with the creole elite of Lima. Areche's hardline reformist stance and brusque leadership style won him few friends, however, and as soon as a crisis befell Peru he too was removed from office.[27]

The crisis that precipitated Areche's downfall was the largest anticolonial revolt in the Americas to date, the Tupac Amaru rebellion (1780–82). This revolt was largely fueled by indigenous resentment over local government corruption, exacerbated by increased taxation and changing commercial policies created by the formation of the viceroyalty of Rio de la Plata. Spawning one additional rebellion near La Paz and coinciding with another in the mining region of Chayanta (near Potosí), the Great Andean revolts lasted three years and involved hundreds of thousands of combatants. Despite the gruesome execution of the uprising's leader, José Gabriel Condorcanqui (who had taken the name of his supposed ancestor, the last Inca, Tupac Amaru), many crown officials blamed Areche's heavy-handedness and administrative incompetence for both inciting the rebellion and delaying its suppression. Gálvez recalled him to Spain in September 1781.[28]

Gálvez charged Areche's replacement as inspector general, Jorge Escobedo, with rectifying one of the other main causes of the Tupac Amaru rebellion, the "tyrannies" of the corregidores de Indios. Corregidores were local governors with direct jurisdiction over the indigenous peoples of the Americas. Low pay, poor supervision, and opportunity had encouraged widespread corruption among these magistrates. By the eighteenth century, corregidores were criticized by almost all levels of colonial society. Indeed, in the aftermath of the Juan Santos Atahualpa rebellion, Manso de Velasco had also blamed corregidores along with corrupt judges and priests as one of the main causes of the uprising.[29] Therefore, in 1784 Escobedo supervised the installation of a system of intendants thought to be less corrupt, since they were better paid, better supervised, and for the most part peninsular Spaniards. But the increased political authority of the office of the intendant threatened the power and prestige of the viceroy.

Into this milieu of change and conflict came another former Gálvez subordinate from Mexico, Teodoro de Croix, as the new viceroy of Peru in April 1784. He was fresh from his tenure as commander of Interior Provinces of New Spain in Mexico's northern frontier region. Croix spent most of his appointment as viceroy quietly struggling with Escobedo, who after his inspection ended in 1785 remained as the *superintendente subdelegado de la real hacienda* (superintendent subdelegate of the royal treasury), essentially the senor intendant and chief officer of the viceroyalty's finances. Escobedo not only represented the other intendants but was answerable not to the viceroy but directly to the minister of the Indies. Though the powers of superintendent were eventually restored to the viceroy after Gálvez's death in 1787, during the entirety of his term of office (1784–90) Croix remained concerned about maintaining viceregal authority.[30]

When it came to frontier missions in Peru, Croix's time in Mexico, it seems, deeply affected his decisions. He had seen that in remote areas of the frontier the "new method" was an utter failure. The crown could not attract enough willing (or even unwilling) colonists for it to work. The "old method," however, was not effective either. Although over centuries the missionaries had "pacified" many frontier areas, disease and the act of forcing the native populations into missions had led, for the most part, to economic and demographic stagnation. This condition would not stand against the incursions of European interlopers who began to push into these peripheral regions in the late eighteenth century as political and military conflicts intensified over control of the Americas. Furthermore, the "old method" gave the regular clergy who manned these missions far too much power. Already obsessed with maintaining the prestige of his office, Croix must have felt the need to have more control over Ocopa, which after the exit of the Jesuits had become the most important religious institution in the frontier of the audiencia of Lima. He, however, had an advantage that his predecessor did not when dealing with Ocopa—Friar Francisco Álvarez de Villanueva.

Viceregal Takeover of Ocopa

The viceregal takeover of Ocopa began with the arrival of Álvarez de Villanueva from Spain in 1785. As apoderado for Ocopa he had spent nearly a decade collecting new missionaries. He clearly saw this as an opportunity to pack Ocopa with like-minded missionaries. Almost from the start, Álvarez de Villanueva attempted to circumvent his enemies in the Ocopa leadership to ensure that these new missionaries would be accepted into service at the college. To do this he created his own seal of the college and began affixing it to new missionaries' licenses, allowing them to incorporate into Ocopa. Though it was standard practice for collectors of missionaries to issue such documents, conditionally incorporating new recruits into the college, once they arrived in Ocopa their licenses had to be ratified by the guardian and affixed with the college's seal. By creating his own seal, Álvarez de Villanueva was attempting to circumvent the guardian's right to approve new missionaries. Even the design of Álvarez de Villanueva's new seal revealed his own regalist attitudes (figure 14). The false seal nearly duplicated Ocopa's official seal by portraying a standing Virgin with Child holding roses, but Álvarez de Villanueva added two royal seals flanking the central figures, suggesting visually the college's subservience to the crown. Though Gonzáles Agueros, then guardian, still accepted the first group of twenty-two missionaries that Álvarez de Villanueva dispatched to Ocopa in 1779 with the false seal, he lodged a complaint about the apoderado's usurpation of his powers to the commissary-general in Spain, who later confiscated and destroyed the counterfeit seals.[31]

Álvarez de Villanueva had been scheduled to follow this first group with a second of forty-four missionaries a few months later, but the war with Britain (related to the American Revolution) caused them to be delayed four years.[32] The delay may have served to reinforce the philosophical bonds that many in this group seemed to share with the apoderado. The 1784 group was also different from previous groups sent from Spain in their regional origins. Previous

FIGURE 14. (*left*) The counterfeit seal created by Álvarez de Villanueva to issue patents to new missionaries bound for Ocopa. This patent was for the later-famous missionary Narciso Girbal (28 November 1783, Cádiz). ESPAÑA. MINISTERIO DE EDUCACIÓN, CULTURA Y DEPORTE, AGI, Arribadas 538. (*right*) The true seal of Ocopa, used on many documents throughout the eighteenth century. This example was taken from Álvarez's own patent, issued by the collector of missionaries Friar Joseph Ampuero but sealed by the then-guardian of Ocopa, Friar Antonio López (13 June 1768, Ocopa). ESPAÑA. MINISTERIO DE EDUCACIÓN, CULTURA Y DEPORTE, AGI, Arribadas 538.

groups had consisted mostly of missionaries from the kingdom of Castile. Only seven of the sixty-three missionaries sent in 1768–69 and only four of the twenty-two Álvarez de Villanueva sent in 1779 were non-Castilians. The 1784 group, however, was split, with nearly half (twenty-two of forty-two) coming from the kingdom of Aragon (sixteen Aragonese, five Catalans, and one Valenciano).[33]

What effect the regional identity of these missionaries had on their philosophical leanings and later actions remains unclear. The regions that made up the kingdom of Aragon had backed the Habsburg claimant in the War of Spanish Succession (1700–13) that brought the Bourbons to the throne in Spain. Therefore, in the wake of the war, regional autonomy suffered greatly as successive Bourbon monarchs attempted to erase the legal distinctions between the two major medieval kingdoms that formed Spain.[34] Unsurprisingly, this process produced few ardent regalists among the Aragonese, Catalans, and Valencianos (the three regions that form the medieval kingdom of Aragon). Perhaps, however, it was simply old animosities between the two principal kingdoms of Spain that allowed Álvarez de Villanueva to turn the Aragonese against the mainly Castilian leadership of Ocopa. Over the previous three centuries, since the unification of the crowns, animosity between the smaller, commercially vibrant Aragon and the larger, politically dominant Castile had festered. Certainly the Aragonese friars (which in the nomenclature of the documents refers to both Catalans and Valencianos as well) spoke Catalan among themselves, further alienating them socially from their Castilian brothers. What is certain is that of the seventeen missionaries considered to be Álvarez de Villanueva's principal "conspirators," nine were from the kingdom of Aragon. Among them the Aragonese Friar Manuel de Sobreviela was widely considered to be Álvarez de Villanueva's coleader in the faction.[35]

In April 1785, Álvarez de Villanueva and the new group of missionaries arrived in Lima, but Álvarez de Villanueva delayed his own departure from the city to meet with Croix. According to the Franciscan commissary-general of the Indies, Álvarez de Villanueva "seduced the viceroy."[36] In their meeting, Álvarez de Villanueva proposed that the viceroy, as the king's representative in Peru and vice-patron of the royal patronage of the Church, should be the person to decide, in consultation of course with the guardian of Ocopa, where the new missionaries would be posted. Álvarez de Villanueva then presented a tentative plan for the distribution of the new missionaries to Ocopa's various posts throughout the viceroyalty. He explained that since he had gotten to know the personalities and abilities of each missionary during their long wait in Spain and their journey to Peru, he might be better suited than the guardian to advise the viceroy on this matter. He added that in September 1783 the commissary-general of the Indies had given him permission to do this in order to "repair the concept of the college that was close to expiring,"[37] an interesting turn of phrase given Ocopa's most recent advancements. Álvarez de Villanueva's proposal must have struck a chord with the viceroy. Not only was he arguing for the supremacy of the crown even in internal religious matters, but he was offering himself as an agent for extending viceregal control to one of the most powerful Franciscan institutions in Peru.

Shortly after his meeting with Álvarez de Villanueva, the viceroy remitted the new plan to the guardian of Ocopa for commentary. Before the guardian could respond, he allowed the missionaries bound for Chiloé to embark, since they had so far to travel. The guardian of Ocopa, Friar Mauricio Gallardo, was an experienced missionary and devoted ally of Gonzáles Agueros, the former guardian who had initially opposed Álvarez de Villanueva over the Mayro expedition. Gallardo had first incorporated into Ocopa in 1745 and had been one of the missionaries expelled from Sonomoro by Juan Santos. Gallardo later returned to Lima, where he taught novices at Lima's principal monastery for many decades. In 1782 he reincorporated into Ocopa, where he served for several months in the Huanta missions before being elected guardian in 1783. When Álvarez de Villanueva's plan for the disposition of missionaries arrived at Ocopa, Gallardo rejected it outright, refusing to recognize the authority of Álvarez de Villanueva or the viceroy to assign the new missionaries to their posts. Croix, disgusted by Gallardo's "discords and dissentions," and in consultation with the audiencia, approved Álvarez's proposal in its entirety within the month.[38] At first Gallardo refused to follow the new plan, attempting to hold off its implementation, but he capitulated on 19 October 1785. Victorious Álvarez de Villanueva began an inspection tour of Ocopa's missionary outposts including Cajamarquilla. He even attempted, though it is unclear whether he was successful, to make it as far as Mayro. Such inspections were not uncommon, but generally they were commissioned by the commissary-general or the guardian of Ocopa, and Álvarez de Villanueva seems to have had no such license.[39]

Meanwhile, even in Álvarez de Villanueva's absence his allies in Ocopa purportedly continued to cause disruptions. On 11 October, just eight days before Gallardo released the missionaries to their new posts, members of the Aragonese faction attempted to enter the guardian's cell forcefully to steal the seal of the college, which would have effectively made it impossible for Gallardo to issue orders to Ocopa's geographically dispersed missions. The guardian had to call up soldiers from Jauja to calm tensions in the college.[40] Four months later on the morning of 16 January, Gallardo woke up violently ill, vomiting, with fever and pustules on his face. Almost immediately he blamed Álvarez de Villanueva's allies for poisoning him, claiming it could not have been someone from outside the college since the door had been sealed all night. As one of Gallardo's supporters stated, "Even though I did not see the poison poured, it is public knowledge" that he was poisoned. Further "proof" that the guardian was indeed poisoned was provided by Ocopa's doctor, who claimed that in addition to his other symptoms Gallardo had a red nose, which, according to the doctor, was a sure sign of poisoning. Álvarez de Villanueva opined that the guardian simply had cholera, a common ailment in the early modern world, though with symptoms similar to arsenic poisoning.[41]

On 16 June 1786, Álvarez de Villanueva finally returned to Ocopa. That same day he confronted Gallardo to again demand the seal of Ocopa.[42] Álvarez de Villanueva later argued that Gallardo's and his predecessor's elections as guardian were invalid, since instead of letting the entire community elect someone to preside over new elections the outgoing guardian and *decretorio* (excutive council) had simply selected one of their political allies, Friar Philip Sanchez, provincial minister of Lima, to do so. In addition, he contended, Gallardo had not spent the requisite year in residence at Ocopa before his election.[43] Gallardo, of course, refused to give up the seal. Unsuccessful, Álvarez de Villanueva attempted to call for a new election immediately. Ringing the bell of the college, he gathered most of the missionaries to the library. Gallardo tried to stop these new elections by threatening to expel all the missionaries who assembled with Álvarez de Villanueva. Some heeded the guardian's warning, but the resulting rump assembly went ahead and picked a date for new elections and selected a new president to preside over them, Friar Antonio Cavallero y Nieto, one of Álvarez de Villanueva's staunchest supporters. Knowing that without the seal of Ocopa Franciscan leadership in Madrid would not recognize the authority of the new president, Álvarez de Villanueva and several of his closest supporters traveled to Lima to get permission from the viceroy and audiencia for a new election.[44]

When he arrived in Lima, Álvarez de Villanueva not only pleaded with the viceroy and the audiencia to approve the election but argued that they should allow him to hold a "clandestine election" so that people "opposed to his ideas" could not vote. The viceroy equivocated, however, when it came to removing Gallardo in this manner. Perhaps he feared the public scandal that it might cause. The bad blood between Álvarez de Villanueva and Gallardo had become "public and notorious," and therefore openly taking sides on the election might cost him political capital elsewhere. Even Álvarez de Villanueva noted that the viceroy's support for him cooled after reports of the guardian's alleged poisoning reached Lima.[45] Croix instead decided to wait for the commissary-general of the Indies, Friar Manuel de Trujillo, to choose a new president for the election. Trujillo selected Friar Andrés Carbajal. Though at first Carbajal's exact alliances in the matter were unclear, he was member of the community at the San Francisco de Jesús monastery in Lima where Gallardo had been in residence for many years. Carbajal seems to have been at least somewhat partial to (or at least not hostile toward) Gallardo. In addition to presiding over the election Carbajal was given judicial powers, in the hope that he could somehow end the schism at Ocopa.[46]

Shortly after the license giving Carbajal his new powers arrived in Lima, he set the date for Ocopa's election for 19 April 1787 and ordered Álvarez de Villanueva and his colleagues back to Ocopa. Álvarez de Villanueva's faction, however, refused to leave until Carbajal changed the date of the election. They complained that since Gallardo's term of office ended on 29 January the election should be held earlier than April. For their disobedience, Carbajal put them "under censure," prohibiting them from voting in the upcoming election. Álvarez de Villanueva again complained to the viceroy, and this time Croix listened. On 4 December 1786 the viceroy and audiencia ordered that the election take place before 20 February1787 and removed the censure on Álvarez de Villanueva and his companions. In addition, the viceroy ordered that the intendant of Tarma, Juan María Gálvez, also be present at the election "with an eye to end any discord or dissension that may occur." With the date set for 12 February, Carbajal, Álvarez de Villanueva, and the core members of the Aragonese faction—now with their censures reversed—left Lima for Ocopa.[47]

Álvarez de Villanueva and his companions arrived the day of the election in the company of the intendant and a detachment of Spanish regulars out of

Jauja. As the voting began, Carbajal remained firm on the censure that he had placed on Álvarez de Villanueva and the other fifteen members of the Aragonese faction, announcing that they would not be allowed to vote. As the voting began, troops filled the room, "causing great terror" among the friars. Intendant Gálvez ordered the troops to present arms. He then read to the assembly the 4 December ruling of the viceroy and audiencia and demanded that Álvarez de Villanueva and the other censured missionaries be allowed to vote. Carbajal refused. Gálvez repeated the order in the name of the king, but Carbajal again refused. After Gálvez gave his ultimatum for a third time, Carbajal's only response was to make silently "a reverent representation," most likely the sign of the cross. In frustration, Gálvez commanded the troops to remove Carbajal forcefully. Confined to his cell and prohibited from communicating with the other friars, he died there ten days later of an unknown illness. With Carbajal gone, Gálvez instructed the missionaries to select a new president and proceed with the election. According to one eyewitness, Gálvez also "ordered his troops to contain the friars even at the risk of death, that [if] they tried to leave the election room, or in case [they] resisted, there was no other reply than the bullet and the bayonet." The missionaries clearly understood the intendant's message. After a complex process typical of Franciscan prelate elections, they selected Friar Manuel de Sobreviela as guardian and three other members of the Aragonese faction as the discretorio. Álvarez de Villanueva himself, though he served as secretary of the election, was not elected to office. He instead stayed for three years to help Sobreviela solidify control of the college and then chose to return to Spain to collect new missionaries.[48]

Consolidating Power

In the wake of the 1787 election, many of the most ardent supporters of the old leadership of Ocopa began to flee the college. Some of Gallardo's backers, particularly those who had completed their ten-year term, simply unincorporated from the community, including the former guardian himself.[49] Those who had not completed their ten-year commitment to Ocopa would either have to serve out their remaining years or somehow escape their "obedience" to the new leaders. Friar Prudencia de Echevarria, for example, assumed a new identity to flee the country. Two days before Carbajal died Echevarria met with the deposed president of the election, and he later claimed that Carbajal gave him permission to leave the college. So Echevarria waited until he was given his new post. Ordered to Trujillo, presumably en route to Cajamarquilla, Echevarria instead went to Payta and embarked on a ship bound for Spain. To avoid the "many spies" that he claimed Álvarez de Villanueva had in the port, Echevarria assumed the name Friar Antonio de

Arostequia and forged a license from the guardian of Ocopa stating that he had completed his ten-year term at the college in order to board the ship.[50]

Ocopa's new leadership also simply forced out friars who had been allied with the old regime. For example, the leadership ordered Friar Vincente de la Torre to leave. He later complained bitterly to the Franciscan commissary-general of the Indies that neither he nor the king could "remove from that throne [the guardianship of Ocopa], the idol of Satan [Sobreviela], that the pride of Álvarez de Villanueva had placed there."[51] With other Gallardo supporters, the new leaders were more heavy-handed, especially with those who attempted to defame them or undermine their authority. Friar Jimenez de Bejarano, like Echevarria, had met with Carbajal just before his death. Carbajal had entrusted Bejarano with all his papers and ordered him to get word to Spain of the events surrounding the election of 1787. Bejarano therefore traveled to Guayaquil, where he sent the papers and a report to the commissary-general in Spain. While waiting for a response he left the coast for Quito, effectively fleeing the audiencia of Lima, where it seems he believed his enemies had more influence. He stayed eleven months in the audiencia of Quito, during which time he accompanied several missionary expeditions into the jungle. Sometime during 1788 he received instructions from the commissary-general to return to the Ocopa missions outside of Huanta. In late September, while making his way to Huanta, he stopped for few days to rest in Huancayo, just 16 miles (27 km) from Ocopa.[52] On the night of the twenty-ninth, he was summoned to give spiritual aid to a soul in need. When he exited the house where he was staying, three Ocopa missionaries and a contingent of militia "too large for the arrest of a friar [*Religioso*]" led by Colonel Pedro Elizalde, the former commander of the Mayro expedition, confronted Bejarano and ordered him arrested "in the name of the king."[53] The soldiers beat him, seemingly severely, shackled him, and temporarily confined him at Ocopa.

The arrest caused a scandal among the locals of Huancayo, who it seems had sympathy for the beleaguered friar. After the arrest, one of the residents reportedly yelled, "Nobody speak with Don Pedro Ilzarbe [Elizalde], he is excommunicated because he beat Father Bejarano."[54] Eventually Bejarano was transferred to Lima along with a group of prisoners from the Tupac Amaru rebellion in Cusco and was imprisoned in La Casa Matas dungeon at the Real Felipe fortress in Callao.[55] His imprisonment in Callao was of course illegal, since as a member of the clergy he should have been held apart from the general population, usually in one of his order's houses. Viceroy Croix stated that he ordered Bejarano's arrest for "disobedience to his superiors." Croix held Bejarano in Callao for about a year before eventually exiling him to Spain.[56]

Even two decades after the election, many accused the Aragonese faction of expelling, or at least distancing, friars from Ocopa who did not agree with their policies. In 1806 the guardian of Ocopa, Geronimo Zurita, ordered Friar

Francisco Campal from his mission in Chaglla to a posting farther north for being a "notorious merchant" of Jesuit bark (from which quinine is extracted). The friar was allegedly forcing the montañeses to harvest the bark against their will.[57] The intendant of Tarma, who most likely was benefiting financially from the trade, mocked this reasoning as a "frivolous excuse."[58] He claimed that the guardian's "efforts on this subject are not the impetus of a justified zeal, but are the necessary recourses that are brought into consideration by the next election [of a new guardian], in which they try to send away critics that are not addicts to supporting the faction controlled by the Aragonese that established rule over the college since the year [1]786, and whose duration [illegible] is the origin of the distraction of so many."[59] The viceroy agreed and Campal stayed in Chaglla.[60] The "frivolous excuse" was even more suspicious considering the new leadership's push for commercial development in the missions.

The 1787 guardian election established almost complete regalist control in Ocopa. For the rest of the colonial period the Aragonese faction dominated the college's leadership. More important, after the election the viceroy became a central figure in the college's decision-making processes. From that point on, the posting of missionaries to any of Ocopa's numerous stations had to be approved by the viceroy. In addition, the office of the viceroy increasingly exercised more subtle forms of control. Ocopa missionaries still lobbied the government in Madrid directly through their apoderado, but more often they turned to the viceroy to advocate on their behalf.

The conflict over the election underlines the complex nature of the Bourbon reform process. On the one hand, it would be easy to simply vilify Francisco Álvarez de Villanueva as a power-hungry clergymen willing to do anything to take control of Ocopa, but this would ignore the larger political and historical context of the election. The 1780s saw the height of the Bourbon reforms, and just a few decades before the Franciscans had seen the Jesuits completely expelled from the Spanish empire—of which Inspector-general José Antonio de Areche, who implemented many of the reforms in Peru during this period, constantly reminded the Franciscans.[61] If the missionaries hoped to move forward, one could argue, then they had to work more closely with the crown, since defying it had obvious and detrimental results. It seems clear that at least at some level the Aragonese faction believed they were acting in the best interest of the college.

At the heart of things, the guardian election of 1787 at Ocopa, and the events leading up to it, demonstrate the importance of individuals to the way reformist ideas unfolded on the ground in the Americas. The extension of royal control over Ocopa came not by way of a mandate from Madrid but from Croix's exploitation of the divisions within the college, created by the adoption of regalist ideas by a few of its members. Croix succeeded where Manso de Velasco had failed, not by an overwhelming display of crown authority but through the exploitation of Álvarez de Villanueva's and the Aragonese faction's beliefs and ambitions. It is still unclear who was manipulating whom. What is clear is that, although the atmosphere of reform provided the context for the divisions at Ocopa and the behavior of viceregal authorities, the changes that occurred were the result of individuals' interpretations of regalism and the Enlightenment and how they acted upon them.

Notes

1. Former guardian Francisco de San Joseph described the Chanchamayo plan in a treatise written probably in 1770s found in RAH 9-9-1731, ff. 434r–40r. The original elaboration of the plan by Joseph de San Antonio is found in San Antonio, Petition to the crown, 11 June 1750, Madrid, JSEI, 146–47.

2. The division between factions can be seen in a letter to the Franciscan provincial minister from Gonzales dated sometime between 1782 and 1784, ASFL, r. 42, n. 12a, b, ff. 273r–76v. See also Libro de Elecciones de Santa Rosa de Ocopa, AO, ff. 43v–45v.

3. Josef de Garmendia, commissary-general of Peru, petition to Real Acuerdo, 4 March 1774, Lima, AGI, Lima 1612.

4. Riva-Agüero, "Los Franciscanos," 15.

5. Álvarez, Report to the crown, 27 June 1785, Lima, AGI, Lima 1610, no. 7; Heras, *Libro de Incorporaciones*, 58 (329); Gonzáles Agueros, Cargos contra Fr. Francisco Álvarez Villanueva, 28 August 1787, San Ildefonso, Lima, AGI, Lima 1607.

6. Gonzáles Agueros, Cargos contra Fr. Francisco Álvarez Villanueva, 28 August 1787, San Ildefonso, Lima, AGI, Lima 1607.

7. Ampuero, Letter to commissary-general of the Indies, 13 June 1778, Ocopa, AGI, Lima 1612; Gonzáles Agueros, Report from the guardian and discretorio of Ocopa to the provincial of the Twelve Apostles about Fr. Caballero, 1782, Lima, ASFL, r. 42, n. 12a, b, ff. 273r–726v.

8. Álvarez, Report to the crown, 27 June 1785, Lima, AGI, Lima 1610, no. 7; Heras, *Libro de Incorporaciones*, 58 (329); Gonzáles Agueros, Cargos contra Fr. Francisco Álvarez Villanueva, 28 August 1787, San Ildefonso, Lima, AGI, Lima 1607. On the illness and removal of Josef Bueno, see Friar Manuel de la Vega, commissary-general of the Indies, Report to the Council of the Indies, 8 November 1775, Madrid, AGI, Lima 881.

9. Friar Manuel Trujillo, commissary-general of the Indies, Report to the crown 16 November 1790, Madrid, AGI, Lima 1610.

10. The entire exchange of letters detailing this proposal, the counter-arguments, and the Council decision are found in ASFL, r. 41, n. 44, ff. 534–74. On Gonzáles Agueros, see chapter 6.

11. Álvarez, Petition to the crown, 5 September 1777, San Ildefonso, AGI, Lima 994.

12. Ibid. Though I found no evidence of Gil's 1768 petition or its viceregal approval, it seems quite plausible that it did occur.

13. To see how closely his reasoning followed that of merchants and colonial officials, see Povea Moreno, "Juan Bezares," 54–57; and Scott, "At the Center of Everything," 395–426.

14. Writ of the Real Acuerdo, regarding the reconquest of the missions of the Cerro la Sal, 30 April 1779, Lima, AGI, Lima 1606.

15. San Joseph, Letter to Viceroy Guirior, 14 September 1779, Santa Cruz de Chanchamayo, AL-MRREE, LEB-12-17 (Caja 94), ff. 0r–1v.

16. Avella Fuertes, Report to Viceroy Guirior, 21 September 1779, Tarma, AL-MRREE, LEB-12-17 (Caja 94), ff. 1v–2v.

17. Declaration of the war council, 26 October 1779, Tarma, AL-MRREE, LEB-12-17 (Caja 94), ff. 7r–12v; Fiscal's report of the council of war in Tarma, 29 September 1779, Lima, AL-MRREE, LEB-12-17 (Caja 94), ff. 13v–14r.

18. San Joseph, Report to Francisco de Robles, with attached reports from Barrantes, Arana, and Carbajal, 12 October 1779, Santa Cruz de Chanchamayo, AL-MRREE, LEB-12-17 (Caja 94), ff. 14r–21v.

19. Writ of the Real Acuerdo, 24 September 1779, AL-MRREE, LEB-12-17 (Caja 94), ff. 21v–23r.

20. Jaurequi, "Relacion que hace," 1784, Lima, RAH, 9-9-3 1706, ff. 24r, 25v.

21. Ibid., ff. 26v–28v; Friar Mauricio Gallardo, Letter to Jose de Gálvez, 28 October 1785, Madrid, AGI, Lima 1609.

22. Both Jorge Escobedo (superintendant of the treasury) and Teodoro de Croix (viceroy) refused to pay it; 7 September 1787, Lima, AGI, Lima 1609.

23. Gonzáles Agueros, Report to the crown, 28 August 1787, San Ildefonso, AGI, Lima 1607.

24. Friar Josef Felix Palacin, minister-general of the province of the Twelve Apostles of Peru, Report to Friar Manuel Maria Trujillo, commissary-general of the Indies, 16 August 1787, Lima, AGI, Lima 1607.

25. Friar Manuel de Trujillo, commissary-general, quotes the archbishop for a letter he wrote to the friar 20 April 1789 (Report to crown, 16 November 1790, AGI, Lima 1610).

26. Kuethe and Andrien, *Spanish Atlantic World*, 290.

27. Fisher, *Bourbon Peru*, 28–35.

28. Ibid.

29. Manso de Velasco, 24 September 1750, Lima, JSEI, 163.

30. Fisher, *Bourbon Peru*, 33–34, 150, 163–64.

31. Gonzáles Agueros, Petition to Friar Manuel de la Vega, commissary-general, 30 January 1781, Santa Rosa de Ocopa, AGI, Lima 1609 (with rescript from Vega, 20 January 1783, Madrid); Friar Manuel de Trujillo, commissary-general, Report, 16 November 1790, AGI, Lima 1610.

32. Spain was drawn into global conflicts related to the American Revolution because of its Family Pact treaty with France yet it never officially allied with the Americans. Villanueva describes the delay in a defense of his actions dated 27 June 1785 from the Convento Grande de Jesus de Lima, AGI, Lima 1610.

33. Heras, *Libro de Incorporaciones,* 48–75.

34. Lynch, *Bourbon Spain,* 28–39.

35. The "conspirators" included friars Francisco Alvarez de Villanueva, Manuel Sobreviela, Agustín Sobreviela, Ramón Aynosa, Martin de Martin, Manuel Pérez, Josef Chaves, Josef Llera, Vicente Gómez, Antonio Díaz, Agustín Alarte, Domingo Romero Fontan, Manuel Ruiz, Agustín Alarte, Josef Tadeo Cavallero, Luis Colomer, Julián Hurtado, and Vicente Aguellas. AGI, Lima 1609; Friar Manuel de Trujillo, commissary-general, Report, 16 November 1790, AGI, Lima 1610.

36. Friar Manuel de Trujillo, commissary-general, Report, 16 November 1790, AGI, Lima 1610.

37. Croix, Report to the crown, 16 August 1788, Lima, AGI, Lima 1611; Consult of the Council of the Indies, 2 November 1793, Madrid, AGI, Lima 1607; Álvarez, "Primeros Antecedentes al Capitulo," n.d., n.p. (but probably after February 1787 from Ocopa), AGI, Lima 1609.

38. Álvarez, "Primeros Antecedentes al Capitulo," n.d., n.p., AGI, Lima 1609.; Writ of the Real Acuerdo, 11 June 1785, Lima, AGI, Lima 1611.

39. Álvarez, "Primeros Antecedentes al Capitulo," AGI, Lima 1609; Gonzáles Agueros, Cargos contra Fr. Francisco Álvarez Villanueva, 28 August 1787, San Ildefonso, Lima, AGI, Lima 1607.

40. Gonzáles Agueros, Cargos contra Fr. Francisco Álvarez Villanueva, 28 August 1787, San Ildefonso, Lima, AGI, Lima 1607.

41. Friar Juan de Marimon, Letter to commissary-general of the Indies, 4 June 1787, Lima, AGI, Lima 1607; Álvarez, "Primeros Antecedentes al Capitulo," AGI, Lima 1609.

42. Gonzáles Agueros, Cargos contra Fr. Francisco Álvarez Villanueva, 28 August 1787, San Ildefonso, Lima, AGI, Lima 1607.

43. Álvarez, "Primeros Antecedentes al Capitulo," AGI, Lima 1609; Croix, "Antecedentes más Próximos al Capitulo celebración de este, y sus resultas," n.d., n.p. (but probably after February 1787 from Lima), AGI, Lima 1609.

44. Friar Manuel de Trujillo, commissary-general, Report, 16 November 1790, AGI, Lima 1610.

45. Álvarez, "Primeros Antecedentes al Capitulo," AGI, Lima 1609; Friar Juan de Marimon, Letter to commissary-general of the Indies, 4 June 1787, Lima, AGI, Lima 1607.

46. Consult of the Council of the Indies, 2 November 1793, Madrid, AGI, Lima 1607; Carbajal, Report to Manuel Maria Trujillo, commissary-general of the Indies, n.d., n.p. (but between April 1786 and Februry 1787 from Lima), AGI, Lima 1609.

47. Croix, Report to the crown, 16 August 1788, Lima, AGI, Lima 1611; Writ of the Real Acuerdo, 4 December 1786, Lima, AGI, Lima 1611.

48. Friar Juan de Marimon, Letter to commissary-general of the Indies, 4 June 1787, Lima, AGI, Lima 1607. The facts of Marimon's story are confirmed by reports on both sides of the schism: Gonzáles Agueros, Cargos contra Fr. Francisco Álvarez Villanueva, 28 August 1787, San Ildefonso, Lima, AGI, Lima 1607; Croix, Report to the crown, 16 August 1788, Lima, AGI, Lima 1611; Consult of the Council of the Indies, 2 November 1793, Madrid, AGI, Lima 1607.

49. Heras, *Libro de Incorporaciones,* 63.

50. Friar Prudencia de Echevarria, Letter to Fr. Manuel Trujillo, commissary-general of the Indies, 25 January 1788, Madrid, AGI, Lima 1607.

51. Friar Vincente de la Torre, Letter to Trujillo, n.d., n.p. (but probably from Lima), AGI, Lima 1609.

52. Gonzáles Agueros, Report to the crown regarding the Bejarano affair, n.d. (probably mid-1789), Madrid, AGI, Lima 1609; Bejarano, Report, n.d. (after 1790), Madrid, AGI, Lima 1609.

53. Etraciano Jose de Thorrez (probably a vecino of Huancayo), Letter to Fray Prudencio, 30 November 1789, Huancayo, AGI, Lima 1609.

54. Friar Francisco Arandaz, Letter to Gallardo, n.d., n.p., AGI, Lima 1609.

55. Gonzáles Agueros, Report to the crown regarding the Bejarano affair, n.d. (probably mid-1789), Madrid, AGI, Lima 1609.

56. Croix, Report to the crown, 13 February 1790, Lima, AGI, Lima 1609.

57. Friar Miguel Andiviela, Letter to Geronimo Zurita, Guardian of Ocopa, 21 June 1806, Huánuco, AL-MRREE, LEB-12-25, Caja 95, f. 6rv.

58. Ramon de Urrutia y las Casas, intendant of Tarma, Letter to the viceroy, 9 May 1806, Tarma, AL-MRREE, LEB-12-25, Caja 95, ff. 3r–5r.

59. Urrutia, Letter to the viceroy, 18 October 1806, Tarma, AL-MRREE, LEB-12-25, Caja 95, f. 8rv.

60. Viceroy to the guardian of Ocopa, 17 November 1806, Lima, AL-MRREE, LEB-12-25, Caja 95, f. 7v.

61. A good example of this is a letter Areche wrote to the principal monastery in Lima, ASFL, r. 6, I. 49, no. 39.

Chapter 6
From Apogee to Collapse

After the 1787 guardian election, Ocopa was a different institution. Though the results would continue to be challenged over the next decade, the shift in the mentality of Ocopa's leadership meant that individual missionaries became more closely aligned with the philosophical and political trends of the colonial government. In this new Ocopa the missionaries strove not just to evangelize but to spread commerce, spur scientific exploration, and occupy and protect Spain's vast eastern frontier in South America against Portuguese encroachment. This shift toward a more "enlightened" focus gave the college both notoriety among intellectuals in the empire and, more important, ever-increasing financial and material support from the crown. At its height, at least on paper, Ocopa was the largest missionary operation in the Americas, serving more than seventy parishes and missions over a vast swath of South America that encompassed approximately 500,000 square miles (1.3 million km^2).

Just as before, however, state largesse came at a cost to Ocopa's autonomy. With increased state funds and support came expanded crown control over Ocopa's missionary enterprise. Just as one of the main factors in the disputes surrounding the 1787 election was the ability of the viceroy to approve the placement of new missionaries to Ocopa, as the crown gave Ocopa more resources it expected a greater hand in the day-to-day governance of the missions. Later expansions of state control would be even more devastating to Ocopa's autonomy, particularly the creation of the diocese of Maynas in 1802, which brought into question the college's pastoral control over its own missions. This meant that, although Ocopa's leaders retained control over the college itself, authority over teaching and liturgy in the missions fell upon a crown-selected bishop. This close association with the crown ultimately led to Ocopa's demise as independence came to Peru.

Evangelization through Science and Commerce

With their hold on the college now firm and the support of the viceregal government at least in the short term unwavering, Ocopa's new leadership set about to remake the missions. Shortly after the election, Sobreviela and Alvarez set off on a grand tour of all of Ocopa's missionary zones (Cajamarquilla,

Huánuco, Huanta) save for the distant Chiloé. The tour was not merely an inspection. Sobreviela supervised new efforts to improve the physical condition and accessibility of the missions. The most important project forged a trail from Huánuco to the river port of Playagrande on the Huallaga River. From Playagrande the river was navigable to Cajamarquilla and, as Sobreviela added in a later report to the viceroy, all the way to the Atlantic. Again according to the guardian, the route reduced the time it took for missionaries to travel from Ocopa to Cajamarquilla from three or more months to only eighteen days.[1]

After the tour, Sobreviela prepared a report for the viceroy in which he pushed for continued and even increased crown assistance for the missions. The report clearly appealed to the pro-commercial, reformist sentiments of the Gálvez-era Spanish American bureaucracy. The guardian attempted to balance the missionaries' spiritual goals and the crown's political and economic aims, emphasizing both "the spiritual and temporal" advantages of Ocopa's enterprise, yet his rhetoric seemed more tilted toward material interests.[2] He suggested many products that the region could export for sale including "cacao, coffee, cinnamon, cotton, tobacco, almonds, pepper, sugar cane, [and] rice." He added that many of the plants had undiscovered medicinal values, and that the region was filled with animal life in all forms, both "bipedal and quadrupedal." He even cited a lecture given on 17 January 1787 in Madrid by the royal botanist Josef Martínez Toledano that advocated the further expansion of evangelization efforts into the Huallaga River valley and on to the Ucayali, where Ocopa's defunct Manoa missions lay. Sobreviela concluded that for the crown it would be "undoubtedly [a] great advantage to facilitate the extension of Catholicism to all the spring-like valleys of the Ucayali" and warned that if they did not the Portuguese would soon claim the area.[3] Sobreviela also included part of a cacao plant, to further convince the viceroy of the economic viability of the missions, as well as a map (figure 15) of the locations of Ocopa's mission stations. Croix was impressed and sent the report along to Spain with his own missive in which he praised Sobreviela. Echoing the guardian's own emphasis on trade, he concluded, "So that those missions increase and do not remain in the same state, as they have until now, there is no other means than to facilitate importation and commerce in those populations."[4]

As with any such work, it is unclear how much Sobreviela (or Álvarez de Villanueva) believed the persuasive rhetoric used in the report. Just as their predecessors had done, the leaders presented a picture that would appeal to their commerce-minded patrons. Had the report not mentioned the economic and security benefits of Ocopa's enterprise, its calls for increased state assistance would have received little attention. Indeed, Sobreviela needed as much political support as he could muster to accomplish his ambitious goals. Just a few months before he issued the report, for example, he asked the crown to consider extending Ocopa's missions to all of the eastern jungle from the equator

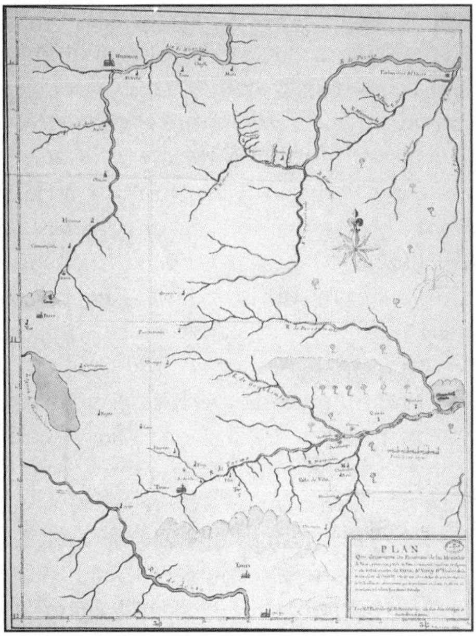

Figure 15. Plan of the frontier of the Montaña. "Plan que demuestra las fronteras de las montañas de Tarma y Huánuco, y el Valle de Vitoc, nuevamente repoblado en el presente año de 1788 de orden del Excelentísimo Señor Virrey Don Teodoro de Croix, Cavallero de Croix, etc., a fin de que sirva de escala para la reducción de 22 pueblos de conversiones que se perdieron en el año de 42, en el alzamiento del rebelde Juan Santos Atahualpa." ESPAÑA. MINISTERIO DE EDUCACIÓN, CULTURA Y DEPORTE, AGI, Mapas y Planos, Peru Chile, 113.

to Cusco, an idea that was gaining support.[5] The report also demonstrated a subtle yet significant change in the rhetoric the missionaries used in their petitions. Whereas before such documents described the commercial and security benefits of the missions as the collateral benefits of evangelization, Sobreviela's report seems to reverse this paradigm of causation. As in the "new method," the report suggested that saving peoples' souls was the natural outcome of commercial advancement and hispanicization, not the obverse.

Sobreviela touted not only the Ocopa missions' commercial value but their scientific importance in a series of articles published in the journal *Mercurio Peruano*. The *Mercurio Peruano* was the product of the intellectual society La Sociedad Académica de Amantes del País (the Academic Society of Lovers of the Country), which was modeled on the salons of Paris. Like its French counterparts, the society consisted of elite members of the limeño citizenry who met in private homes to discuss Enlightenment-inspired philosophy and the scientific advancements of the day. In 1790 the society began to produce articles in journal form under the title *Mercurio Peruano*. Society members published under their own names or pseudonyms on topics ranging from geography and economics to natural and moral philosophy. Over the five years of its existence, the society produced twelve volumes of the journal consisting of 3,568 pages of text. Many historians have argued that these articles provided the seed for Peruvian creole (if not national) identity. Though initially sanctioned by the viceroy in 1792 and by royal decree in 1793, in 1795 the society disbanded and publications ceased after several of its volumes were banned. With the specter of the French Revolution gripping Europe, many of the members of the society feared arrest.[6]

Sobreviela's involvement in the society and the *Mercurio Peruano* seems to have begun sometime around early 1791. Encouragement for the guardian to publish on the natural geography, flora, and fauna of the Ocopa missions, along with their commercial benefits, came in part from Viceroy Croix himself. In June 1791 the first article on the Ocopa missions appeared in the *Mercurio*, titled "Historia de las Misiones de Caxamarquilla: Origin and pérdida de las de Manoa" (History of the missions of Cajamarquilla: Origin and loss of those of Manoa). It was published under the name Aristio, the nom de plume for one of the society's central figures, Hipólito Unanue. The article promised more to come.

A month later Aristio again produced an article on the missions, this time in collaboration with Sobreviela. The article, "Peregrinación por el río Huallaga hasta la Laguna de la Gran Cocama, hecha por el padre predicador apostólico fray Manuel Sobreviela en el año pasado de 1790" (Peregrination along the Huallaga river until the Gran Cocama lagoon, written by the apostolic preacher father friar Manuel Sobreviela this last year of 1790), was the edited version of a diary Sobreviela had written on his last inspection of the Ocopa missions from Huánuco to Cajamarquilla. Whereas Sobreviela's original diary was saturated with religious rhetoric and musings on the evangelical potential of the region, Aristio's version focused almost exclusively on scientific considerations: the geography, animal and plant life, as well as the ethnography of the native peoples.

In September another account of an expedition by an Ocopa missionary, Narciso Girbal y Barceló, appeared in the *Mercurio*, again edited by Aristio, titled "Peregrinación por los ríos Marañón y Ucayali a los pueblos de Manoa, hecha por el padre predicador apostólico fray Narciso Girbal y Barceló en el año pasado de 1790" (Peregrination along the Marañón and Ucayali rivers to the village of Manoa, done by the apostolic preacher father friar Narciso Girbal y Barceló this last year of 1790), with the same basic scope and focus as the previous piece. Again in October Aristio published another piece on Ocopa, this time focusing almost exclusively on ethnography, titled "Noticia de los trages, supersticiones, y exercicios de los indios de la Pampa del Sacramento, y Montañas de los Andes de Perú" (Information on the dress, superstitions, and exercises of the Indians of the Pampa del Sacramento and the jungle of the Andes of Peru).

Sobreviela's participation in the *Mercurio* culminated in late October with the publication of a map titled "Plan del Curso de los Ríos Huallaga y Vcayali, y las Pampas del Sacramento" (Plan of the course of the Huallaga and Ucayali rivers, and the Pampas of Sacramento), believed to be the first published in Peru, which represented the bulk of the territory serviced by Ocopa (figure 16). According to Mariselle Meléndez the map expressed the desires of both the publishers, the Academic Society for the Lovers of the Country, and Ocopa. For the society, it was an attempt to demonstrate to the crown the rich, fertile, and diverse areas of Peru yet to be brought under Spanish dominance but ready to be exploited for commercial gain. It was an invitation for the crown not to disregard the Peruvian Amazon as an impenetrable stretch of vegetation best left to the seemingly barbaric inhabitants (actually depicted on the map with an inviting stare outward toward the viewer) but to see it as a place where the crown should invest its time and resources. The map emphasized one of the principle goals of the society: to advocate for Peru, to put such spaces on the map, both literally but also in the minds of the colonial decision makers. For Ocopa, the map was intended to underscore the grand scope of its missionary efforts in Peru, demonstrating that only it could help lead the way to bringing such a vast trove of material resources to the empire.[7] To further drive home this concept, the map included a table that listed Ocopa missions and the number of inhabitants in each one. According to the table, as of 12 October 1791 the missions of Ocopa had 31,671 people living within their confines.[8] This impressive piece of propaganda, along with subsequent articles in the *Mercurio,* had profound consequences for Ocopa. The names of Sobreviela and Narciso Girbal became well known not just in Lima but in Madrid. The articles, map, and tables seem to have transformed Ocopa from an institution that appeared to many reformers as a liability to border security and a lag on frontier commercial development to a model of how a regular religious institution could be adapted to meet regalist objectives.

Ocopa's advancements were not just propagandist fiction. As one of the titles of the articles in the *Mercurio* suggests, in 1790 the missionaries reentered Manoa under the leadership of Friar Narciso Girbal. Upon arriving at the site of one of their old missions, they found a community of eighty individuals still attempting to practice Catholicism under the direction of the missionaries' old ally and guide, Ana Rosa. With this community as a base, they continued to evangelize, but this time to the Cunibo and Pano (Paño or Pino) nations instead of the Shipibos and Setebos as before. Within a few years the missionaries had built up four mission stations.[9] The area remained, however, volatile, and Girbal made several requests for soldiers and arms. This brought

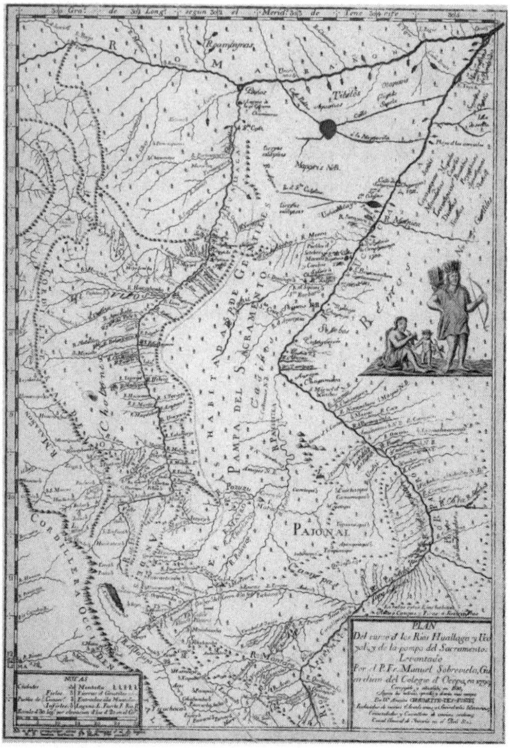

FIGURE 16. Plan of the course of the rivers Huallaga and Ucayali. "Plan del Curso de los Ríos Huallaga y Vcayali, y las Pampas del Sacramento," originally printed in the *Mercurio Peruano* in October 1791. This image is a reproduction of the original printed by Amadeo Chaumette des Fossés in 1830 that now resides in the Biblioteca Nación de España.

him into direct contact with the local governor of the province (Maynas), Francisco Requena, an up-and-coming Spanish bureaucrat who later advocated for both Girbal and Ocopa.[10]

Mounting Opposition

Praise of Ocopa's new regime was not universal. As Sobreviela began to exercise authority as guardian, opposition mounted not just against the manner in which he took power but also the way he ran Ocopa's various enterprises. In the wake of the 1787 election, reports of Sobreviela's overreaching use of power and inappropriate conduct by the Ocopa missionaries began to proliferate. Whether accurate or not, these complaints clearly cast dispersions on Ocopa's new leaders. One notable example was the rancor surrounding the new missionaries assigned to Cajamarquilla. As soon as they arrived at their highland staging point, the hospicio of Huaylillas, prominent citizens, including a local priest, complained to the bishop of Trujillo about the missionaries' "affinity for gambling, drink, and sensuality." Several witnesses even reported that one of the missionaries, Friar Francisco Obiol, had brought a mistress from Cajamarca.[11] When the missionaries finally descended to Cajamarquilla, the friars already stationed there also began to gripe bitterly about their new companions. They claimed not only that the converts viewed these missionaries with "less veneration and respect," but that the new missionaries were inciting the natives in the mission to rebellion against the old ones. The new missionaries, the old missionaries affirmed, went without their habits, danced "all hours of the night," and sold European goods to the local population. At some point it seems one of the new missionaries and one of the old even had some sort of physical altercation. To protest their new brothers' behavior and the lack of material support for the Cajamarquilla missions from Ocopa, the old missionaries left, heading to the hospicio of Huaylillas. But the president of that hospicio, Friar Valentin Lopez, newly appointed by Sobreviela, barred them from entering, though one of them was ill. Even after Sobreviela personally visited the missions, according to the old missionaries, he defended the new missionaries' actions. Without any other recourse, the old missionaries simply left Ocopa's service without the guardian's permission.[12]

Another example of the mounting criticisms of Sobreviela's leadership of Ocopa came from closer to home, in the parishes surrounding Ocopa. Although the main focus of the Apostolic Institute was to preach to the "infidels," the missionaries had a commission to fortify the faithful spiritually as well. Highland Andeans congregated regularly in the college church and other parishes controlled by Ocopa. Those with the inclination and sufficient wealth joined the Franciscan third order that the college operated out of these churches. Members of the Franciscan third order were lay, generally married, congregants who did not take vows as friars or nuns but participated in the good works and civic ceremonies of the order. Membership brought social status, and perhaps some were even emulating the late King Charles III, who was also a Franciscan tertiary. Members must have been relatively wealthy, since the price for entry was three pesos a year, much too high for a common laborer.

Sometime after coming to office, Sobreviela ordered Friar Antonio Romero Colas to extend the Ocopa missionaries' preaching along with their third order outside their own houses of worship to the surrounding parishes. Romero began to give sermons at local festivals, near devotionary chapels dedicated to local patron saints, and even at the parish churches themselves. These gatherings caused the third order based at Ocopa to surge in popularity, as Romero began leading members in what witnesses called "spiritual exercises," perhaps akin to those previously practiced by the Jesuits. Local parish priests protested what they saw as a blatant overreach of Ocopa's mission. They claimed that the third order bore "little fruit" and worried that such an organization "separated the Indians from their immediate pastors." The third order also seems to have encouraged its members to travel to Ocopa to confess, hear mass, and, though its critics never openly stated it, give alms. The archbishop agreed and in 1791 ordered Ocopa's third order suppressed in all secular parishes.[13]

Ocopa's new leadership's most virulent and dangerous opponent, however, was the commissary-general of the Indies, Friar Manuel Maria Trujillo. In truth, the election of 1787 was more of a threat to Trujillo's power than to any other friar's in the Franciscan order. By both Church and crown law elections in the order had to be authorized by the commissary-general to be valid. When the intendant, with the consent of the viceroy, dismissed Carbajal, the commissary-general's hand-picked president for the election, the viceregal government had indeed usurped Trujillo's power. Once he learned of the election, the commissary-general was livid. He immediately voided the election of Sobreviela and called for a new election. He asked the crown to confirm his decision and order the arrest of Sobreviela, Álvarez de Villanueva, and Luis Colomer, who served as president of the election after Carbajal's dismissal. He stipulated that they be confined in separate monasteries and be tried for sedition and that the intendant of Tarma, Juan María Gálvez, be investigated as well.[14] Trujillo stopped short, however, of accusing Viceroy Croix directly, stating in a separate letter that Álvarez de Villanueva made "bad use of his natural goodness."[15] The Council of the Indies and the king agreed and on 6 July 1788 ordered the viceroy to carry out the annulment and arrests.[16]

News of the annulment did not go over well at Ocopa. In a rather melodramatic letter to Intendant Gálvez, the missionaries describe the shock that they experienced upon receiving the order of annulment in late April 1788, including crying and fainting. They seemed most disturbed by the implication that some of the missionaries tried to poison the former guardian.[17] The intendant for his part was more resolute, simply stating that such an order would only disrupt the good works that the missionaries had recently accomplished.[18] Viceroy Croix immediately ordered the annulment's implementation delayed and by 18 May had convinced the rest of the audiencia of Lima to revert the case back to the Council of the Indies, despite a suggestion by González Agueros, one of the former guardian's most staunch allies, that the majority of the audiencia's members favored its implementation.[19]

To defend his own position, within two months Croix had gathered an impressive eight volumes of documents, organized and indexed, filled with correspondence, testimonies, and decrees regarding the 1787 election, which he dispatched to Spain ahead of the hearing before the Council. As a preamble to these documents, Croix included his own account of the election to explain the reasons for his actions. Not surprisingly, Croix attacked Gallardo, stating that the former guardian demanded "obedience in a gross and disrespectful manner." At the same time, he did not completely spare Álvarez de Villanueva either, admitting that the missionary had a reputation for "little religiosity" even before arriving in Peru. Croix explained that despite these rumors he decided to support Álvarez de Villanueva's plan because he carried a royal order issued by the minister of the Indies, José de Gálvez, which authorized the viceroy, as vice-patron of the royal patronage, to decide, in consultation with the guardian of Ocopa, where the new missionaries who accompanied Alvarez should be posted. He argued that it was Gallardo's initial resistance to this order that made him suspicious of his motives and led him to instruct the intendant to intervene in the election if the guardian or any of his allies caused "dissentions." These suspicions, he reasoned, were justified when Carbajal prohibited some of the missionaries from voting in defiance of his own viceregal decree.[20]

Certainly Carbajal had defied the viceroy, but the royal order that Alvarez presented to Croix giving him power to place the new missionaries seems to have never existed. Alvarez did carry an order from the minister, which Croix cited and included in the eight volumes that he sent to the Council, but the document in question said nothing about the power of the viceroy to distribute missionaries. It was simply a license for Alvarez to escort missionaries to Peru.[21] Croix's tactic worked, however, delaying a final decision on the annulment for another five years.

Ocopa before the Council of the Indies

Both sides used the long delay to get representatives back to Spain to help strengthen their positions with the Council. In many ways, the traditionalist faction already had the upper hand. Sobreviela's expulsion of Gallardo's supporters meant that several of them were already in Spain or were making their way there. Friar Prudencio de Echevarria, who had used an assumed identity to board a ship in Paita, arrived in early 1788.[22] Shortly thereafter Friar Bernardo Bejarano joined him after being freed from his imprisonment in Callao. Perhaps foreseeing the coming political imbroglio, Gallardo had already sent González Agueros as Ocopa's new apoderado at court in 1785, two years before the election had even taken place.[23] It was these missionaries who had first reported the election to the commissary-general, and their opinion appears to have weighed heavily on the prelate's initial decision to annul the election.[24] Sobreviela, however, had powerful advocates as well. In 1790 he dispatched Álvarez de Villanueva himself, who not coincidentally traveled to Spain on the same ship as the recently recalled Viceroy Croix.

The arrival of Álvarez de Villanueva created a new problem: there were now two apoderados for Ocopa at court. González Agueros obviously had the advantage. He had already been representing Ocopa for five years at court and had the backing of the commissary-general who had nullified the election of the guardian that had selected Álvarez de Villanueva. Even though Álvarez de Villanueva arrived in the entourage of the former viceroy, he received a cold reception from Commissary-general Trujillo, who balked at the missionary's "audacity" in appearing before him. Trujillo complained that allowing him to come to Spain "does not have precedent" and demonstrated "a positive contempt for the most sacred rights of the sovereign, of his ministers, and of religious subordination."[25] Trujillo therefore immediately stripped Álvarez de Villanueva of his title and had him confined to a monastery in Guadalajara.

Unfortunately for González Agueros, this did not settle the question. When González arrived in Spain, he had lacked the proper license to act as apoderado for Ocopa from the viceroy. This was because when he attempted to leave Peru in 1784, Juan Maria Gálvez, the future intendant of Tarma and then secretary to Viceroy Croix, denied González's request to travel to Madrid in an official capacity for Ocopa. Gálvez allowed González to travel to Spain only if he unincorporated from the college and thereby abdicated any authority to act in Ocopa's name once he returned to the peninsula.[26] When he arrived in Spain, González must have thought that his lack of a license from the viceroy would not be an impediment since he enjoyed the support of the commissary-general. He was so confident that, at Trujillo's insistence, he published two missionary tracts with the promise that the printing costs, amounting to more than 2,600 pesos, would be paid for from the 500-peso annual stipend that Ocopa's apoderado received at court. Without the proper license, however, González Agueros found it difficult to draw the money.[27] The lack of a license also gave ammunition to Álvarez de Villanueva's criticisms of González Agueros, calling him a "pretend apoderado" and painting him as simply a disgruntled former missionary who was able to trick the commissary-general of the Indies into nullifying the 1787 election with his "machinations" and "secret reports."[28] The fiscal of the Council of the Indies seemed unconvinced by Álvarez de Villanueva's characterizations, but he concluded that this matter could not be decided until the Council ruled on the election itself.[29]

On 2 September 1793 the Council finally sat down to decide the fate of the increasingly notorious 1787 election at Ocopa. Ostensibly the Council upheld the commissary-general's nullification and ordered that a new election be conducted by the proper authority. Sobreviela was ordered to be removed from Ocopa and Álvarez banned from ever returning to the Americas or engaging in any business in Spain on the college's behalf. The Council asked the king to censure Viceroy Croix, the audiencia of Lima, and in particular the intendant of Tarma, Juan María Gálvez, whom they agreed had overstepped his authority. The Council additionally ruled that González Agueros and Bejarano could return to the Americas and later recommended that the latter be selected to head the new college de propaganda fide in Tarata (in modern-day Bolivia). To avoid further conflicts, however, they also forbade González Agueros from returning to Ocopa and stripped him of his title as apoderado. Gallardo was similarly barred, although he had already comfortably reincorporated into the Franciscan province of the Twelve Apostles in Lima. King Charles IV not only agreed with the Council's recommendations but was apparently "very content" with the way it handled the case "in restoring tranquility to the college."[30]

On the surface, the ruling was seemingly a victory for the traditionalists at Ocopa. Though Gallardo and González Agueros could not return to the college, their faction had been proven correct and their enemies punished. Over the next year, however, the Council began to equivocate and this victory became less one-sided. After the initial ruling, González Agueros pressed the Council for the funds reserved for the apoderado of Ocopa to pay his debts. On 20 June 1795 the Council finally agreed to pay the costs of printing the two tracts, despite González's lack of a proper license, but it also stipulated that the money left over, some 2,995 pesos, be given to Álvarez for services rendered as apoderado, who despite the controversy did have a proper license.[31] Nine days later the Council agreed to allow Sobreviela to remain at Ocopa. It seems that it had been swayed by a report from the friar presiding over the new guardian election convened at Ocopa a year earlier. The friar, who was presumably hand-picked by Commissary-general Trujillo, had refused to expel Sobreviela. He argued to the Council that Sobreviela was simply an innocent bystander during the contentious election of 1787 and that as guardian he had spearheaded a massive expansion of Ocopa's missionary program. Additionally, the president noted the great "tranquility" in the college (aided no doubt by the expulsion of all of Sobreviela's enemies).[32] Álvarez de Villanueva, the principal provocateur of these events, was never allowed to return to Ocopa. Even before the Council upheld the election nullification, however, he seems to have made inroads with Trujillo. The commissary-general told the Council that Álvarez had "humbled himself," and the Council eventually agreed to allow him to remain as a "collector" of new missionaries for the college in Spain. In 1797, Álvarez dispatched a new group of missionaries to Ocopa.[33] Even as late as 1812, Álvarez was described as "the commissary and procurator general of Ocopa." At the time he was working for the French occupation government in Seville at the Archive of the Indies, where he certified a death warrant for a man condemned to die by firing squad for aiding Spanish forces after the battle of Talavera.[34]

Ocopa and the Creation of the Comandancia and Diocese of Maynas

As the disputes settled from the Council's ruling regarding the election of 1787, Ocopa continued to push its evangelization efforts northward to the Ucayali River valley. These efforts led them farther and farther into the province of Maynas, an amorphous territory created in the early seventeenth century to govern Jesuit missions in the tropical forests in what is now eastern Ecuador. As missionizing efforts expanded during the seventeenth and eighteenth centuries, spearheaded mostly by the Jesuits, its borders expanded to encompass most of the upper Amazon basin including parts of modern-day Ecuador, Colombia, and Peru (figure 17), though its exact borders, particularly to the east, were ill defined. With the expulsion of the Society in 1767, other regular orders were given charge of its missions, including Ocopa, which took over Cajamarquilla after the Jesuits left. Most of these abandoned missions, however, were turned over to the Franciscan province based in Quito, since Maynas was under the jurisdiction of its audiencia. Not only were the quiteño Franciscans notoriously undisciplined, but many friars were sent to Maynas as a form of punishment. As a result, the province swelled with some of the most indolent and recalcitrant friars in the Americas. The quiteño friars did no evangelization and little pastoral work, performing mass irregularly and rarely hearing confession. Many government and ecclesiastical officials judged them to be parasites on the mission converts. Unsurprisingly, one by one these friars were forced to abandon the Jesuits' former missions as their native converts fled rather than suffer the missionaries' malfeasance and neglect.[35]

Worrisome for many Bourbon bureaucrats, this virtual collapse of the Maynas missions coincided with the Spanish state becoming more interested in developing Maynas as a buffer zone between the Portuguese and its more valuable highland possessions in the Andes. As the missionaries themselves had reported, Portuguese traders and slavers had begun making their way farther up the Amazon basin and were encroaching on territory traditionally seen as Spanish. Although several treaties between the Spanish and Portuguese delineated the borders between the two European powers in South America, from the Treaty of Tordesillas in 1494 to the Treaty of Madrid in 1750, the exact line of demarcation in this relatively unexplored corner of the continent remained unclear. Alarmed, Spain scrambled to negotiate a new treaty. In 1777 it signed the Treaty of San Ildefonso with Portugal, finally solidifying the colonial boundary between Portuguese Brazil and Spanish South America.[36]

To assure that the treaty was honored by the Portuguese, the Spanish crown sent military engineer Francisco Requena y Herrera as a boundary commissary (*comisario de limites*) and later named him governor of Maynas. Requena, who boasted more than two decades of experience in the New

FIGURE 17. Viceroyalty of Peru in 1810. Taken from Raúl Porras Barrenechea, *Historia de los límites del Perú: texto dictado a los alumnos del Colegio anglo-peruano de Lima, conforme al programa oficial.* Lima: Librería francesa científica y casa editorial E. Rosay, 1930.

World, began to study Maynas to understand better how it could be developed both commercially and militarily to be a more effective source of revenue for the crown and a buffer against the Portuguese. Requena noted with disgust the undisciplined, corrupt manner that the Franciscans of Quito comported themselves. He was, however, impressed with the missionaries of Ocopa, in particular the expeditions of Friar Narciso Girbal into the Ucayali River valley. It became clear to Requena that Ocopa was the only religious institution expanding in Maynas, and the governor aided these expeditions with supplies and troops.

When Requena finally returned to Spain in 1799, he submitted a report on the state of Maynas, along with recommendations on how to develop the region and improve its utility to the crown. He recommended the creation of a military district, the Comandancia General de Maynas, to streamline multiple political, military, and religious jurisdictions that had existed in the province of Maynas into one clearly defined politico-religious entity. If created in the manner Requena suggested, the Comandancia would have several important implications for Ocopa. Most important, Requena urged that Ocopa be given exclusive pastoral rights to all of Maynas's missions and parishes and that all other religious institutions, particularly the friars of Quito, be expelled. To help Ocopa control the region's missions more effectively, he recommended that it be granted two additional frontier parishes as well as two small highland monasteries to serve as staging points for missionaries going into the jungle. These included the monastery of Huánuco, which Friar Álvarez had fought so hard to annex a decade earlier. For its services Ocopa would be paid 6,000 pesos per year from the crown, the same amount that the Jesuits had received previously, in addition to its current 6,000-peso stipend. Requena added that it should be granted more new missionaries as well. To simplify further Ocopa's problems working in multiple political and religious jurisdictions, Requena made two suggestions. He argued that all of Ocopa's missionary zones in Peru be annexed into the new district and that within this district the Church create a new diocese. The erection of a new episcopate was meant to simplify issues of ecclesiastical jurisdiction. Even Ocopa's existing missions fell within two Catholic dioceses, Lima and Trujillo. The additional territory it would be working in fell under two more, Quito and Cuenca. This meant that to receive licenses to function in pastoral matters Ocopa friars would have had to appeal to four different bishops. The missionaries had gotten around these complications previously with the creation of a prefect, who in certain cases could act in behest of a bishop, but such dispensations would have to be sought in each jurisdiction. Requena reasoned that having Maynas fall under one local bishop would be more convenient. The bishop, he argued, should have no cathedral and would travel around the district as needed. Of course, for this plan to work, he cautioned, the bishop would have to be from Ocopa, and he suggested giving the new mitre to Friar Narciso Girbal.[37]

The recommendation with the longest-lasting impact on the region, however, was that Maynas should be transferred from the audiencia of Quito to that of Lima. It seems that the idea for the shift in territorial jurisdiction originally came from Girbal and Sobreviela, who argued that since Ocopa's headquarters lay in the Peruvian highlands having all of its missions under the same jurisdiction would be more convenient for the college. Requena cited two additional reasons for the switch. First, the shift from Quito to Lima recognized a change in transportation patterns into the province of Maynas. During the seventeenth and early eighteenth centuries under the Jesuits, missionaries tended to enter via Quito or Cuenca through the Napo River valley. As missions along the Napo fell apart during the transfer of the region to the Franciscans, however, the main access to the tropical lowlands of Maynas came through Moyabamba or Jaen in the Lima jurisdiction. The second reason was that Lima, as the viceregal capital and major trading hub, had a larger military garrison than Quito and could more easily provide assistance in the case of a rebellion. The crown's later implementation of this suggestion led to no less than six wars between Peru and Ecuador over ownership of Maynas, the last ending in 1998.[38]

After several years of debate, the crown codified most of Requena's suggestions in a royal decree dated 15 July 1802. The decree created the Comandancia General de Maynas, incorporating almost all the upper Amazon basin including the Ucayali, Napo, Putumayo, Marañón, and Huallaga river valleys and many of their tributaries up to the edge of the Andean highlands in the west and to the line of the Treaty of San Ildefonso in the east into one political-military entity. Save for a few regions in the northernmost reaches of the Comandancia, the crown granted Ocopa exclusive rights over all the missions and parishes in Maynas, including the various small convents and parishes in the highlands suggested by Requena. Any cleric who wanted to continue his service in the region had to incorporate into Ocopa. The decree also called for the creation of a diocese under the archbishop of Lima, pending papal approval.[39]

Ocopa's missionaries rejoiced as they began to make preparations to take charge of the new territories. Quickly, however, Ocopa's leaders began to realize the massive scope of their new responsibilities as the Franciscans from Quito, upon learning of the decree, began abandoning their posts. At the same time other institutions, even Franciscan ones, jealous of the college's massive acquisition, began squabbling over the implementation of the decree.[40] The local Franciscan province, for example, agreed to forfeit the monastery at Huánuco, but it demanded that it retain the religious adornments and images as well as any incomes from mortmain donations. With the religious cohesiveness of the Comandancia at stake, much of the ability of Ocopa to manage the territory and defend it against outside institutions depended on the selection of the new bishop of Maynas.[41]

On 19 September 1803 a select committee within the Council of the Indies charged with recommending royal appointments, the Cámara of the Indies, met to consider the selection of the new bishop. The royal patronage, conferred upon the Spanish monarch in stages over the late fifteenth and early sixteenth centuries, gave the crown virtual control over selecting new bishops. In its advisory capacity the Cámara considered worthy candidates and created a list of three in ranked order for the monarch's consideration. The Cámara weighed several options, including the former Franciscan provincial minister of Lima, Friar Juan Marimon, but they ultimately agreed with Requena's assessment of the new diocese, that the new bishop had to come from Ocopa, and unanimously selected as their top choice Friar Narciso Girbal (figure 18, top). When the king's decision came back to the Cámara, however, he had selected Juan Antonio Mantilla, chaplain of San Felipe Neri in Valladolid. Man-

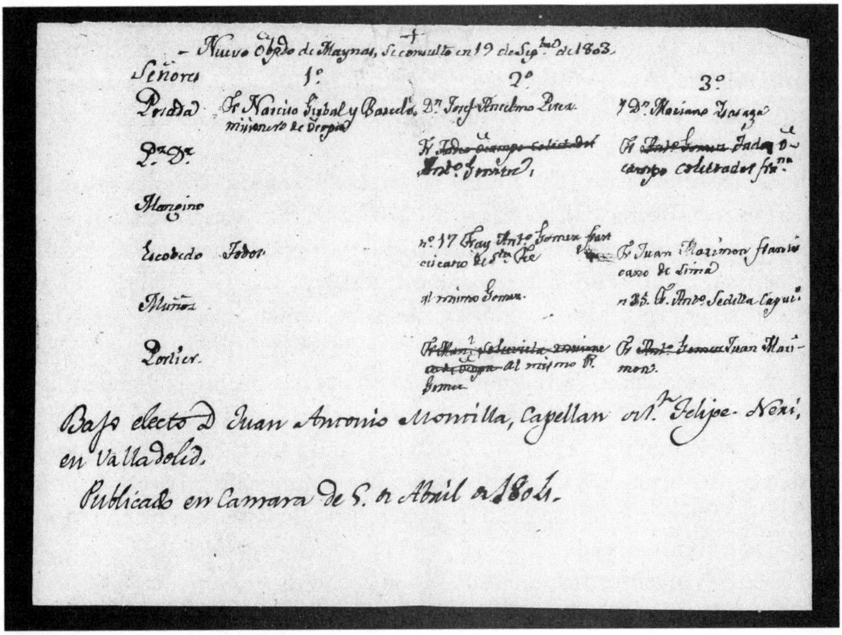
Nuevo Obpdo de Maynas, se consultó en 19 de Sepre. de 1803.

Señores | 1º | 2º | 3º

Baso electo D. Juan Antonio Montilla, Capellan del Sr. Felipe Neri, en Valladolid.

Publicado en Camara de 5 de Abril de 1804.

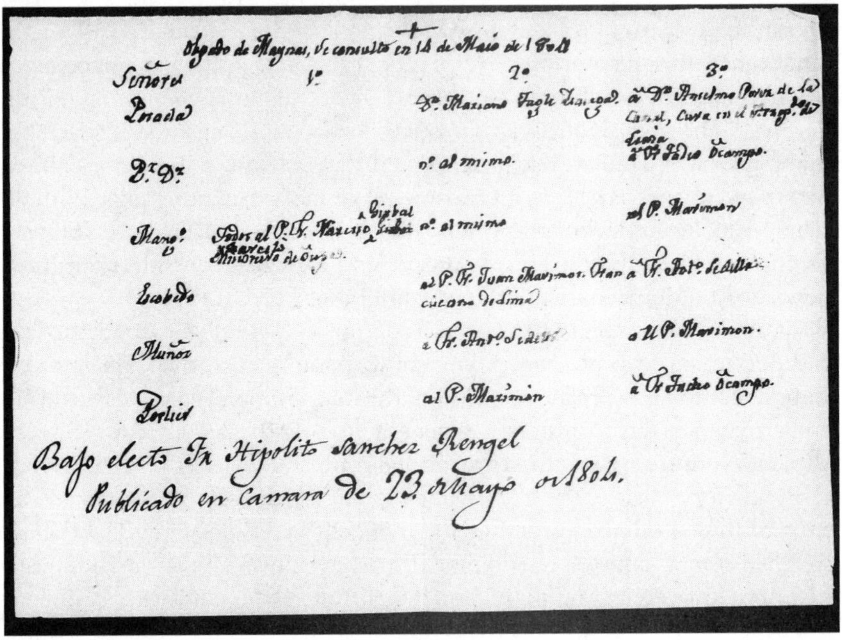
Obpdo de Maynas, se consultó en 14 de Mayo de 1804

Señores | 1º | 2º | 3º

Baso electo Fr. Hipolito Sanchez Rengel

Publicado en Camara de 23 de Mayo de 1804.

FIGURE 18. Results for the Cámara de Indies selection of the new bishop of Maynas, 19 September 1803 (*above*), and 14 May 1804 (*below*). ESPAÑA. MINISTERIO DE EDUCACIÓN, CULTURA Y DEPORTE, AGI, Lima 1580.

tilla had not been on the list of candidates. He had no connection to Maynas or Ocopa and was not even a Franciscan. No rationale accompanied the decision. Mantilla, however, declined the post, citing health problems.[42] Certainly the rigors of taking over a new, unorganized diocese in the sweltering tropical forests of the Amazon would have seemed less desirable than a comfortable sinecure back in Spain. The Cámara once again convened, on 14 May 1804, to present a new slate of names for the king's consideration, and again they unanimously selected Girbal in first place (figure 18, bottom). Charles IV (or perhaps his royal favorite, Manuel Godoy) again selected a person who was not on the list or affiliated with Ocopa. The choice, Friar Hipólito Sánchez Rangel, was a Franciscan and his current posting in the notoriously undesirable tropical port of Havana made him more likely to accept, which he did. A papal decree confirmed his appointment September 10, 1805.

It is unclear exactly what the king was doing in not appointing Girbal, given the lack of documented evidence, but there is only one logical possibility. Although the king had been willing to give Ocopa, a well-respected institution, several large concessions, he must have feared the missionaries' power. Though it is possible that Charles IV, widely known for being a rather passive individual, was taking direction from his royal favorite, Manuel Godoy, who though he had obtained high office was less than impressive when it came to actual governance. This situation was a classic dilemma that the kings of Spain had faced time and time again, and one that only intensified with the Bourbon reforms. The monarch had to give certain individuals and groups sufficient authority to accomplish tasks and govern so far away from the metropole, but he feared giving up too much power. The reforms only exacerbated this problem. As the crown tried to take more direct control, it had to endow some person or institution with increased political authority and material sufficient to implement it. But in doing so the crown was acting counter to its centralizing goal. It was an impossible paradox. The vast distances that separated Spain from its colonies made the type of oversight the Bourbons sought unattainable and in many cases destabilizing. Indeed, this was an empire that had flourished because of the consensus of institutions and communities at its periphery. In most cases, as in this, failure to recognize the importance of these institutions in governance usually only ended in disaster.

Problems with Maynas

As Requena's report had implied, not selecting a bishop from Ocopa would have deleterious consequences. In 1807, Rangel arrived in Quito, where he was anointed by that city's bishop, and on 20 February 1808 he finally entered Maynas. Despite Rangel's previous experience with tropical regions, he complained bitterly about the climate, stating in a letter just a year later that he was sick and covered with sores. He seemed surprised at the disorder that reigned in the region and begged the crown to be released from his new see. By far one of his most pressing problems was Ocopa's lack of cooperation. The royal decree that had created Maynas required that Ocopa provide most of the manpower for the diocese, but the college refused to recognize the authority of the new bishop in most matters. Rangel, on the king's recommendation, had selected Girbal as one of his principal assistants, perhaps in an attempt to ease the college's resentment toward the new bishop. Girbal had initially reported for duty at the new diocesan seat at Concepción de Jeberos, but after a short time he had abandoned his post, in the words of Rangel "like a fugitive."[43]

At the heart of the conflict was an uncertainty over who had pastoral oversight of the missions and parishes in Maynas. Both the papal bulls creating the Apostolic Institute and colonial law had allowed missionaries to have pastoral control of their own missions. This was because missions usually lay so far from the episcopal seat that expecting a bishop to oversee such enterprises was impractical. Instead the Church followed the practice of creating prefects, generally older missionaries, who would tend to all the duties of a bishop in their stead, such as performing confirmations, giving dispensations to couples with too close an affinity to get married, and, most important, licensing and supervising mission and parish priests. The crown and the archbishop of Lima had granted Ocopa a prefecture almost fifty years earlier. Previously the prefects in Ocopa's missions worked closely with its guardians and were effectively subordinate to them. The 15 July 1802 and subsequent decrees did not seem to clarify the issue. Perhaps it was assumed that since the bishop would be from Ocopa delineating such ecclesiastical jurisdictions would be unnecessary. Rangel, however, argued that the whole purpose of creating the diocese was to have a bishop present to see to all the duties formally performed by the prefect and attempted to dissolve the office. This effectively meant that all missionaries leaving Ocopa for their respective missions or parishes should receive license from Rangel. According to Rangel, it also signified that he could inspect and remove friars from their missions and even punish them if he deemed it necessary. Rangel argued that the Ocopa missionaries should engage in "the conquest of the Gentiles, under the authority of the bishop, nothing more."[44]

Friar Luis Colomer, former guardian and current prefect of Ocopa, countered Rangel's arguments with a nuanced response. Colomer agreed that in regards to the parishes of Maynas the bishop was correct in asserting pastoral oversight, but he observed that according to both canon and colonial law the missions still fell under the control of Ocopa. In making this argument he also conceded that those same laws recommended that after ten years all missions should be converted into parishes, but he was quick to point out that this clause had largely been ignored because of the slow development of most frontier zones and the lack of secular clergy to staff them. Certainly in this case, he argued, the missions in question were not strong enough in the faith to make such a change. Colomer also strongly disagreed with Rangel regarding his ability to restrict the movements of, punish, or remove Ocopa's missionaries without the guardian's permission. Though the bishop had the right to inspect parishes and even missions, he had no power over the missionaries since "the regular [clergy] are exempt and independent from the lord bishops in their persons and their monastery."[45]

Two additional factors weakened the bishop's authority. One was funding. Rather than give the pay for the Maynas missions and parishes to the bishop to disperse, as was typically done in other dioceses, the 15 July 1802 royal decree directly granted the funds to the Ocopa missionaries. In 1807, perhaps to force the two parties to work together, Requena suggested that missionaries be forced to submit a budget to the bishop for his approval. This idea, however, never came to fruition.[46] Although the viceroy of Peru, José Fernando de Abascal y Sousa, refused to disseminate the funds until the new bishop arrived, it appears he did so after 1808. Rangel complained bitterly about this discrepancy, but it seems that he never saw any of the crown funds marked for his diocese.[47]

The other factor weakening Rangel's authority was viceregal control over the placement of missionaries. Though the guardian of Ocopa claimed authority to decide in which missions and parishes his missionaries should be placed, after the 1787 election he had to submit his plan to the viceroy for approval. This meant that to get the viceroy to side with him over pastoral authority and funding Rangel would have to submit a plan to him as well. Ocopa had the advantage of a head start: two years before the bishop had even arrived in Maynas it had submitted its list, and Abascal had allowed the missionaries to begin making preparations for the new expansion.[48] When Rangel arrived in 1808 he submitted his own plan, but instead of waiting for approval he expected the missionaries to implement it immediately. Abascal seems to have largely ignored the bishop's request.[49]

The ultimate effect of Rangel's weakened authority was that the missionaries of Ocopa simply ignored him. Only one missionary, Girbal, ever even met with him personally. Ocopa maintained the missionary zones that it already occupied, but it never sent friars to service the new missions granted it by the 15 June 1802 royal degree.[50] Ocopa's inaction was not, however, motivated solely by its disregard for Rangel's episcopal authority. Nor indeed was Abascal's indifference to the bishop's pleas. By 1808, events in Spain and throughout its American possessions conspired to turn the attention of colonial administrators elsewhere, relegating the problems in Maynas to be dealt with later.

The Crisis of 1808

The outbreak of the French Revolution in 1789 deprived Spain of its most important ally in Europe. Since the French Bourbon dynasty had come to rule Spain in 1700, the two countries, bound by blood, had worked out a series of treaties that tightly joined the nations both militarily and politically. With the abdication and later execution of his cousin, French king Louis XVI, Charles IV attempted to respond militarily to the growing revolutionary threat in France. Political corruption caused in part by a weak-willed Charles and exacerbated by his incompetent royal favorite, Godoy, led to a series of humiliating Spanish defeats. Quickly Spain found itself on the losing end of a war with France and sued for peace. The resulting treaties not only forced Spain to recognize the new government of France but made it a virtual puppet of French foreign policy. Spain's vulnerability only intensified after the British routed a combined French and Spanish fleet at Trafalgar (off the southwest Spanish coast) in 1805. The defeat prompted Napoleon Bonaparte, now emperor of France, to establish the "continental system," which attempted to bar British merchants from trading with continental Europe. One of the lone holdouts of the system was longtime British ally Portugal. Without a navy, which had been crippled at Trafalgar, the only route available for France to conquer Portugal was through Spain. In 1807, Godoy negotiated an agreement that would allow French troops to pass through the country. Napoleon, however, saw an opportunity in the political chaos caused by the rivalry between Godoy and Charles' heir, Ferdinand. Instead of merely passing through Spain, French forces invaded it. After luring both Charles and Ferdinand to France, Napoleon forced them to abdicate in May 1808. Within a few months, French forces controlled most of Spain, except for a few pockets of fierce local resistance. Napoleon had his brother, Joseph Bonaparte, crowned king of Spain. A small rump of Spanish government officials fled to Cádiz, where that city's location on a peninsula and the British navy kept the French forces at bay. There Spain established a government in exile, first forming a ruling council (Junta Supremo) and later a national assembly (Cortes).[51]

The French invasion and subsequent abdication of the king of Spain caused a crisis of legitimacy in Spain's American possessions. The debates that followed centered on the question of who had sovereignty in the absence of the king. Political elites in the Americas almost universally rejected Joseph Bonaparte's claim, but without a legitimate king in power some began to question the authority of their own colonial administrators. Without a king how could a viceroy (quite literally a vice-king) or audiencia claim authority? The town councils of several viceregal and provincial capitals such as Quito and Buenos Aires, instead of letting colonial officials continue in office, set up their own ruling councils (*juntas*) to govern in the name of King Ferdinand VII, *el deseado* (the desired one). These cities did not fully accept the authority of the government in Cádiz either, but they did send representatives to the newly formed Cortes. Peru, as a bastion of colonial conservatives, experienced no such shift in governance. Some credit for this intransigence has to be given to Abascal's ironfisted rule of the viceroyalty. During the six years of the crisis, he put down numerous rebellions and attempts at autonomous government, including the brutal suppression of the junta of Quito, many of whose members were massacred. He prevented upper Peru (now Bolivia) from falling under the influence of the Buenos Aires government by having it annexed to the viceroyalty of Peru.[52]

Though Abascal completely ignored the liberal ministers in Cádiz, the government in exile did eventually try to intervene in the conflict between Ocopa and the bishop of Maynas. At first, as in most matters of government regarding Peru, officials in Cádiz left the decision of who ultimately should have pastoral control of the diocese to the viceroy.[53] It seems, however, that one or both of the factions pushed for Cádiz to adjudicate the matter, perhaps because the viceroy seemed to ignore the issue. After the formation of the Cortes in 1812, the new government attempted to resolve the conflict by siding completely with Ocopa. Citing the 15 July 1802 royal decree, the Cortes argued that the whole purpose of creating the diocese was to aid Ocopa's evangelization efforts. Following Friar Colomer's logic, it proclaimed that "all governors, bishops and other superiors in the Indies . . . should not interfere but leave [evangelization] completely to the discretion of the missionaries, or the college can in no way progress in the missions."[54] This, of course, did little to fix the problem, since the Cádiz government could not enforce its decision across the Atlantic.

The issue was taken up once again after the restoration of the monarchy in March 1814. Ferdinand VII, hoping to renew the type of royal absolutist government of his grandfather, Charles III, within a few months ordered the Cortes in Cádiz disbanded and annulled the extremely liberal 1812 constitution it had promulgated.[55] Rangel, who for several years had been residing outside of his diocese in the highlands, wrote to the king lamenting the poor state of the missions in Maynas and begged the crown to transfer him to a new episcopate. He blamed these conditions in his diocese on the Ocopa missionaries' lack of deference and inability to man all the Maynas missions.[56] In 1816 the Council of the Indies began to collect reports to make recommendations to the king on how to solve the matter definitively. As the guardian of Ocopa admitted, "I believe only our sovereign will be able to redeem such great evils."[57] The fiscal, in his report to the Council, suggested a simple solution: just let Bishop Rangel transfer to another diocese, as he had requested multiple times, and choose someone from Ocopa to replace him.[58] The Council's recommendations, which the king later approved, failed to heed the fiscal's opinion and instead produced a vaguely worded, partial reversal of the decision made by the Cortes of Cádiz. They confirmed the bishop's right to inspect the missions and parishes in Maynas but did not clarify completely the question of pastoral control. To confuse the matter further, they instructed the bishop and the governor of maynas to defer to the expertise of friars Girbal and Colomer on all military matters in the province.[59]

The overall effect of war in Spain, civil strife in Peru, and more specifically the conflict between the missionaries and the bishop was the "complete abandonment of the missions."[60] As one missionary described Maynas, "There are many abuses and superstitions; sins and scandals of all unspeakable types and ignorance of the mysteries [of God]." He hoped that another Saint Francis or Saint Dominic would come teach in the New World but concluded that it appeared that the earth was preparing itself for "God's last wrath."[61] In 1816 the guardian of Ocopa reported that the missionary zones of Huánuco, Cajamarquilla, and Maynas were all "forsaken" and without missionaries save two because of the "differences" between the bishop of Maynas and Ocopa.[62]

Even if these "differences" had not existed, however, and Ocopa had wanted to man all the missions and parishes of Maynas, it would have been impossible. The crisis of 1808 not only disrupted the crown's supervision of the Maynas project but cut off the literal lifeblood of Ocopa—the flow of missionaries from Spain. Even before Ocopa was granted the responsibility of servicing Maynas, the size of the groups of missionaries coming from Spain had been in decline. In 1797 only nine missionaries made the journey to replace those who had completed their ten-year term from the previous group in 1784. After the 15 July 1802 royal decree the crown promised that a significant number of missionaries would be provided for Ocopa, but the three groups that came between 1802 and 1805 totaled only forty friars.[63] This was not nearly enough to service the fifty-seven missions and parishes of Maynas, which according to papal decree had to be staffed by at least two missionaries each.[64] By 1816 the manpower situation had become desperate; of the nine missionaries who came in 1797 only two remained, and of the forty from the 1802–5 groups only fifteen.[65] The college was in fact forced to abandon the monastery at Huánuco because it had neither the manpower to maintain the physical facilities nor enough staff to meet the liturgical needs of the community.[66]

The Cádiz government had recognized the problem of too few missionaries at Ocopa, but because of the exigencies of war had few resources to help. In 1813 it asked for the bishops of the audiencia of Lima to give money to Cádiz so that Spain could send back missionaries, but nothing came of the idea.[67] After the restoration of the monarchy the crown optimistically promised one hundred new missionaries for Ocopa but admitted that it had few funds to pay for their journey.[68] The bigger problem, however, was recruitment. It seems that few friars in war-torn Spain were willing to make the journey to the Americas. The last group to leave, in 1818, consisted of only fourteen missionaries, two of which had already served in Ocopa, with one lay friar considered too old for service.[69] In 1819, Ocopa's collector of missionaries in Spain, Friar Joseph Lasala, attempted to send another group of sixteen missionaries but complained that he could not find a "national ship" bound for Callao, and that he was forced to look for a "neutral" vessel.[70] Those missionaries never left Cádiz. In 1822, crown officials in Cádiz ordered Lasala to stop collecting missionaries "due to occurrences overseas," but they added optimistically in the margin that it was only "for now."[71]

The Suppression of Ocopa and the End of Spanish Peru

The "occurrences overseas" that had ended the collection of new missionaries was nothing less than the collapse of the Spanish colonial government in most of the Americas. After the restoration of the monarchy, the practically autonomous governments that had survived the previous six years were unwilling to accept crown rule once again. Their defiance was only solidified by Ferdinand's attempt to move the colonial government back to a strictly regalist model. They had never fully accepted the legitimacy of the Cortes of Cádiz. Now, the king's annulment of the 1812 constitution demonstrated his unwillingness to negotiate a power-sharing agreement with creole elites. In South America, independence movements continued in the viceroyalties of New Granada and Rio de la Plata. As these regions began to win their independence, their leaders came to understand that there would be no permanent peace in the continent without removing the royalists from their stronghold in Peru.[72]

Independence leaders in Buenos Aires were the first to realize the threat Peru posed and as early as 1811 had begun campaigns in upper Peru to dislodge royalist forces. These expeditions, however, met with disaster. Further plans to invade Peru floundered as the independence movement in the Rio de la Plata region fractured. In 1814 one of the movement's most gifted military generals, José Francisco de San Martín y Matorras, made plans to attack Peru once again. San Martín concluded that the best route to the royalist heartland of South America was through Chile, not upper Peru. In 1817 he gathered an army of five thousand men in Mendoza (in what is now Argentina) and from there marched in several columns across the high mountain passes of the Andes (with the highest almost 12,000 feet) to surprise, along with their Chilean allies, the royalist army near Santiago. From Chile they launched an expedition to Peru, landing in Pisco in September 1820. By July 1821, San Martín had captured Lima and declared independence on the twenty-eighth of that month.[73]

In an attempt to gain local support, San Martín had prolonged his march toward Lima, and the delay allowed most of the royalist army to escape to the highlands. Trapped on the coast with the arduous task of dislodging a numerically superior force from the Andes, San Martín's expedition stalled. The general's problems were further exacerbated by the conservative local elites who remained unconvinced by the cause of independence. Many creole elites, particularly in the wake of the Tupac Amaru rebellion of the 1780s, feared that independence could lead to a race war that the indigenous majority of Peru would inevitably win. The fact that San Martín's army consisted mostly of freed blacks and indigenous peoples did little to calm their anxieties. San Martín's only hope lay in the other great rebel army in South America, led by General Simón Bolívar. Bolívar, over the previous half decade, had liberated all of the viceroyalty of New Granada (the modern-day nations of Venezuela, Colombia, and Ecuador) from royalist forces. Bolívar and San Martin met in Guayaquil in July 1822. What transpired between the two liberators is not known, but Bolivar's victory at Pichincha just a few months before gave him the negotiating advantage. Also, his control of the Ecuadorian highlands meant that his army was not penned in against the sea and was free to march south and face the Spanish on even terrain. It seems San Martin understood the weakness of his position and agreed (perhaps at Bolivar's insistence) to leave Peru entirely and give Bolívar command of his army.[74]

After almost a year spent gathering strength, in 1824 Bolivar's army made the arduous journey down the Andean cordillera. On 6 August the liberation army faced royalist forces on the plateau of Junín, only 85 miles (135 km) from Ocopa, where they inflicted a major defeat on the royalists, sending the Spanish army into full flight. On 8 December they completed their victory at the battle of Ayacucho, capturing the last viceroy of Peru, José de la Serna y Martínez de Hinojosa.[75]

As Bolívar's army passed through the Mantaro Valley from Junín to Ayacucho, they came upon the College of Ocopa. On 1 November, Bolívar ordered the community suppressed, their goods confiscated, and the missionaries sent to Lima under arrest.[76] The Liberator's heavy-handedness with the friars was probably due to three factors. For one, though Ocopa was a center of spiritual reflection and learning, the college was also headquarters of a large missionary operation that by the early nineteenth century had a recognizable military component. As late as 1817 the viceregal government had provided the college with arms, two cannons, thirty-nine rifles, and 6,876 cartridges to be distributed to their missionary outposts.[77] A second factor was that the missionaries were peninsular Spaniards, who were at least perceived as being unfavorable to the independentist cause, though there is no record of them opposing it. Finally, among the goods confiscated from the college were one hundred ounces of gold and 275 silver pesos, hard currency that was certainly useful to the Liberator's army.[78]

As a consequence of the suppression, Ocopa's network of missions completely collapsed. Not all the friars were captured by Bolivar's forces. The missionaries along the Ucayali were somehow able to slip away and made their way back to Spain. Those in Huanta followed the Spanish army into upper Peru and ultimately returned to Europe. One missionary, Manuel Plaza, simply stayed in his mission for twenty years, reappearing in Lima in 1844. For such dedicated service, Plaza was made the bishop of Cuenca (in Ecuador). The missionaries caught by the Liberation army, however, had a humiliating fate. Once they arrived in Lima, they were forced to try to rejoin their fellow Spaniards in the still besieged Real Felipe fortress in Callao. As the friars crossed the no-man's land between the two forces, the starving defenders in the fort began to fire at them to prevent them from entering. Peruvian officials eventually had pity on the friars and allowed them to incorporate into the Franciscan province in Lima.[79]

During the early nineteenth century the scope of Ocopa's territory and resources were unparalleled among the religious institutions in the New World. Ocopa oversaw, at least in theory, most of the missions and parishes in the Spanish Amazon and received a staggering stipend from the crown of nearly 12,000 pesos per year. This was in addition to vast property holdings in the Mantaro Valley and a separate missionary enterprise in Chiloé. This power was built upon the close relationship Ocopa had fostered with the state during the latter half of the eighteenth century and solidified with the election of its guardian in 1787.

These events demonstrate the ways changes in the Atlantic world affected Ocopa, but they also show how Ocopa and other actors on the ground shaped the politics of the empire. The fact that Maynas passed into the audiencia of Lima, and that a diocese was established there, had much to do with Ocopa's influence and relationship with Requena and ultimately bureaucrats back in Spain. Such interactions, as different groups vied for power, were the cornerstone of the Bourbon reform process despite its purported goal of centralizing authority. No matter how much the crown desired complete control, it had to govern through groups like Ocopa.

In the case of Ocopa, however, this relationship eventually created a dependency that tied the mission to the fate of the Spanish crown. As the king himself attempted to vie for more power, he refused to select one of the college's own as bishop of Maynas. Perhaps had he done so the college would have been able to maintain some autonomy and some semblance of a missionary program during the crisis of 1808. As it was, Ocopa was forced to rely on the adjudication of the viceroy, who was too busy to care, and a crown bureaucracy in Spain that no longer existed. Therefore, even before Bolivar arrived and suppressed the community, Ocopa and its missions were in shambles. As Ocopa pushed the crown for more resources, it was forced to reconstitute itself in a way that lacked the flexibility necessary to deal with the great changes surging through the Atlantic world during the early nineteenth century and under such pressure ceased to function.

Notes

1. Sobreviela, Report to the viceroy, 20 June 1789, Ocopa, AGI, Lima 686 (also found in Lima 1610).
2. Sobreviela, Letter to Croix, 11 March 1788, Ocopa, AGI, Lima 677.
3. Sobreviela, Report to the viceroy, 20 June 1789, Ocopa, AGI, Lima 686 (also found in Lima 1610).
4. Croix, Report to the crown, 5 May 1788, Lima, AGI, Lima 1607.
5. Sobreviela, Petition to the crown, 17 March 1789, Ocopa, AGI, Lima 686.
6. Clément, *El Mercurio Peruano*, vol. 1, 9–36, 261–67.
7. Meléndez, "Cultural Production of Space," 183–87; see also Arbesmann, "Contribution of the Franciscan College."
8. Joan Manuel Morales Cama, "Fray Manuel, guardián del Colegio de Ocopa, en el *Mercurio Peruano,*" in Morales Cama, *Diario de visita*, 5–21.
9. "Relación del Gobierno de la Exmo Señor Virrey del Perú, Fray Don Francisco Gil de Tobada y Lemus presentado a su sucesor el Señor Varon de Villanari," 1797, Lima, RAH 9-9-3 1707, ff. 129–55; AGI, Lima 703, c. 14, contains the "diarios" of two Girbal expeditions to Manoa.
10. Friars Buenaventura Marques, Manuel Haza, and Pedro Pablo Garcia, Petition to the viceroy, 10 July 1803, Sarayacu, MRREE-AL, LEB-12-5, ff. 1r–2r; Friar Luis Colomer, Petition to the viceroy, n.d., n.p., MRREE-AL, LEB-12-5, ff. 2r–6v; Fr. Manuel Gil, Letter to the bishop of Quito, 7 October 1795, Lima, CVU, Mss. Tomo 11, no. 20.
11. Francisco Pober, vecino of Trujillo, before the bishop of Trujillo, 3 July 1788, Trujillo, MRREE-AL, LEB-11-39, ff. 1r–3v; Don Josef de Castro, vecino of Asiento de Parcos, before the bishop of Trujillo, 3 July 1788, Trujillo, MRREE-AL, LEB-11-39, ff. 3r–5v; Licenciado Padre Martin Prieto, parish priest of Challas, before the bishop of Trujillo, 19 August 1788, Trujillo, MRREE-AL, LEB-11-39, ff. 6r–7v.
12. Christobal Gonzales, Letter to the bishop of Trujillo, 19 July 1788, MRREE-AL, LEB-11-39, 1r; Licenciado Padre Martin Prieto, parish priest of Challas, before the bishop of Trujillo, 19 August 1788, Trujillo, MRREE-AL, LEB-11-39, ff. 6r–7v.
13. Father Dr. Jose Antonio de la Via Orcasitas, parish priest of Jauja, Petition to the archbishop, 20 October 1790, Jauja, AAL, Sección San Francisco, X-1, f. 1rv; La Via y Orcasitas, Declaration, 19 October 1790, Jauja, AAL, Sección San Francisco, X-1, ff. 3r–5r; Father Buenaventura de Tagle Ysasaga, parish priest of Huancayo, Petition to the archbishop, 16 January 1791, Huancayo, AAL, Sección San Francisco, X-1, f. 6rv; La Via Orcasitas, Decree, 22 February 1791, AAL, Sección San Francisco, X-1, f. 7r.
14. Trujillo, Petition to the Council, 10 September 1788, Madrid, AGI, Lima 1609.
15. Trujillo, Report, 6 October 1790, Madrid, AGI, Lima 1607.
16. Fiscal's report, 6 July 1788, Madrid, AGI, Lima 1607; the fiscal notes the king's ascent to the consulta that same day at the end of the document.
17. Missionaries of Ocopa, Letter to the Juan María Gálvez, intendant of the Tarma, 19 April 1788, Ocopa, AGI, 1609.
18. Gálvez, Letter to the viceroy, 24 April 1788, Tarma, AGI, 1609.
19. Decree of the Real Acuerdo, 18 May 1788, Lima, AGI, Lima 1609; González, Report to the crown, 7 July 1788, Madrid, AGI, Lima 1609.

20. Croix, Letter to His Majesty through the Council of the Indies, 16 August 1788, Lima, AGI, Lima 1611. (AGI, Lima 1611 and 1612 comprise the whole eight volumes.)

21. Croix cites the first and second documents of the second cuarderno as these royal orders. They are royal orders, signed by the minister of the Indies, José de Gálvez at San Lorenzo, 16 October 1778, and two at San Ildefonso, 7 October 1783, AGI, Lima 1611.

22. Echavarria, Report to the commissary-general, 25 January 1788, Madrid, AGI, Lima 1607

23. Council of the Indies, Consult, 20 June 1795, Madrid, AGI, Lima 1607.

24. Trujillo mentions the testimony of these men in several correspondences and petitions, such as Trujillo, Petition to the Council, 10 September 1788, Madrid, AGI, Lima 1609; and Trujillo, Report, 6 October 1790, Madrid, AGI, Lima 1607.

25. Trujillo, Report, n.d. (sometime between 1790 and 1795), Madrid, AGI, Lima 1609.

26. González, Petition to the crown, 7 January 1794, Madrid, AGI, Lima 1607.

27. Council of the Indies, Consult, 20 June 1795, Madrid, AGI, Lima 1607; González, Petition to the crown, 28 October 1785, Madrid, AGI, Lima 1607. Of the two missionary tracts, one focused on the Franciscan missionary activity in Chiloé, advocating the construction of a new college de propaganda fide on the island to directly manage its mission parishes. The second, titled *Calamores Apostólicos,* was a tract intended to recruit new missionaries in Spain for service in the Apostolic Institute in the Americas and Philippines. A special thanks to the library at Ohio Dominican University for providing me an electronic copy of this tract.

28. Álvarez, Report to the crown, 4 December 1790, Madrid, AGI, Lima 1609.

29. This note from the fiscal appears at the end of a petition from Álvarez, 29 October 1790, Madrid, AGI, Lima 1607.

30. Council of the Indies, Consult (with a note from the king's secretary attached), 2 September 1793, Madrid, AGI, Lima 1607. Bejarano's posting to Tarata is noted in Council of the Indies, Consult, 17 December 1794, Madrid, AGI, Lima 1607.

31. Council of the Indies, Consult, 20 June 1795, Madrid, AGI, Lima 1607.

32. Ibid.

33. Council of the Indies, Consult, 2 September 1793, Madrid, AGI, Lima 1607. The list of missionaries collected by Villanueva in 1797 is found in AGI, Arribadas, 241.

34. Death warrant for Don Manuel Antonio Perez, 16 November 1812, Madrid, AGI, Indiferente 962.

35. Francisco Requena, Report to the crown, 29 March 1799, Madrid, AGI, Lima 1580; Espinoza, *Amazonía del Perú*, 128–29, 335–52.

36. Espinoza, *Amazonía del Perú*, 326–27.

37. Ibid., 352–58; Francisco Requena, Report to the crown, 29 March 1799, Madrid, AGI, Lima 1580.

38. Espinoza, *Amazonía del Perú*, 352–58.

39. Ibid,. 365–72; Royal decree, 15 July 1802, Madrid, AGI, Lima 1580.

40. Diego Calvo, governor of Maynas, Petition to the crown, 12 January 1803, AL-MRREE, LEB-3-26, Caja 88.

41. Casimiro de Sotomayor e Yparraquirre, Summary, Lima, 21 January 1806, AL-MRREE, LEB-12-9, Caja 94, ff. 2r–7v.

42. Cámara of the Indies, Consult, 19 September 1803, Madrid, AGI, Lima 1580; Juan Antonio Mantilla, Letter to the crown, 14 April 1804, Valladolid, AGI, Lima 1580.

43. Rangel, Letter to José Fernando Abascal y Sousa, viceroy of Peru, 2 January 1809, n.p., AGI, Lima 1580; Espinoza, *Amazonía del Perú*, 405–6.

44. Fiscal's summary of three letters from Rangel dated 10 May 1808, 23 September 1808, and 8 April 1809, Madrid, AGI, Lima 1580; Rangel, Letter to the guardian of Ocopa, 14 December 1810, Jeberos, AGI, Lima 1580.

45. Colomer, Letter to Viceroy Abascal, 1 December 1809, Ocopa, MRREE, LEB-3-30, Caja 88, ff. 18r–21r.

46. Fiscal's report, 20 June 1807, Madrid, AGI, Lima 1580.

47. Junta Superior de Real Hacienda [headed by the viceroy], Edict, 28 March 1806, Lima, AL-MRREE, LEB-3-25, Caja 88; Rangel, Letter to Colomer, 5 May 1808, Jeberos, AL-MRREE, LEB-3-30, Caja 88, ff. 11r–16v; Rangel, Letter to Abascal, 3 March 1810, Jeberos, AL-MRREE, LEB-3-30, Caja 88, ff. 52r–54v.

48. Several letters regarding the submission of this plan and the negotiation between the viceroy, the intendant of Tarma, and Ocopa are located in AL-MRREE, LEB-12-2, Caja 94, and LEB-12-25, Caja 95.

49. Rangel, Letter to Abascal, date illegible, copied 21 May 1810, AL-MRREE, LEB-3-29, Caja 88.

50. Rangel, Letter to Abascal, 2 January 1809, n.p., AGI, Lima 1580; Rangel, Petition to the crown, 15 April 1814, Jeberos, AGI, Lima 1580.

51. Lynch, *Bourbon Spain*, 375–421.

52. Lynch, *Spanish-American Revolutions*, 157–84.

53. Junta Supremo de Cádiz, 23 December 1810, Cádiz, AGI, Lima 1580.

54. Manuel Plaza, Letter to the assessor general, 13 April 1814, Lima, AL-MRREE, LEB-12-11, Caja 94, ff. 1r–4v.

55. The Constitution of 1812 was remarkably radical legal framework for its time. Among other things, it granted almost universal male suffrage throughout Spain and its colonies.

56. Rangel, Petition to the crown, 15 June 1814, n.p., AGI, Lima 1580. The guardian of Ocopa, Friar Geronimo Zurita, reveled in Rangel's absence in a letter to Friar Pablo de Moya, commissary-general of Indies, 14 August 1816, Ocopa, AL-MRREE, LEB-12-15, Caja 94.

57. Friar Geronimo Zurita, Letter to Friar Pablo de Moya, commissary-general of Indies, 14 August 1816, Ocopa, AL-MRREE, LEB-12-15, Caja 94.

58. Fiscal's report, 13 August 1816, Madrid, AGI, Lima 1580.

59. Council of the Indies, Consult, 19 June 1818, Madrid, AGI, Lima 1580.

60. Friar Geronimo Zurita, Letter to Friar Pablo de Moya, commissary-general of Indies, 14 August 1816, Ocopa, AL-MRREE, LEB-12-15, Caja 94.

61. Friar Francisco Andiviela, Letter to the archbishop of Lima, 1 November 1816, Ocopa, AAL, Sección San Francisco, XI-24, ff. 1r–2r.

62. Ibid.

63. Royal decree, 15 July 1802, Madrid, AGI, Lima 1580; Heras, *Libro de Incorporaciones,* 75–85.

64. Espinoza, *Amazonía del Perú*, 422–23.

65. Heras, *Libro de Incorporaciones,* 75–85.

66. Council of the Indies, Letter to the viceroy of Peru, 28 February 1820, Madrid, AL-MRREE, LEB-12-8, Caja 94, f. 2rv.

67. Cortes of Cádiz, Royal order, 2 June 1813, Cádiz, CVU, Papeles Varios, Mss. Tomo 24, no. 32.

68. Royal decree, 20 July 1816, Madrid, AGI, Lima 1606.

69. Fiscal's report, 18 April 1818, Madrid, AGI, Lima 1608; List of missionaries embarking for Peru, 17 March 1818, Cádiz, AGI, Lima 1808.

70. Friar José Lasala and Friar Antonio Boria, Letter to Juan Buenventa Bestard, commissary-general of Indies, 1 April 1819, Cádiz, AGI, Lima 1608.

71. Accountant general of Cádiz, Report, 27 November 1822, Cádiz, AGI, Indiferente 2979A.

72. See Lynch, *Spanish-American Revolutions*, chaps. 2, 5–8.

73. Ibid., 137–40, 171–73.

74. Ibid., 175–87.
75. Ibid., 271–72.
76. Riva-Agüero, "Los franciscanos en el Perú," 20–21.
77. Josef Gomala de Prado, Letter to Friar Timoteo Delgado, guardian of Ocopa, 21 April 1817, Huánuco, AL-MRREE, LEB-12-16, Caja 94, f. 17r.
78. Padre Rafael Castro, List of the goods from Ocopa, signed by Félix Balega, 9 March 1822, AGN, Sección Republicana, Ministerio de Hacienda, OL-57-2; Delgado, Letter to the minister of Hacienda, 24 June 1825, AGN, Jauja, Ministerio de Hacienda, OL-131-425.
79. Riva-Agüero, "Los franciscanos en el Perú," 20–21; Jorge Benevente, archbishop of Lima, Declaration, 30 January 1738, Lima, AAL, Sección San Francisco, XV, ff. 1r–2r.

Conclusion

Many aspects of Ocopa's trajectory within Spain's colonial empire reveal the nature of the Bourbon reform process. When the Apostolic Institute entered Peru, it was the darling of many early reformers, particularly in Madrid. Ocopa's popularity among Bourbon bureaucrats may have seemed contradictory to the goals of the reforms, since part of the reform process sought to wrest power away from traditionally powerful nongovernmental institutions such as the Church. Yet the Apostolic Institute's dedication to expanding Spain's hegemony to its vast American borderland aligned almost perfectly with many of its other aims. Furthermore, its missionaries, and the Apostolic Institute writ large, consisted of mostly peninsular Spaniards. Bourbon reformers saw these peninsulars as free of the impediments and local corruption many government administrators believed characterized the then creole-led regular religious institutions throughout the Americas. For these reasons, early on Ocopa's missionaries were able to occupy a tenuous middle ground, where they presented enough positive change to receive crown support. This is not to say that they did not have their critics, particularly within the viceroyalty of Peru. They were still a powerful regular religious institution in a time when curtailing the clergy's political and economic power was becoming increasingly popular. At least at first, however, their critics had to remain relatively silent, opposing them through neglect rather than out-and-out hostility. Though in many cases indigenous groups were able to exploit the instability caused by the friction between the college and viceregal authorities, as well as the missionaries' tenuous position in the Montaña, these smaller rebellions seem to have had little effect on the larger balance of power between Ocopa and Lima.

The Juan Santos Atahualpa rebellion changed that equilibrium, opening up the missionaries to harsh criticisms. Juan and Ulloa's *Noticias Secretas de América* was probably the most direct, but not the most damaging. Although Viceroy José Antonio Manso de Velasco seems to have at first wanted to support the missionaries, at least publicly, whether out of genuine interest or simply duty, this desire disappeared as soon as the missionaries became involved with Friar Calixto. Implications of Calixto's involvement in the Lima conspiracy seem to have signaled to Manso de Velasco that Ocopa was just as potentially treasonous as its Franciscan brothers elsewhere.

Ocopa, however, was able to weather this opposition. This fortitude had to do, in large part, with its ability to present a unified front. More than anyone, Friar Joseph de San Antonio probably deserves credit, staying in Spain and continuing to lobby the crown despite attacks against the college. He was able to convince crown authorities in Madrid that, despite their desire to curtail the "excesses" of the regular clergy, Ocopa was still an exception to the failures other Franciscans were experiencing. The lack of dissension among Ocopa's ranks further bolstered its ability to resist a viceregal takeover or perhaps even suppression. Once political conditions improved after the fall of Ensenada and the "Jesuit party," Ocopa's adroit lobbying and tight ranks allowed it to be reborn.

As Ocopa entered the 1760s, it again began to take advantage of two competing narratives in the empire. Though it still fulfilled Spain's religious mandate to spread the word of God to the "infidels," it also had enough elements that reformers could support. This was only magnified by the ascension of Charles III, whose more pro-Franciscan tendencies helped Ocopa sell its narrative that it was indeed strengthening the empire. Furthermore, the expulsion of the Jesuits aided the college in this cause, presenting it as one of the only viable solutions for controlling Peru's Amazonian frontier. Ocopa's seemingly invulnerability to criticism among the colonial bureaucracy can be demonstrated in the aftermath of the Manoa rebellion. Manoa had resulted in more friars' deaths than the Juan Santos Atahualpa rebellion. Certainly, though the circumstances of the two uprisings were distinct, the relative reaction of colonial administrators is telling. Whereas after the Juan Santos Atahualpa rebellion viceregal officials' reports were thick with innuendo and even outright accusations that the missionaries' misconduct caused the uprising, virtually no such blame was evident after Manoa.

Again this situation could not last, as a second wave of reforms began during the 1770s and '80s. In particular, the introduction of the "new method" had changed much of the rhetoric in the empire regarding the proper way to evangelize the frontier. What actual effect this had on frontier zones is debatable, but Ocopa certainly would have been a possible target for this reform had its powerful influence at court not kept it above most debates regarding the "new method," at least in the short term. In the long term, however, Ocopa's resistance could not last. This was because, unlike the situation during the Juan Santos Atahualpa rebellion, Ocopa was not unified. The addition of Friar Francisco Álvarez de Villanueva and the Aragonese faction gave the viceregal government the tool by which it could fracture and at least partially subdue Ocopa.

Still, the Aragonese faction did not give over some of Ocopa's autonomy for nothing. In exchange for increased viceregal control and acquiescence to more of the principles of the "new method," the college received unprecedented crown support. This largesse culminated in the granting of ecclesiastical jurisdiction of almost the entirety of the Comandancia General of

Maynas, which included most of the Peruvian Amazon. Though the missionaries could have not known it at the time, this great endowment was ultimately worthless. True control of Maynas was contingent upon one of Ocopa's brothers being named bishop over the newly created diocese. This effectively extended control of Ocopa's internal workings beyond just the viceroy and to the monarch himself. Though most within the government (and without) saw one of Ocopa's own receiving the bishop's mitre as the best possible outcome, the king (or perhaps Godoy) did not. He (whoever he was) must have seen Ocopa's control over the distant province as a threat to his own power, rather than as a practical administrative matter, and thus twice named someone from outside the college as bishop. The selection of an outsider and indeed Ocopa's absolute dependence on the monarch to control even its most basic internal workings eroded any gains it had made through the election of 1787. The suppression of Ocopa in 1824 perhaps would have occurred independent of these events, but certainly by the time Bolivar's armies arrived it was in a diminished state. Without funding, manpower, or control of the missions, all at this point derived from the crown, the college, save for a few enclaves, had effectively ceased to function in its principal goal of missionizing the Montaña.

Broadly, the arc of Ocopa over 115 years was the result of the overall trends in the Spanish empire and the Atlantic world, but these movements were not the reflections of some sort of invisible philosophical force but rather those of the interaction of myriad groups and individuals engaged in multiple, mutually reconstituting encounters. If the history of Ocopa demonstrates anything, it is the importance of groups at all levels—how they grapple with new ideas and new pressures from other groups and then act upon their new circumstances. In the process of changing themselves and others to meet ever-shifting cultural contexts and find new spaces in constantly evolving political, social, and economic landscapes, the missionaries wanted to continue their evangelization, aided by the crown, while remaining free of its control. Viceregal officials hoped to curtail the power of large religious institutions in the hinterland of their jurisdiction where they struggled to exert control. They also wanted to keep their masters back in Madrid pleased. Crown officials in Spain wanted to exert more control over a vast empire, but in this they saw Ocopa not as a problem but as a solution, hoping that the peninsular friars could develop the region economically and secure the border against Portugal. As for the montañeses, though some seemed to accept the teachings of the friars, other rejected mission life and worked to maintain their autonomy, through violence if necessary. Each of these groups pursued its own agenda and inevitably had to change that agenda according to the pressures exerted by the others.

Ultimately the Bourbon reformers failed to understand that the great strength of their empire lay not in absolute devotion to royal authority but in allowing local political actors to interpret and negotiate the terms of their service to the crown. In this way they could serve the needs of the empire while fulfilling local necessities. Therefore, under pressure the far-flung parts of the empire remained for the most part loyal, since local leaders could still convince the people of the benefits of being part of the system. In this way groups such as Ocopa were critical as mediators between the crown and the populace. Not only did the missionaries attempt to instill Hispanic values, they tried to demonstrate the benefits of participation in the empire through material, such as steel tools and European wares; protection from European rivals, such as the British; and, most important in the friars' view, salvation. As the Bourbon government attempted to destroy or coopt these groups, it worked only to undo this framework, which had proven its resilience time and time again. When the crisis of 1808 struck, therefore, the empire lacked the institutional resources to cope and eventually disintegrated.

Ocopa, as a center of missionary activity and place of instruction for friars (or aspiring friars), did not end with the colonial period. As an institution it would rise and fall throughout the next two centuries, just as it had done in the previous. In 1836 the college was reformed by order of Peruvian president José de Obregoso and once again began missionary activities in the Peruvian Amazon. This period produced many famous missionaries, still remembered in Peru today, including Father Pío Sarobe, whose case for beatification and canonization remains ongoing. In 1908, Ocopa ceased to function as an independent college de propaganda fide and was subsumed into the Franciscan province of San Francisco Solano. Ocopa continued, however, to be an important center of ideas and learning. In 1928 it became the principal seminary for the province, training a generation of Franciscans. Its students included Juan Landázuri Ricketts, later a cardinal and archbishop of Lima. Cardinal Landázuri was a proponent of liberation theology and in the 1960s a major player in both the Conference of Latin American Bishops and the Second Ecumenical Council of the Vatican. In 1973 the seminary at Ocopa closed. The former college now houses a museum and research library. A small community of friars still live there, servicing the spiritual needs of the nearby communities of the Mantaro Valley.

Appendix: Individuals Important to the Events Described

(Persons are listed by the name most frequently used in the text.)

Álvarez de Villanueva, Friar Francisco. Controversial procurador and apoderado for Ocopa. Álvarez de Villanueva was recruited for Ocopa in 1768. As he passed through Chile en route to Ocopa, he was retained by an army captain to be his chaplain. After the captain died, Álvarez de Villanueva finally incorporated into Ocopa, in 1770. Within a month, he returned to Lima as Ocopa's procurator. In 1775, Álvarez de Villanueva returned to Spain as the apoderado for Ocopa in order to collect a new group of missionaries. While in Madrid he made numerous proposals that eventually infuriated Ocopa's new leadership (Gallardo and González Agueros) back in Peru. When he returned to Peru in 1785, he attempted to gain control of the college, principally with the backing of missionaries he had himself recruited, the so-called Aragonese faction. Initially unsuccessful, he was able to get the backing of the viceroy, and in the election of 1787 one of the Aragonese faction, Manuel de Sobreviela, was elected Ocopa guardian. Álvarez de Villanueva returned to Spain, where he remained as Ocopa's apoderado until at least 1812.

Amat y Junyent, Manuel de. Viceroy of Peru from 1761 to 1776. Amat's term of office signaled a reprieve for Ocopa from the neglect of previous administrations. He lacked the personal animosities that Castelfuerte and Manso de Velasco had harbored against the clergy and adhered more closely than his predecessor to decrees emanating from Madrid regarding Ocopa.

Assia, Mateo de. Cacique for the mission towns of Metraro and Eneno. At first Assia was one of the most loyal caciques to the missionaries of Ocopa. In 1727 he helped Friar Juan de la Marca explore the Pajonal. Assia was also brother-in-law to Antonio Gatica, an African servant (possibly slave) of the missionaries. Assia seems to have had a falling out with the missionaries when he was whipped for interfering with the punishment of his brother Bartolomé, who was accused of polygamy. He along with Gatica became one of Juan Santos's principal generals.

Calixto de San José Túpac Inka. Lay friar and missionary and possible member of the 1750 Lima conspiracy. Calixto was born in Tarma in 1710 of noble

Inca descent. In 1727 he entered the Franciscan order in Lima as a donado. Calixto spent almost two decades in Lima working for various Franciscan institutions, principally as a procurador. He also spent a few years working as a missionary for Ocopa. In 1744, Calixto began to meet with indigenous leaders who were upset that natives were not allowed to become priests. Sometime before 1748, after working in Cusco and Quillabamba, Calixto returned to Lima, where he illegally printed a polemical treatise against the established colonial order known as the *Representación Verdadera,* which advocated the creation of an indigenous clergy. In 1749 he left Lima and traveled with a license to Madrid, where he presented the *Representación Verdadera* to King Ferdinand VI. After the treatise was initially well received and Calixto was elevated to a lay friar, word of the 1750 Lima conspiracy and Huarochirí rebellion reached Madrid and royal interest in his proposals cooled, especially since the viceroy had blamed both events on Calixto's rabble-rousing. Consequently, Ocopa's relationship with Calixto seems to have had a negative impact on the college's relationship with the viceroy, possibly leading to a cessation in crown campaigns against the Juan Santos Atahualpa rebels. Calixto eventually returned to Lima but was arrested by Viceroy Manso de Velasco on suspicion of fomenting rebellion and exiled to Spain in 1759.

Castelfuerte, Marqués de, José de Armendáriz y Perurena. Viceroy of Peru from 1724 to 1736. Castelfuerte was a highly aggressive regalist who attempted to use the royal patronage to the full extent possible. Given the vicissitudes of the political climate of the early Bourbon reform period, his ability to curtail the clergy was limited, but it set the stage for later reforms. His attitude toward Ocopa was more neglectful than malevolent.

Charles III. King of Spain from 1759 to 1788. Charles is remembered as Spain's most absolute and reformist monarch, but he did have a proclivity for the Franciscans. Consequently, the first few decades of his reign were a period of growth and crown largesse for Ocopa, which was seen as one of the most effective and pious Franciscan communities in Peru.

Croix, Teodoro de. Viceroy of Peru from 1784 to 1790. Croix spent much of his energies obsessed with his own authority as he fought off challenges from other royal officials sent from Madrid to help reform Peru. He backed Álvarez de Villanueva in his attempt to gain control of Ocopa, most likely seeing it as a way to extend his own authority into one of the most powerful regular religious institutions in the viceroyalty.

Ensenada, Marques de la, Zenón de Somodevilla y Bengoechea. Minister of finance, war, navy, and the Indies from 1743 to 1754. Ensenada was already an important force at court, but with the ascension of the relatively weak-willed Ferdinand VI he became an even more powerful figure within the inner circle of the royal government. He was also the patron of Manso de Velasco and most likely secured his appointment as viceroy in 1745. Ensenada along with two other important ministers, secretary of state José de Carvajal y Lancaster and José de Rávago, the king's confessor, constituted what was known as the "Jesuit party." Not only did they advocate for the Society of Jesus, they sought to curtail what they saw as the excesses of the other regular clergy. After the death of Carvajal, Ensenada was unable to hold onto power and was eventually accused of secretly trying to start a war and exiled from court in 1754.

Gallardo, Friar Mauricio. Guardian of Ocopa from 1783 to 1787. Gallardo first incorporated into Ocopa in 1745 and was one of the missionaries expelled from Sonomoro by Juan Santos. He later returned to Lima, where he taught novices at Lima's principal monastery for many decades. In 1782 he reincorporated into Ocopa, where he served for several months in the Huanta missions before being elected guardian in 1783. Gallardo clashed with Álvarez de Villanueva, who attempted to oust him on several occasions, over the direction of Ocopa. After the election of guardian in 1787, Gallardo left Ocopa and reincorporated into Lima's monastery.

Gatica, Antonio. African (possibly the Ocopa missionaries' slave) and sergeant major of the mission village of Eneno. Gatica's exact origin is not known. A man named Antonio (no last name) was listed as a godfather in the Eneno registry in 1732 and was said to be from Mina (el Mina), along the Gold Coast of Africa. Gatica held a prominent position in the community. He was married to Margarita Appinur, an Asháninka woman and the sister of Eneno's cacique, Mateo Assia. As sergeant major, Gatica was tasked with the training of the local militia. He personally performed two baptisms on two separate occasions when the individuals were at the point of death and no friar was present in the mission, which was permissible by canon law under such circumstances. Nonetheless, when the rebellion broke out, Antonio Gatica, along with his brother-in-law, became one of Juan Santos's principal captains.

Girbal, Friar Narciso. Ocopa missionary and member of the Aragonese faction. Girbal became one of the most famous Ocopa missionaries when several expeditions he led were featured in series of articles in the *Mercurio Peruano.* In 1803 and again 1804 he was considered for the position of bishop of Maynas and received unanimous support from the Council of the Indies. The crown ultimately chose someone else, perhaps out of fear of giving too much power to Ocopa.

González Agueros, Friar Pedro. Guardian of Ocopa from 1780 to 1783. González Agueros along with Gallardo was one of the most ardent opponents of Álvarez de Villanueva and the Aragonese faction. Shortly before the election of 1787, Ocopa's guardian (Gallardo) made González Agueros Ocopa's apoderado, but the viceroy refused to recognize the appointment and instead allowed him to travel to Spain only if he officially left the community. When the new guardian (Sobreviela) appointed a new apoderado (Álvarez de Villanueva), González Agueros contested the appointment before the Council of the Indies and lost. He was later allowed to return to the Americas, but not to Ocopa.

Manso de Velasco, José Antonio, Conde de Superunda. Viceroy of Peru from 1745 to 1761. Manso de Velasco is often credited with overseeing the reconstruction of Lima and Callao after the earthquake and tsunami of 1746. As part of these efforts, he targeted the regular clergy, attempting to limit their resurgence in the city. Although he was unsuccessful in many aspects, he did impede Ocopa's efforts to retake its missions lost in the Juan Santos Atahualpa rebellion. Though at first he had promised to help, Manso de Velasco eventually ordered an end to all expeditions against the rebels and in 1756 cordoned off the region. He also for a time cut the Ocopa missionaries' funding in half, justifying it by the loss of the majority of their mission villages. Manso de Velasco ultimately had to back off from his attacks against the missionaries after the fall of his political patron, the marqués de la Ensenada.

Rangel, Friar Hipólito Sánchez. Bishop of Maynas from 1805 to 1824. Rangel was selected for the diocese in 1804 over the objections of clergymen and crown officials who worked in the Peruvian Amazon and believed that only a member of the College of Ocopa could successfully be bishop of Maynas. In February 1808 he finally entered Maynas. Despite Rangel's previous experience with tropical regions, he complained bitterly about the climate. Consequently, he spent most of his term of office outside his diocese. The Ocopa missionaries gave him little help, but after the French invasion of Spain in 1808 there was little help to be found anywhere.

Rosa, Ana. Setebo translator and guide. Ana was captured in an expedition to the Ucayali in 1757. When the Ocopa missionaries returned in 1760, she guided and translated for them throughout the region. She eventually introduced them to a local cacique, Runcato, who for a time became their ally. She remained in the Ucayali River basin after the Manoa rebellion in 1766 and once again aided the missionaries when they returned in 1790.

Runcato. Setebo cacique. In 1766, Runcato initially invited missionaries into his village, perhaps to gain access to their tools. Runcato's village, Manoa, had become the Ocopa base of operations along the Ucayali, from which Ocopa established two other stations over the next six years. In 1766, however, he had a falling out with the friars and eventually rebelled against them, resulting in the deaths of sixteen missionaries.

San Antonio, Joseph de. For several decades Ocopa's collector of new missionaries in Spain and then eventually the college's first apoderado at court. San Antonio came to Ocopa in 1730 in one of the first groups to come directly from Spain. After serving in the mission villages, he began escorting groups of new missionaries from Spain to Ocopa. Although he had essentially acted as such up to that point, in 1762 he became Ocopa's apoderado, allowing him to act in the college's name while in Spain. Over decades, he sent numerous petitions to the crown on behalf of Ocopa.

San Joseph, Francisco de. Founder of the community of Apostolic missionaries that would eventually occupy the College de Propaganda Fide of Santa Rosa de Ocopa. Born Melchor Francisco Jiménez in 1654 in the Spanish village of Mondéjar near Toledo, he served six years as a soldier in the Spanish army in Flanders, including during Spain's involvement in the Franco-Dutch war of 1672–78. He took the habit of a Franciscan in the monastery of San Julián near Burgos, renaming himself Francisco de San Joseph. In 1692 at the age of thirty-eight, San Joseph sailed to Mexico in the service of the Apostolic Institute. He stayed two years at Querétero before leaving for Guatemala City, where he aided in the establishment of a community of missionaries that later became Ocopa. San Joseph stayed in Guatemala City only a few months before leaving to proselytize among the "infidel" nations of modern-day Costa Rica. In 1708, he left for Lima with six other missionaries to extend the Apostolic Institute into Peru. In 1709 he established two small mission reductions at Quimirí and Cerro de la Sal. He led the missionaries until 1736, when he died suddenly at Ocopa.

San Joseph II, Francisco de. Guardian of Ocopa from 1767 to 1770. Born Francisco Antonio Josef de Mora Fernández in 1721 in the Castilian village of Manzanares, La Mancha, San Joseph was most likely part of the local hidalgo class. At age sixteen he took the habit of a Franciscan at a college near Cartagena and was later ordained a priest in the diocese of Cuenca. In 1751, San Antonio recruited San Joseph. After arriving in Peru in 1752, San Joseph distinguished himself as an able missionary and was part of the first expedition to the Manoa region. His biographer claimed that he had been referred to as *el Apóstol de las Montañas del Perú* (the Apostle of the Peruvian Jungle) but admits that he was vulgarly known as *el quatro ojos* (four eyes), probably because he wore spectacles. After his election to guardian of Ocopa in 1767, San Joseph II enacted a series of reforms aimed at controlling the missionaries under his charge more effectively as well as improving the college's reputation for diligence and obedience, which had been tarnished during the turbulent 1740s and '50s. (*Note: Since this Francisco de San Joseph shares the same vocational name as Ocopa's founder, I have added "II" to his name to avoid confusion.)*

Santos Atahualpa, Juan. Leader of the rebellion of the same name from 1742 to 1752. The Franciscan chronicler José Amich described Santos as a mestizo. He reportedly spoke or had knowledge of at least four languages: Spanish, Latin, Quechua, and Asháninka. He claimed to have been the servant of a Jesuit priest, whom he had accompanied to Europe and Africa. According to Amich's account, Juan Santos then entered the Ocopa missions in May 1742 in an attempt to flee justice after he had killed a man in Huamanga (modern-day Ayacucho). While wandering through the high jungle he encountered the cacique of Quisopango, Mateo Santabangori, who guided him to his village, where he began his rebel movement. More contemporary reports refute Amich's version written several decades later, instead indicating that between 1729 and 1730 Santos traveled along the Peruvian Andes attempting to rally support for his cause, then made his way to the missions. Considering Santos's fluency in the local dialect and his widespread local support, it is more likely that he had spent considerable time among the montañeses before the outbreak of hostilities in 1742. Santos ultimate goal was to extend his rebellion to the more populous highlands and to the rest of Peru. Despite his successes, he was never to accomplish his goal, as demonstrated by his inability to hold the highland village of Andamarca in 1752. Santos most likely died as a result of internal conflicts within his own alliance sometime around 1755.

Sobreviela, Friar Manuel de. Guardian of Ocopa. One of the Aragonese faction, Sobreviela was elected guardian in 1787. His time in office is seen as one of the greatest periods of expansion and exploration for the college and, when the Council of the Indies ruled in 1795 that his election was illegal, he was allowed to stay in the community.

Troncoso, Benito. Frontier governor of Jauja involved in two expeditions to quash the Juan Santos Atahualpa rebellion in 1743 and 1746. Troncoso had close ties to the College of Ocopa. His wife, Teresa Apolaya, donated a large portion of her dowry to the community, and he served as it financial agent for several years in the 1750s.

Notes

Abbreviations

AAL	Archivo Arzobispal de Lima
AGI	Archivo General de Indias, Seville
AGN	Archivo General de la Nación, Lima
AHN	Archivo Histórico Nacional, Madrid
AL-MRREE	Archivo de Limites, Ministerio de Relaciones Exteriores, Lima
AO	Archivo del Convento de Santa Rosa de Ocopa
ARJ	Archivo Regional de Junín, Huancayo
ASFL	Archivo San Francisco de Lima
BNE	Biblioteca Nación de España, Madrid
BNP	Biblioteca Nación del Perú, Lima
BRPR	Biblioteca Real del Palacio Real, Madrid
CVU	Colección Rubén Vargas Ugarte, Lima
JSEI	Loayza, *Juan Santos, el invencible* (1942)
RAH	Biblioteca de la Real Academia de Historia, Madrid

Unless otherwise noted, translations of archival documents and secondary literature not in English are those of the author.

Bibliography

Manuscripts

Archivo Arzobispal de Lima, Peru
    Sección San Francisco
Archivo de Limites, Ministerio de Relaciones Exteriores, Lima, Peru
Archivo del Convento de Santa Rosa de Ocopa, Santa Rosa, Peru
Archivo General de Indias, Seville, Spain
    Arribadas de Cádiz
    Audiencia de Lima
    Contaduría
    Escribanía
    Indiferente General
    Mapas y Planos, Peru-Chile
Archivo General de la Nación, Lima, Peru
    Sección Colonial
        Caja Real de Jauja
        Caja Real de Pasco
        Gobierno Superior
        Real Audiencia, Causas Criminales
    Sección Republicana
        Ministerio de Hacienda
Archivo Histórico Nacional, Madrid, Spain
Archivo Regional de Junín, Huancayo, Peru
Archivo San Francisco de Lima, Peru
Biblioteca de la Real Academia de Historia, Madrid, Spain
Biblioteca Nación de España, Madrid, Spain
Biblioteca Nación del Perú, Lima
Biblioteca Real del Palacio Real, Madrid, Spain
Colección Rubén Vargas Ugarte, Lima, Peru

Published Primary Sources

Amat y Junient, Manuel de. *Memoria de gobierno.* Edited by Vicente Rodriquez Casado and Florentino Perez Embid. Seville: CSIC, Escuela de Estudios Hispano-Americanos, 1947.

Amich, José. *Historia de las misiones del convento de Santa Rosa de Ocopa.* Iquitos, Peru: CETA, 1988.

González de Agüeros, Pedro. *Clamores Apostólicos dirigidos a todos los religiosos del órden de nuestro padre San Francisco, en estas provincias de España, Solicitando Operarios Evangélicos, zeloso del bien de la almas, se alienten fervorosos á pasar á las Misiones de Indias, para emplearse en la conversión de la Gentiles que habitan en aquellos montes: con advertencias prácticas para los que quieran dedicarse á este Apostólico Ministerio: Y un Estado de la Religión Seráfica en las dos Américas é Islas Filipinas para mejor conocimiento de aquellas partes.* Madrid: Oficina de Don Benito Cano, 1791.

Heras, Julián, ed. *Comienzos de las misiones de Ocopa (Perú): documentos inéditos para su historia (1724–1743): con introducción y notas.* Lima: Convento de los Descalzos, 2001.

———, ed. *Libro de Incorporaciones del Colegio de Propaganda Fide de Ocopa (1753–1907).* Lima: Imprenta San Antonio, 1970.

Juan, Jorge, and Antonio de Ulloa, *Discourse and Political Reflections on the Kingdoms of Peru. Their Government, Special Regimen of Their Inhabitants and Abuses Which Have Been Introduced into One and Another, with Special Information on Why They Grew Up and Some Means to Avoid Them.* Edited with introduction by John J. TePaske, translated by John J. TePaske and Besse A. Clement. Norman: University of Oklahoma Press, 1978.

Loayza, Francisco A., ed. *Juan Santos, el invencible, manuscritos del año de 1742 al año de 1755.* Lima: Editorial D. Miranda, 1942.

Manso de Velasco, José Antonio. *Relación y documentos de gobierno del virrey del Perú, José A. Manso de Velasco, Conde de Superunda (1745–1761).* Edited with introduction by Alfredo Moreno Cebrían. Madrid: Consejo Superior de Investigaciones Científicas, Instituto "Gonzalo Fernández de Oviedo," 1983.

Morales Cama, Joan Manuel, ed. *Diario de visita de fray Manuel Sobreviela a las misiones de los ríos Huallaga y Marañón.* 2 vols. Lima: Ministerio de Relaciones Exteriores, 2010.

San José, Francisco de. *Cartas e informes sobre Ocopa y sus misiones.* Edited by Julian Heras. Lima: Convento de los Descalzos, 1997.

TePaske, John Jay, Herbert S. Klein, and Kendall W. Brown, eds. *The Royal Treasuries of the Spanish Empire in America.* Durham, N.Car.: Duke University Press, 1982.

Secondary Literature

Andrien, Kenneth J. *Crisis and Decline: The Viceroyalty of Peru in the Seventeenth Century.* Albuquerque: University of New Mexico Press, 1985.

———. "The Coming of Enlightened Reform in Bourbon Peru: Secularization of the Doctrinas de Indios, 1746–1773." In Gabriel Paquette, ed., *Enlightened Reform in Southern Europe and Its Atlantic Colonies, c. 1750–1830*, 183–202 (Farnham, U.K.: Ashgate, 2009).

———. "The Noticias Secretas de América and the Construction of a Governing Ideology for the Spanish American Empire." *Colonial Latin American Review* 7, no. 2 (1998): 175–92.

Arbesmann, Rudolph. "The Contribution of the Franciscan College of Ocopa in Peru to the Geographical Exploration of South America." *Americas* 1, no. 4 (1945): 393–417.

Barbier, Jacques A. "The Culmination of the Bourbon Reforms, 1787–1792." *Hispanic American Historical Review* 57, no. 1 (February 1977): 51–68.

———. "Peninsular Finance and Colonial Trade: The Dilemma of Charles IV's Spain." *Journal of Latin American Studies* 12, no. 1 (May 1980): 21–37.

Bernales Ballesteros, Jorge. "Fray Calixto Tupac Inca, Procurador de Indios, y la 'exclamación' revindicacionista de 1750." *Historia y Cultura* 3 (1969): 5–18.

Block, David. *Mission Culture on the Upper Amazon: Native Tradition, Jesuit Enterprise and Secular Policy in Moxos, 1660–1880*. Lincoln: University of Nebraska Press, 1994.

Burkholder, Mark A. *Biographical Dictionary of Councilors of the Indies, 1717–1808*. Westport, Conn: Greenwood Press, 1986.

Burns, Kathryn. *Colonial Habits: Convents and the Spiritual Economy of Cuzco, Peru*. Durham, N.Car.: Duke University Press, 1999.

Castro Arenas, Mario. *La rebelión de Juan Santos*. [Lima,] Peru: Carlos Milla Batres, 1973.

Clément, Jean-Pierre. *El Mercurio Peruano, 1790–1795*. 2 vols. Frankfurt: Vervuert, 1997.

Deeds, Susan M. *Defiance and Deference in Mexico's Colonial North: Indians under Spanish Rule in Nueva Vizcaya*. Austin: University of Texas Press, 2003.

Dueñas, Alcira. "Andean Scholarship and Rebellion: Indigenous and Mestizo Discourses of Power in Mid- and Late-Colonial Peru," Ph.D. dissertation, Ohio State University, 2000. Durston, Alan. *Pastoral Quechua: The History of Christian Translation in Colonial Peru, 1550–1650*. Notre Dame, Ind.: University of Notre Dame Press, 2007.

Elliott, John H. "A Europe of Composite Monarchies." *Past and Present*, no. 137 (November 1992): 48–71.

———. *Empires of the Atlantic World: Britain and Spain in America, 1492–1830*. New Haven, Conn.: Yale University Press, 2006.

Espinoza Soriano, Waldemar. *Amazonía del Perú: historia de la gobernación y comandancia general de Maynas (hoy regiones de Loreto, San Martín, Ucayali y Provincia de Condorcanqui): del siglo XV a la primera mitad del siglo XIX*. Lima: Fondo Editorial del Congreso del Peru, 2007.

Estenssoro, Juan Carlos, and Gabriela Ramos. *Del paganismo a la santidad: la incorporación de los indios del Perú al catolicismo, 1532–1750*. Lima: IFEA, Instituto Francés de Estudios Andinos, 2003.

Fisher, John R. *Bourbon Peru, 1750 – 1824*. Liverpool: Liverpool University Press, 2003.

———. "Soldiers, Society, and Politics in Spanish America, 1750–1821." *Latin American Historical Review* 18, no. 1 (1982): 177–22.

Glave, Luis Miguel. "El Apu Ynga camina de nuevo: Juan Santos Atahualpa y el asalto de Andamarca en 1752." *Perspectivas Latinoamericanas,* no. 6 (2009): 28–68.

Grafe, Regina, and Alejandro Irigoin. "Bargaining for Absolutism: A Spanish Path to Nation-State and Empire Building." *Hispanic American Historical Review* 88, no. 2 (May 2008): 173–209.

———. "The Spanish Empire and Its Legacy: Fiscal Redistribution and Political Conflict in Colonial and Post-Colonial Spanish America." *Journal of Global History* 1, no. 2 (2006): 247–67.

Greenblatt, Stephen. *Marvelous Possessions: The Wonder of the New World*. Chicago: University of Chicago Press, 1991.

Gregory, Brad S. *Salvation at Stake: Christian Martyrdom in Early Modern Europe*. Cambridge, Mass: Harvard University Press, 1999.

Hackel, Steven W. *Alta California: Peoples in Motion, Identities in Formation, 1769–1850*. Berkeley, Calif: Published for Huntington–USC Institute on California and the West by University of California Press, Berkeley, California, and Huntington Library, San Marino, California, 2010.

Heras, Julián, and Laura Gutiérrez Arbulú. *Archivos franciscanos de Lima*. Madrid: Fundación MAPFRE Tavera, 2004.

Hyland, Sabine. *The Jesuit and the Incas: The Extraordinary Life of Padre Blas Valera, S.J.* Ann Arbor: University of Michigan Press, 2003.

Izaguirre, Bernardino. *Historia de las misiones franciscanas y narración de los progresos de la geografía en el oriente del Perú; relatos originales y producciones en lenguas indígenas de varios misioneros . . . 1619–1921*. Lima: Talleres tipográficos de la Penitenciaria, 1922–29.

Kuethe, Allan J. *Cuba, 1753–1815: Crown, Military, and Society*. Knoxville: University of Tennessee Press, 1986.

———. "La deregulación comercial y la reforma imperial en la época de Carlos III: los casos de Nueva España y Cuba." *Historia Mexicana* 41 (October–December 1991): 265–92.

Kuethe, Allan J., and Kenneth J. Andrien. *The Spanish Atlantic World in the Eighteenth Century: War and the Bourbon Reforms, 1713–1796.* New York: Cambridge University Press, 2014.

Langer, Erick D. *Expecting Pearls from an Elm Tree: Franciscan Missions on the Chiriguano Frontier in the Heart of South America, 1830–1949.* Durham, N.Car.: Duke University Press, 2009.

Langer, Erick, and Robert H. Jackson. *The New Latin American Mission History.* Lincoln: University of Nebraska Press, 1995.

Latasa Vassallo, Pilar. "Negociar en red: familia, amistad y paisanaje; el virrey Superunda y sus agentes en Lima y Cádiz, 1745–1761." *Anuario de Estudios Americanos* 60, no. 2 (2003): 463–92.

Lehnertz, Jay Frederick. "Lands of the Infidels: The Franciscans in the Central Montaña of Peru, 1709–1824." Ph.D. dissertation, University of Wisconsin–Madison, 1974.

Lynch, John. *Bourbon Spain, 1700–1808.* Cambridge, Mass.: Basil Blackwell, 1989.

———. *The Spanish American Revolutions, 1808–1826.* New York: Norton, 1986.

Mahoney, James. *Colonialism and Postcolonial Development: Spanish America in Comparative Perspective.* Cambridge: Cambridge University Press, 2010.

McEnroe, Sean F. *From Colony to Nationhood in Mexico: Laying the Foundations, 1560–1840.* Cambridge: Cambridge University Press, 2012.

Meléndez, Mariselle. "The Cultural Production of Space in Colonial Latin America: From Visualizing Difference to the Circulation of Knowledge." In Barney Warf and Santa Arias, eds., *The Spatial Turn: Interdisciplinary Perspectives,* 179–91. New York: Routledge, 2009.

Metcalf, Alida C. Go-Betweens and the Colonization of Brazil, 1500–1600. Austin: University of Texas Press, 2008.

Miller, Joseph C. "Retention, Re-invention, and Remembering: Restoring Identities through Enslavement in Africa and under Slavery in Brazil." In José C. Curto and Paul E. Lovejoy, eds., *Enslaving Connections: Changing Cultures of Africa and Brazil during the Era of Slavery,* 81–121. Amherst, New York: Humanity Books, 2003.

———. *Way of Death: Merchant Capitalism and the Angolan Slave Trade, 1730–1830.* Madison, Wis.: University of Wisconsin Press, 1988.

Mills, Kenneth. *Idolatry and Its Enemies: Colonial Andean Religion and Extirpation, 1640–1750.* Princeton, N.J.: Princeton University Press, 1997.

Navarro, José María. *Una denuncia profética desde el Perú a mediados del siglo XVIII: El Planctus indorum christianorum in America peruntina.* Lima: Pontificia Universidad Católica del Perú, 2001

O'Phelan Godoy, Scarlett. "'Ascender a al estado eclesiástico': la ordinación de indios en Lima los medianos del siglo XVIII." In Jean-Jacques Decoster, ed., *Incas e indios cristianos: elites indígenas e identidades cristianas en los Andes coloniales.* Cuzco, Perú: Centro de Estudios Regionales Andinos Bartolomé de Las Casas, 2002.

———. *La gran rebelión en los Andes: de Túpac Amaru a Túpac Catari.* Cuzco, Perú: Centro de Estudios Regionales Andinos "Bartolomé de las Casas," 1995.

Pallarés, Fernando, Vicente Calvo, and José Amich. *Noticias históricas de las misiones de fieles é infieles del colegio de propaganda fide de Santa Rosa de Ocopa.* Barcelona: Impr. de Magriña y Subirana, 1870.

Paquette, Gabriel B. *Enlightenment, Governance, and Reform in Spain and Its Empire, 1759–1808.* London: Palgrave Macmillan, 2008.

Parker, Geoffrey. *El siglo maldito: clima, guerras y catástrofes en el siglo XVII.* Barcelona: Planeta, 2013.

Pearce, Adrian J. "Early Bourbon Government in the Viceroyalty of Peru, 1700–1759." Ph.D. dissertation, University of Liverpool, 1998.

Pérez-Mallaína Bueno, Pablo Emilio. *Retrato de una ciudad en crisis: la sociedad limeña ante el movimiento sísmico de 1746.* Sevilla: Consejo Superior de Investigaciones Científicas, Escuela de Estudios Hispano-Americanos, 2001.

Porras Barrenechea, Raúl. *Historia de los límites del Perú: texto dictado a los alumnos del Colegio anglo-peruano de Lima, conforme al programa oficial.* Lima: Librería francesa científica y casa editorial E. Rosay, 1930.

Povea Moreno, Isabel. "Juan Bezares y la apertura de un camino en la montaña real: defensores y opositores." *Temas Americanistas,* no. 22 (2009): 54–77.

Quecedo, Francisco. *El ilustrísimo fray Hipólito Sánchez Rangel: primer obispo de Maynas.* Buenos Aires: Impresor y casa editora Coni, 1942.

Quiñones Tinoco, Leticia. "Los funcionarios de Dios: la reforma de la Iglesia del Perú a fines del siglo XVIII." In Ilana Lucía Aragón, Carlos Pardo-Figueroa Thays, and Joseph Dager Alva, eds., *El virrey Amat y su tiempo.* Lima: Pontificia Universidad Católica del Perú, Instituto Riva-Agüero, 2004.

Radding, Cynthia M. *Wandering Peoples: Colonialism, Ethnic Spaces, and Ecological Frontiers in Northwestern Mexico, 1700–1850.* Durham, N.Car.: Duke University Press, 1997.

Riva Agüero, José de la. *Los franciscanos en el Perú y las misiones de Ocopa.* Barcelona: Tipografía católica Casals, 1930.

Rodríguez Tena, Fernando. *Crónica de las misiones franciscanas del Perú, siglos XVII y XVIII.* Iquitos, Peru: CETA, 2005.

Saignes, Thierry. *Los Andes orientales: historia de un olvido.* Cochabamba: CERES, 1985.

Saiz Diez, Félix. *Los colegios de Propaganda Fide en Hispanoamérica*. Lima: CETA, 1992.

Santos-Granero, Fernando. "Anticolonialismo, mesianismo, utopía en la sublevación de Juan Santos Atahualpa." *Amazonía Indígena*, no. 19. (January 1992): 33–44.

———. "Epidemias y sublevaciones en el desarrollo demográfico de las misiones Amuesha del Cerro de la Sal, siglo XVIII." *Histórica* 11, no. 1 (July 1987): 33–35.

Santos-Granero, Fernando, and Frederica Barclay. *Selva Central: History, Economy, and Land Use in Peruvian Amazonia*. Washington, D.C.: Smithsonian Institution Press, 1998.

Scott, Heidi V. "At the Center of Everything: Regional Rivalries, Imperial Politics, and the Mapping of the Mosetenes Frontier in Late Colonial Bolivia." *Hispanic American Historical Review* 95, no. 3 (2015): 395–426.

Smith, Gene A., and Sylvia L. Hilton. *Nexus of Empire: Negotiating Loyalty and Identity in the Revolutionary Borderlands, 1760s–1820s*. Gainesville: University Press of Florida, 2010.

Spalding, Karen. *Huarochirí, an Andean Society under Inca and Spanish Rule*. Stanford, Calif: Stanford University Press, 1984.

Stavig, Ward. *The World of Túpac Amaru: Conflict, Community, and Identity in Colonial Peru*. Lincoln: University of Nebraska Press, 1999.

Stein, Stanley J., and Barbara H. Stein. *Apogee of Empire Spain and New Spain in the Age of Charles III, 1759–1789*. Baltimore, Md.: Johns Hopkins University Press, 2003.

———. *The Colonial Heritage of Latin America: Essays on Economic Dependence in Perspective*. New York: Oxford University Press, 1970.

———. *Edge of Crisis: War and Trade in the Spanish Atlantic, 1789–1808*. Baltimore, Md.: Johns Hopkins University Press, 2009.

———. *Silver, Trade, and War: Spain and America in the Making of Early Modern Europe*. Baltimore, Md.: Johns Hopkins University Press, 2000.

Stern, Steve J., ed. *Resistance, Rebellion, and Consciousness in the Andean Peasant World, 18th to 20th Centuries*. Madison: University of Wisconsin Press, 1987.

Taylor, William B. *Drinking, Homicide and Rebellion in Colonial Mexican Villages*. Stanford, Calif: Stanford University Press, 1992.

Tibesar, Antonine. "The Alternativa: A Study of Spanish-Creole Relations in Seventeenth Century Peru." *Americas* 11, no. 3 (January 1955): 229–83.

———. "San Antonio de Eneno: A Mission in the Peruvian Montaña." *Primitive Man* 25, nos. 1/2 (January–April 1952): 22–39.

———. "The Suppression of the Religious Orders in Peru, 1826–1830; or, The King versus the Peruvian Friars: The King Won." *Americas* 39, no. 2 (October 1982): 205–39.

Torre Curiel, José Refugio de la. *Twilight of the Mission Frontier: Shifting Interethnic Alliances and Social Organization in Sonora, 1768–1855*. Stanford, Calif: Stanford University Press, 2012.

Torres Sánchez, Rafael. *La llave de todos los tesoros: la Tesorería General de Carlos III*. Madrid: Sílex, 2012.

Varese, Stefano. *Salt of the Mountain: Campa Asháninka History and Resistance in the Peruvian Jungle*. Norman: University of Oklahoma Press, 2002.

Walker, Charles F. *Shaky Colonialism: The 1746 Earthquake-Tsunami in Lima, Peru, and Its Long Aftermath*. Durham, N.Car.: Duke University Press, 2008.

———. "The Upper Classes and Their Upper Stories: Architecture and the Aftermath of the Lima Earthquake." *Hispanic American Historical Review* 83, no. 1 (2003): 53–82.

Weber, David J. *Bárbaros: Spaniards and Their Savages in the Age of Enlightenment*. New Haven, Conn.: Yale University Press, 2005.

Index

Note: Page references in *italic type* refer to illustrative matter.